D1596920

Howard County Library
Big Spring, Texas

B
N491

Marble
Dust

The Life of Elisabet Ney:
An Interpretation

Marjory Goar

Edited by Thomas Goar

EAKIN PRESS
Austin, Texas

Howard County Library
Big Spring, Texas

078448

Library of Congress Cataloging in Publication Data

Goar, Marjory, 1918–
    Marble dust.

    Bibliography: p.
    Includes index.
    1. Ney, Elisabet, 1833–1907. 2. Sculptors—Germany—Biography.
3. Sculptors—Texas—Biography. I. Goar, Thomas. II. Title.
NB588.N4G6   1984   730'.92'4 [B]   83–20773
ISBN 0-89015-430-9

Copyright © 1984
By Marjory Goar

Published in the United States of America
By Eakin Press, P.O. Box 23066, Austin, Texas 78735

ALL RIGHTS RESERVED

ISBN 0-89015-430-9

Dedication

To Thomas,
my son and editor,
and to
"my best friend,"
my husband Tom.

Contents

Dedication   iii
Foreword   vii
Preface and Acknowledgments   xi
Part One: The Old World
  1 Childhood in Münster   1
  2 Munich Art Academy   13
  3 Edmund and Heidelberg   24
  4 Study with Rauch   33
  5 Deaths in Berlin   43
  6 Schopenhauer and King George V   52
  7 Berlin and Münster   65
  8 Edmund in London   73
  9 Marriage in Madeira   85
 10 Garibaldi and *Prometheus*   92
 11 Berlin and Munich   102
 12 Travel in the Near East   112
 13 King Ludwig II   119
Illustrations   131
Part Two: The New World
 14 Flight to Thomasville   147
 15 Travel in America   160
 16 Plantation in Texas   173
 17 Death of a Son   184
 18 A Son in Rebellion   198
 19 Commissions in Austin   209
 20 Return to Europe   223
 21 Success and Catastrophe   233

22 Recognition in Texas 248
23 Seravezza, Italy 254
24 Lady Macbeth 262
Epilogue 274
Appendix 277
    Chart of Chronology of Elisabet Ney
    Simplified Chart Showing Elisabet Ney's
        Relationship to Marshal Michel Ney
Notes 281
Bibliography 297
Index 301

Foreword

The complete, true story of Elisabet Ney is one of history's unfinished mysteries, so fascinating that it will be told again and again, using conjecture and analysis, until all the pieces of the puzzle have been placed in proper order. Marjory Goar has presented here another piece of the composite picture of this Texas artist. With excellent research into new facts brought to light in Germany, she has filled with factual materials some of the shadowy areas concerning Ney's early life in Europe. The author's own suppositions concerning the thoughts and personality of this unusual pioneer complete her version of "Ney." *Marble Dust* adds new components to history's complex portrait.

Elisabet Ney must be viewed from many vantage points, because, like a true intellectual, she continued to grow philosophically and to espouse new ideologies. Once she had made a decision, she acted on it, welcoming change and new circumstances. Her actions, emotionally and psychologically self-centered, often overwhelmed the lives of friends, family, and the public, producing incredulity, sometimes personal disaster, and, usually, a great misunderstanding of her real motivations.

As an artist, Ney overcame all obstacles to gain admittance to and graduate from an art academy for men, where she excelled so rapidly that she was famous all over Europe before she was twenty-five. Trained in Neo-Classicism, influenced by Goethe and Shelley, she was a participant in the intellectual "enlightenment" which swept Europe in the wake of Darwin, Huxley, Schopenhauer, and she infused her sculpture with the new theory of "natural" realism. Unfortunately, her artistic growth could not continue without stimuli in the rural surroundings of her new world home, but the products of her genuine talent and energies attest to the success of her artistic experiment.

To become a woman, according to her own ideas of what a woman should be, Ney produced, one hundred years ahead of her time, a true personal revolution and the unconventional behavior that made her life and the lives of those around her a nightmarish struggle. Some of her efforts to bring independence to women resulted in a plethora of bizarre tales — her strange mode of dress, her reckless determination to drive her own carriage at top speed, and to travel about unescorted. But, above all, she was persecuted, by the church and by her neighbors, for stubbornly refusing ever to admit that she had actually married her "friend" and lover, Dr. Edmund Montgomery.

She became, through her admiration of Texas history, one of the state's first historians. By immortalizing the heroes Stephen F. Austin and Sam Houston, she assured herself a place in Texas annals. Not so widely known are her other contributions to the state's cultural and social development. How great her influence was on her friend Gov. Oran Roberts is not known, but, when the university opened its doors in 1883, it opened them to women as well as men. She preserved for us in marble excellent portraits of many of the state's most prominent men and women, as well as the portly face of the "silver-tongued" William Jennings Bryan.

Ney was asked to serve on the governor's committee to plan the state capitol building, and she presented to the university its first gift on the day of dedication, a bust of Governor Roberts. Unsuccessful as her attempt was to open a department of fine arts at the university, she did, however, organize the first state association for the fine arts, The Texas Association for Fine Arts, which is still in existence today. "Formosa," her studio/home, became the state's first museum.

Spurning the opportunity for a "comeback" of her extraordinary career in Europe in her late years, she returned to Austin, to work and to die in the studio which she had built for herself — in her real home. Her sculpture, personal records and library, she left to the state university. Perhaps, towards the end, she may have felt she had achieved some of the Utopian dream she had longed for.

Marjory Goar's part fiction, part fact, heroine now belongs to the intricate mosaic which is the legend of this unique individual.

Ney was, in her own eyes, first an artist, next an idealist, then a free woman. She was confidante of kings, a spy, and a humanitarian. All that she was has not been fully explored even yet.

Kathleen Hjerter Gee
Austin, Texas

Preface and
Acknowledgments

Elisabet Ney was born at least a hundred years ahead
of her time. As a liberated woman in nineteenth-century
Germany, she was unorthodox, but later as a free spirit
in Texas shortly after the Civil War, she was unprecedented. A brilliant, romantic, and idealistic woman, she
was also difficult, egotistical, and contradictory; further,
she was a gifted artist who sculpted marble portraits of
some of the major figures of her time in Europe, such as
Schopenhauer, Garibaldi, Bismarck, and King Ludwig II
of Bavaria, and in the United States, where she sculpted
portraits in marble of Sam Houston, Stephen F. Austin,
and other Texas heroes, as well as such other notable
Americans as the orator William Jennings Bryan. The
major collection of her approximately seventy works is
currently exhibited in the Elisabet Ney Museum, with
various others scattered in capitols, palaces, museums,
universities, and private collections in the United States
and Europe.

When I undertook the project of relating Elisabet
Ney's life story, I wanted to describe her as accurately
as historical research would allow, but also to present

her as a living person who experienced a life-long love affair, fame as an artist, and heartbreak as a mother. Unfortunately, the correspondence of fifty years between "Miss Ney" (as she called herself) and her "best friend" (as she called him) and secret husband, Dr. Edmund Montgomery, without which the complicated pattern of her life can never be correctly woven, was apparently destroyed after their deaths by their housekeeper and companion of forty years, to protect their privacy.

To create a realistic portrait of Elisabet Ney in view of the void left by these missing letters, I decided to write a researched historical novel; however, to enable the reader to identify the documented facts, I have cited references in the end notes and have endeavored to point out discrepancies found in some of the acquired information. In the undocumented portions of the manuscript, based on my research of the period, places, characters, and events of Elisabet Ney's life, I have exercised literary license to invent situations and dialogues that portray my conception of the spirit of Elisabet Ney.

I am grateful for the special assistance of Kathleen Gee, Curator of the Humanities Research Center Art Collection, University of Texas at Austin, for reading and advising as to the form of the completed manuscript. Both she and Jim Fisher, Supervisor of Museums, City of Austin Parks and Recreation Department, allowed me the full use of their collections of Elisabet Ney material. The personnel of the Barker Texas History Center, University of Texas at Austin, the Austin-Travis County Collection of the Austin Public Library, the Daughters of the Republic of Texas Archives, Fondren and DeGolyer Libraries, Southern Methodist University, the Texas State Library Archives, City of Munich Archives, and other libraries provided cooperation and assistance.

I am also grateful to my friends Ana Marie Grundner Lee for her excellent German translations, Ruth May for her generous help in editing and proofreading, Frances McIntosh and Edna Grace Trotti for their interest and encouragement, and Mr. and Mrs. Carl Detering for their hospitality at Liendo.

I

The Old
World
1833–1871

Childhood in Münster

*If ... he hears a different drummer, let him step to
the music which he hears ....*

Henry Thoreau

One morning in the year 1850, in the ancient town of
Münster, Westphalia, Elise (as Elisabet Ney was called as a
girl) appeared at the Ney family's breakfast and announced: "I
will eat no more food until you allow me to study sculpture in
Berlin with Christian Rauch. Now I must go, while Germany's
master craftsman is still living. If you continue to refuse, I'll
starve myself to death." The red-headed seventeen-year-old
marched upstairs to her room and slammed the door.[1]

Her parents and her brother Fritz looked at each other in
disbelief. Such an ultimatum was unprecedented. "This *Mädchen* will send me to my grave," wailed Elise's mother. "Herr
Ney, what do we do now?"

Adam Ney usually sided with his daughter in family dis-
putes, at least he had until her present defiance of his order
that under no circumstances should she consider leaving home
to study art. A woman sculptor? The idea was unthinkable.
"Just ignore her," he told his wife Anna. "It's a gesture she

thinks will intimidate us. But I, for one, will *not* be bullied."
With this declaration, he also stalked out of the dining room
without finishing breakfast.

For months before she announced her hunger strike, Elise
had begged, cajoled, stormed, and cried in her efforts to make
her parents understand her burning ambition to become a
sculptor. The happiest times of her childhood were occupied in
her father's dusty stonemason's atelier, littered with dirty tar-
paulins and riggings, wires and ropes for building armatures,
pots for modeling clay, and pieces of wood and marble for carving. She even liked the shop's musty smell. Certainly she was
not interested in playing with silly little *Mädchen,* who only
wanted to make-believe with dolls and to imitate their moth-
ers in cooking, sewing, cleaning, going to mass, and gossiping,
nor was she interested when her mother tried to teach her domestic skills. Even as a child, she knew that she did not intend
to grow up to become like all the other Münster *Hausfrauen.*

After spending most of her seventeen years absorbed in
her father's workshop, she was obsessed by a vision of becoming a famous *sculptor* — not a sculptress. The fact that no
well-known, accomplished woman sculptor existed in Germany only increased her determination to become one. To
achieve greatness, she must have a great teacher; so to discover her tutor, she had read newspapers and made inquiries,
"Who is the most famous sculptor in Germany?" The answer:
"Christian Daniel Rauch of Berlin."

At age seventy-three, Rauch was at the height of his career. When Elise learned that Rauch accepted a few very talented students, she promised herself that she would be one of
them. When she had made this decision, she was aware that
her parent's lack of understanding and their opposition presented a barrier that she must overcome.

Although her father encouraged her work in his studio, she
knew only too well how he felt about a woman as a sculptor. He
was proud of being considered a respectable burgher in Münster; the prospect of his daughter studying sculpture was not
socially acceptable. Elise recognized that her mother, as a duti-
ful, submissive wife, unquestioningly followed her husband's
judgments, but Elise wanted other things for her life than to
become a Münster *Hausfrau* like her mother, who could not
imagine how Elise could think of being anything else.

As she pondered upon some new approach to solving her problem with her parents, she remembered that the nuns, who had taught her basic academic subjects and the catechism at Saint Martin's Girls Seminary,[2] had told stories about the Christian martyrs who were willing to die for their beliefs. These tales had inspired Elise with the idea that if she threatened to fast, until death if necessary, her parents should be convinced that she was as sincere as the Christian martyrs in her determination to reach her goal. Because no other strategy she had tried had been successful, she had bolstered her courage and announced her hunger strike.

For two days after Elise began her self-starvation, her parents argued and pleaded with her to eat, but refused to compromise their stand *not* to allow her to leave home to study sculpture. Her brother Fritz, with whom Elise often argued, laughed and told her, "This 'hunger strike' is your craziest notion so far." Elise had expected her family's reactions and was determined that they would not defeat her. As she gazed from her window to the street below and watched her neighbors laughing, talking, and strolling about in the sunshine, she became conscious of contractions in her stomach. She was hungry. Perhaps she could sneak a *Kasebrötchen* from last night's supper. *Nein!* If she meant to starve herself, she must really starve herself. Cautiously she settled her stomach with sips of fruit juice.

After the third day of her self-imposed abstinence, Elise no longer felt hungry. Whenever she was weak or dizzy, she sipped fruit juice or tea. That night, after turning and tossing restlessly, she dozed and dreamed that she was a baby again, standing amid slivers of marble and shavings of wood in her father's atelier. A shaft of sunlight from the window transfigured spiraling particles of marble dust into a scintillant angel with fluttering wings. When she reached out her arms and toddled toward the delightful illusion, it disappeared into the marble of one of her father's gravestones. In bafflement, she beat her hands against the stone, then tried to catch the magic marble dust, that was swirling around her, while her dream faded into exhausted slumber.

As Elise's hunger protest continued, she became the target of concern of the Neys' friends and neighbors who brought Elise special dishes of food to entice her to eat. Her mother left

a freshly baked *Apfelstrudel* on the table beside her bed that
tempted Elise to sample one small mouthful. Then her father
came into the room, sat beside her, and said, "Of course you
know, *Tochter,* that some of your obstinancy comes from our
Ney ancestors. My cousin Marshal Ney may have been Napoleon's most courageous general; yet he was also red-headed
and impulsive. He was brave but stubborn; however, you don't
want to end as he did in front of a firing squad."

"But *Vati,* so many times I've explained I must study
with Rauch. Why can't you understand?" pleaded Elise.

Her father said that he could understand only because she
was a hard-headed Ney. He could give her a comfortable future; she could work with him in his studio, study art in Münster, marry a promising young man, and lead a happy life. Elise
insisted that he did *not* understand. How could she become a
sculptor unless she could learn the technique and excellence
that only an artist like Rauch could teach. Herr Ney sighed
and left the room.

He told Anna that Elise would not listen to reason and
called her a stubborn obstinate Ney. "Although she has your
good looks, her disposition apparently comes from my side of
the family."

Elise regretted that her father could not appreciate her
compelling ambition. She knew that he loved her, and she had
affection for him in return. She closed her eyes and recalled her
pride and enjoyment as a little girl in accompanying him almost every Sunday after mass on a promenade through the
town. Although such a walk accorded with the widely observed
custom in Münster, where Adam Ney had a reputation as a
solid, conservative citizen, he was true to the heritage of Marshal Ney in his eccentricity of style on their promenades: he
wore Sunday clothes that he had designed for himself—a great
cloak upon his shoulders, a large hat with gold tassels upon his
head, and in his hand, an ornate hand-carved walking stick.
That this costume set him apart from the other male inhabitants, who wore traditional overcoats and derbies or top hats,
had seemed not to matter to him as he strolled proudly erect
along the narrow cobblestone streets, displaying these indica-
tions of his Ney ancestry.[3]

Elise remembered telling her father on one of these Sunday perambulations that she liked his dressed-up clothes and

wished that she had clothes that looked distinctive, as did his. Her father then suggested that she ask her mother to make the sort of clothes that she wanted. When he said this, Elise began to design them in her mind even before they had finished their walk. She would have no tight waist, no full skirt, no starched petticoats, no embroidered pinafore, no prim bonnet, no high-laced shoes: such clothes as she was wearing had seemed ridiculous to her compared to the soft, flowing, form-fitting draperies that she had watched her father carve on the statues of saints and madonnas on his gravestones.

When she had returned home, Elise remembered that she had painstakingly sketched a dress and cloak and eagerly showed her mother her designs. Her mother had been horrified and told Elise that if she wore such clothes the other children would poke fun and laugh at her.

"That gives me no concern," Elise had replied. *Vati* pays no attention to what anyone thinks about his Sunday clothes, so if these clothes are what I want to wear, why should I?"

"Your father as head of the household can make his own decisions, whereas you're a child under our supervision," her mother had informed her. This refusal had upset Elise to the extent that she stormed out of the room in tears.

Elise was interrupted in this reverie by an intense hunger pain such as she had not known since the first two days of her fast. Yesterday had seemed almost easy, and today she had for a short while forgotten hunger altogether. To ease her renewed discomfort, she sipped some fruit juice as she gazed at the white flowers gently bobbing in the box outside her window. She brought her mind back to her retrospections, recalling the soft, white woolen material that she had selected, and how her mother had most reluctantly but obediently acceded to her father's wishes and made it into a dress such as Elise had sketched, draped in Grecian style with a sash at the waist and with a matching cloak loosely hung from the shoulders.

When she and her father had sauntered forth for their Sunday walk, she had been proud of her appearance. Soon after they had emerged from the church, Elise reminisced, they had come face to face with an acquaintance of Elise's age strolling with her mother. The properly dressed *Mädchen* had pointed to Elise and laughed. "*Mutti*," the child said, "look at her funny clothes!" With this remark, the child and her mother had walked briskly past Elise and her father.

Her father had chortled, but Elise had been indignant. She had run from her father to overtake the two, had stood directly in front of the little girl and her mother and had forced them to stop. With a haughty stare, Elise had turned around slowly and deliberately, as though modeling her new clothes. Then, with a supercilious look, she had made a graceful bow. "Wouldn't you like clothes this becoming? Now laugh, you stupid *Mädchen*," Elise had demanded. The terrified child had burst into tears and had hidden her face in her mother's skirts. Triumphantly Elise had rejoined her father, who had been watching in apparent amusement.[4]

"You acted like a true Ney, *meine Tochter*. I'm proud of you," her father had said. "But I wonder what that *Hausfrau* will be telling her friends."

In looking back on this incident and her disagreement with her mother about her clothes, Elise realized that she had managed by perseverance to achieve what she wanted. If she could successfully apply the same technique in her hunger strike, she could win her objective this time also. Now that she was in the fourth day of her fast, daily she was aware that her parents were increasingly concerned about her health. If she could hold out long enough, they might relent.

Rather than thinking of relenting, however, her parents were downstairs discussing a new plan for convincing Elise to end her hunger strike. Being good Catholics (especially the devout Anna), the Neys customarily turned to the church for guidance in time of trouble. Naturally Elise's mother related her distress to the parish priest, whom Elise refused to see. Because of the seriousness of the situation the priest suggested that the Neys consult with Bishop Johann Georg Müller, the presiding Bishop of Westphalia.

Although Elise knew that her mother would consult with the priest again, she watched from her upstairs window in disbelief when she saw her father also leave his shop in the middle of a work day dressed in his Sunday clothes and walk with her mother toward the center of town. While her parents were gone, Elise dozed and tried to surmise what they had told the priest about her; yet she never imagined that they would consult the Bishop at the *Dom* (Cathedral).

When the Neys returned from their visit to the Bishop, Anna told Elise that Bishop Müller wanted to talk with her at the Cathedral if she were willing and strong enough. That her parents conferred with the Bishop surprised Elise, but she was even more surprised to learn that the Bishop wanted to talk with her.

Elise knew that Bishop Müller was an important person in Westphalia, that he had a reputation for being very learned, and that he was more liberal than the other Bishops. For Elise, the Bishop's crowning attribute was his interest in and appreciation of art. On looking back on her school days, she remembered that she had rarely encountered Bishop Müller from the time that she had entered Saint Martin's Girls Seminary at age six until she had completed the Cathedral School at seventeen. She had seen Bishop Müller only when he officiated at mass for holy days or some special occasion.[5] This chance to meet the Bishop was a rare opportunity, and she would also take some religious figurines that she had modeled in her father's shop to show him.

When she awakened the next day, the fifth day of her fast, her excitement over the prospect of an interview with the Bishop was heightened by the mentally intensifying effect of her lack of food. With self-control, she dressed carefully and becomingly (no Grecian-styled dress for the Bishop). She observed herself in the mirror, brushed her auburn curls back from her high forehead, admired her large hazel eyes and aquiline nose, and appreciated the fact that, in spite of the paleness of her naturally light skin, she was attractive. She informed her image that if she expected to lead the Bishop to understand the reason why she must study away from Münster, she must not only *look* the role that she intended to play, but she must *act* the part as well.

With a heart full of hope, Elise, accompanied by her parents, walked along the cobblestone streets toward the Cathedral, which was situated in the *Domplatz,* surrounded by stalls where tradesmen peddled their wares. As she approached the impressive thirteenth century edifice which contained a 1520 altarpiece of Saint John and a statue of Saint Paul, "the minister" for whom Münster was named,[6] she could scarcely believe that she was actually entering the *Dom* for a talk with the Bishop.

A priest conducted her into the Bishop's commodious, richly furnished study. Bishop Müller, a large kindly man

dressed in his robes, greeted Elise with an open smile. He offered her a chair and opened a ledger on his desk before him: "I
read from our baptismal records that you, christened Franciska Bernadina Wilhelmina Elisabeth Ney in Saint Martin's
Church and named in honor of your god–mother and relatives,
were born on January 26, 1833, which confirms that you are
now seventeen.[7] I must tell you that, after talking with your
parents, I expected to find you thin and emaciated from hunger. Instead, you're a poised, beautiful *Fräulein,* whose refusal
to eat has upset her parents very much. Why do you feel that
you must leave Münster to study art?"

Elise explained that no famous sculptor, or school of sculpture existed in Münster; furthermore, she intended to study
under the greatest sculptor that she had heard about — Christian Daniel Rauch of Berlin.

"But why choose sculpture? Is not that a man's vocation?"
asked the Bishop.

"Ever since I can remember," Elise began, "I've watched
my father in his studio chiseling forms in marble for a gravestone or monument, or working with wood, carving a mantel,
figurines, a baptismal fount, or making furniture. Most of all,
from him I've learned to model in clay. As I watched him create
so many beautiful objects with his hands, I wanted to become a
sculptor myself and to create noteworthy works of art."

"Have you ever heard of a woman sculptor?" the Bishop
asked.

"I have, *ja,*" Elise related with enthusiasm: "When I was a
child, my mother read to me about Sabine von Steinbach, who
worked with her father, an architect and sculptor who built the
Strasbourg Cathedral in the fourteenth century. When her father, Erwin von Steinbach, died before the work was completed, Sabine and her brothers finished the Cathedral and decorated it with statues of wise and foolish virgins. At the end of
the story, one of the statues of a virgin stated, 'I am grateful
for Sabine's piety, through the power of which, I, out of hard
stone have been made into a figure.' "[8]

The Bishop smiled. "I'm afraid your mother was reading
the story to inspire your piety rather than to inspire you to become a sculptress." The Bishop asked her why she thought
that Rauch, the most eminent sculptor in Germany, would ac-

cept her, an unknown student, also a female, to study with him. Elise had learned her facts. "Didn't he accept Wilhelm Achtermann from Münster, who was a peasant with no training? After Achtermann studied with Rauch, he became such a fine sculptor that you commissioned his *Pieta* and *Descent from the Cross* for our Cathedral."[9] She quickly followed with her next point. "You know, Bishop Müller, that Rauch is seventy-three years old. If I am to study under his guidance, I must begin soon or it could be too late." From a pouch she was carrying, she took several small statuettes of saints and madonnas for his inspection, which he did carefully and approvingly.

"*Dänke schön, Fräulein,*" the Bishop said, "and now that you have told me your reasons for this impasse with your parents, suppose you go home, start eating, then come to see me tomorrow. With prayer, Our Lord will give us an answer."

After this interview with Elise, Bishop Müller consulted with the Neys about his proposal that, because Elise was so young, she should be willing to agree to wait a year before leaving Münster. If, after a year, she were still determined to study sculpture, he suggested that she attend the Bavarian Art Academy in Munich, an excellent art school, although an all-male academy. He selected Munich as opposed to free-thinking, militaristic, Protestant Berlin because Munich was not only a center of culture, but also a Catholic city. Because the Neys respected the Bishop's authority, they agreed to accept his recommendation, as it appeared to be their only hope of ending Elise's abstinence.[10]

In spite of some weakness after six days of fasting, Elise still refused to eat, but she was able to return to the Cathedral the next morning, eager for another interview with the Bishop. He received her kindly, but when he asked if she had started to eat, she only shrugged her shoulders. The Bishop told her that while he appreciated her ambition, he believed that seventeen was a very young age for a well-brought-up *Fräulein* to leave home, particularly to live in a city as large and as wicked as Berlin. The Bishop suggested that she enroll in the Münster School of Art for a year. After that time if she were *still* determined to leave to study sculpture, she could consider attending the excellent Bavarian Art Academy in Munich — if they would accept a female.

The Bishop paused and leaned back in his big chair. "Fräulein Ney, your parents love you very much and want only what they believe is best for you. I can remember how happy they were when you were born to have another daughter, especially because your brother's twin sister died in infancy. You should be more considerate and understanding of your parents. End your fast. Don't be so impatient. You have a lifetime ahead to achieve what you want to accomplish."

After hearing the Bishop's proposition, Elise realized that her only hope of going away to study was to accept his suggestion; so she unenthusiastically agreed to remain in Münster for a year. Later in the evening, when the Neys were seated at the dining table, Elise appeared with a new demand, "I want three raw eggs with sugar and some dry bread."

This requested menu startled Elise's mother, but she did not protest because she was happy that Elise finally had decided to eat. Her father smiled broadly as he laced the eggs with cognac to lift her spirits. After downing the food with great satisfaction, Elise observed, "From now on I'll no longer eat meat. Eating animal flesh is repugnant and unhealthy."

Fritz, who had been impassively eating his meal while appraising his sister's capitulation from her hunger strike, heard her renunciation of meat and exclaimed, "Now you're a vegetarian. I suppose your next project will be a trip to the moon on a broomstick. As usual everything you say and do seems idiotic to me."

Elise glared at him. "You'll see. Because of the *idiotic* things I do and want to do, I'll be a great artist while you'll be a dumb schoolmaster in Münster for the rest of your life." With these words, she stamped upstairs to her room, flung herself exhaustedly on her bed, and felt that she had at least made a beginning in her career.

After a good night's sleep and food, Elise was revitalized. At least now she had a chance of studying with Rauch, even if she must go by the route of Munich to achieve it. She realized that the year that she had promised to wait would be long and frustrating; however, to keep learning and practicing she enrolled in the art school of Theodor Emmerich, a local portrait painter, because it was the only art training available, and she resumed her work in her father's studio.[11]

After the hunger strike and her agreement to study in Münster for a year, her life took on a slower pace. She studied

art, assisted her father, and on Sundays attended mass with
her family at St. Martin's Church. Their Gothic-styled church
was begun in 1187, but was not completed until two centuries
later. When Elise worshipped in the quiet and solitude in the
musty air of this ancient edifice, she imbibed the music, the ritual of mass, and especially the beauty of the marble statues.
After Sunday mass, she and her father took their customary
stroll along the "Ramparts Promenade," which consisted of a
ring of small parks and well-kept, landscaped flower gardens
and old moats, which were now ponds for ducks and swans.
This "promenade" replaced the ancient fortifications which
had once enclosed the town when it was the prosperous Han-
seatic capital of Westphalia in the thirteenth and fourteenth
centuries.

Often on these walks, Elise observed the many artists who
came to Münster to capture the town's medieval quaintness on
canvas. She watched as a woman set up her easel to paint the
Old Saint Lambert's Church, surrounded by the city's medieval architecture with its four and five-storied houses with
sharply gabled roofs and latticed half-timbered upper stories.
Often she paused to admire the elaborate carvings on the doors
and the centuries-old statues scattered about the streets when
she walked or shopped in the *Prinzipalmarkt* or along the Bog-
enstrasse. Many homes, such as that of the Ney family, had
shops on the ground level with living quarters in the upper
floor. In the spring and summer, Elise enjoyed the color and
gaiety of the many-hued geraniums, pink and scarlet roses,
and purple clematis which dripped from window boxes of practically every house along the downtown streets.[12]

While biding her time in Münster, Elise continued her lessons in drawing and spent much time in her father's workshop.
Herr Ney enjoyed talking while he worked. Born in Lorraine,
he often spoke French, which Elise had studied in the Cathedral School. She enjoyed his stories of the exploits of Marshal
Ney and of the achievements of the other Ney ancestors, many
of whom had been stonemasons, artists, even sculptors. "We
Neys can know the great persons of the world," he told Elise,
who never forgot his prophesy.

One morning in the shop, Elise looked around for a suitable subject to model and spied the Neys' little dog, Tyrus, in
the corner, curled up on a pile of shavings. Wagging his tail at

078446   **Howard County Library**
                                 Big Spring, Texas

Elise's attention, he appeared to be a willing enough model; so she gathered her materials. She fashioned an armature of wire, nailed it to a wooden base at the height and dimensions of the small animal, dipped her hands into a bucket of wet clay and shaped the clay upon the armature until she had formed it into the likeness of the dog. Then she embedded metal shims along the center line of the clay to make it possible later to split the mold in half. To form the mold, she covered the clay model with wet plaster. When this dried, she used a chisel to pry the halves of the mold apart at the shims, filled both sides of the mold with wet plaster and joined the halves together again. When the plaster hardened, Elise chipped the mold away with a hammer and chisel to release the portrait of Tyrus.[13]

Herr Ney, however, would not allow Elise to carve duplicates of her plaster models into marble because the stone was too expensive to be used for anything except a work for which he had a commission. As Elise admired one of the figures that her father had chiseled on a marble monument, she remarked, "You know, *Vati*, I believe that any marble form becomes like a living thing. When I saw Achtermann's *Descent from the Cross* in the Cathedral with the light from the stained glass windows shining on the marble figure of Christ, I understood what the Sisters meant when they explained that Christ did not die on the cross, but lives eternally. He's alive in His marble statue. Someday my statues will be living in beautiful white marble."

Herr Ney was amazed by her seriousness; yet he knew the heartbreaks and disappointments ahead if she continued her determined course. "Why not stay here, *Tochter*, and work with me. I can not comprehend why you must leave your home to go to Munich to study."

Although Elise had evaded this question many times before, this time she answered, "Because, *Vati*, I've already learned all that you can teach me."

In his heart he knew that she did know all that he could teach her. He admitted to himself that even though he was a Ney, he was actually a stonemason — not a sculptor. Sadly he returned to his chisel as Elise walked out of the atelier.

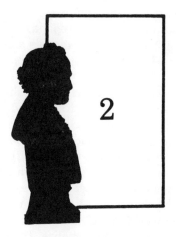

Munich Art Academy

She fell in love with Munich.

Vernon Loggins

During these months in Münster, Elise never wavered in her determination to study sculpture; her mother felt it her duty to try to dissuade her daughter from making the terrible mistake of leaving home to pursue a career. Although she realized that Elise was resolved to study art, she explained to Elise what she would be giving up. Anna reminded her that her grandparents had been forced to leave Poland because of political turmoil, and to flee to Germany. When the family had hurriedly left, all the possessions that they had been able to bring with them they carried in one large chest. Elise's grandfather had to start over to earn a living in a new country. Because Anna had experienced hardships and difficulties in the past, she cherished her good home and good life in Münster and wanted Elise to also appreciate it.

She opened a heavily carved wooden chest, which Herr Ney had made and took out an exquisitely handworked tablecloth that she had embroidered for Elise's hope chest. Anna said, "Believe me, Elise, the only way any woman can find happiness is through marriage and children."

"*Nein,* such is not for me," Elise replied. "I'll never marry. Marriage would only handicap my work as a sculptor. You'll never convince me to become a Münster *Hausfrau* like yourself."

Although Elise considered this time that she had promised to remain at home as time wasted, she fulfilled her part of the bargain by attending the local art classes and modeling various figurines, including some religious figurines. On one occasion when Elise brought some of her work to Bishop Müller, he asked her what was the strongest motive behind her determination to become a sculptress. After gazing for a moment into space beyond him, she answered: "Because I want to know the great persons of the world. When I become a famous artist, they will come to me to immortalize their portraits in marble." [1] Her reply impressed the Bishop, but did not surprise him.

As the end of Elise's year in Münster grew near and her mother realized that her hope of persuading her daughter to remain at home was impossible, Anna reluctantly wrote to trustworthy friends in Munich, Karl and Emma Dietrich, who were good Catholics, and made arrangements for Elise to board in their home when she arrived. [2]

Now that Elise was leaving home, to make himself appear more important, Herr Ney repeated the often-told story about the "Napoleonic lace," which had been presented as a gift to Napoleon, who had awarded it to Marshal Ney, who, in turn, had included the lace among presents that he had sent to his relatives in Lorraine. From the time that her father had acquired this heirloom, he regarded it as one of his most valued possessions. [3] Because Elise knew how highly her father prized this souvenir, she was surprised when he suggested that if she excelled in her studies in Munich, he would give her this family keepsake.

It was not until September 1852, two years after she had graduated from the Cathedral School, that Elise finally found herself, at the age of nineteen, on the way to the railroad depot bound for Munich. As the Neys rode in the carriage that her father had hired for the occasion, her mother had her qualms but sat quietly, while Herr Ney made boisterous conversation and slipped a purse of money into Elise's hand. Even Fritz, whom Elise accused of coming only to make sure that she boarded the train, said that he wished her well. With her head high and her heart thumping, she began her journey with the resolute certainty that she would succeed.

Elise's train chugged southward across the plains and marshes beyond Münster into the Bavarian plateau to the foothills of the Alps to Munich. Frau Dietrich, as she had promised her friend Anna Ney, was at the depot when Elise arrived. After the long train ride, Elise was glad to greet this stout, middle-aged, pleasant-faced *Hausfrau,* who started chatting about her home above their bakery on the *Karlplatz.* She informed Elise that she had promised her mother to be an *Anstandsdame* (chaperon) for her because her mother was afraid for Elise to go about alone, especially in a city as large as Munich. Elise explained to Frau Dietrich that she had applied for admittance to the Royal Bavarian Art Academy.

Frau Dietrich gulped in surprise, "But that is an all-male Academy."

"Nevertheless, that's where I've applied and where I intend to study," Elise stated.

Elise was already excited by what she observed on her ride through the city, by the bigness and beauty of Munich, a city of 115,000 population, in contrast to the ancient appearance and slow moving pace of provincial Münster, a town of less than 30,000. Before exploring the city, however, Elise wanted to go to the Art Academy. Although Frau Dietrich had strong misgivings that Herr von Kaulbach would consent to talk with Elise, at Elise's insistence, Frau Dietrich agreed to accompany her. Surprisingly, Herr von Kaulbach did agree to see Elise on her first visit. He explained to her that he did so because of her persistence in coming to Munich from Münster, and also because of his curiosity to know what sort of *Fräulein* would have the audacity to think that she could be accepted in his institution — especially as a student of sculpture.

"Fräulein Ney," Kaulbach patiently explained, "I've written emphatically, in reply to your application, that this is strictly an *all-male* academy. Now I'm *telling* you in person. I can't understand why an individual of your appearance and intelligence would want to subject herself to the scorn and ridicule of being the only woman in an institution for men." He paused, raising an eyebrow as he looked at Elise, "And, further-more, you would disrupt my classes to the extent that nothing could be learned. How could the students concentrate with such a *hübsch* (pretty) *Fräulein* in the same room? I'm sorry, but once again, *nein,* you may not be admitted to this Art Academy."

Elise was discouraged, but would not admit defeat. She realized, however, that it might be some time before she could gain permission to attend the Academy. Because the school term had already begun, and because she did not want to fall behind, she asked Johann Baptist Berdellé, a painter specializing in portraits and Biblical subjects, for lessons in drawing and design. He informed Elise that he did not usually accept female students, because he did not believe that they would take their lessons seriously. He had, however, accepted one other female student, Fräulein Johanna Kapp, who seemed to have some talent. Because drawing and design were Elise's weaknesses, she insisted that she was serious and would prove herself by what she produced. After some persuasion, she convinced Berdellé to accept her as a student.[4]

She was happy in the ambience of Munich, now that she was enrolled in an art course, even though she was not yet accepted by the Academy. She wanted to become better acquainted with the artistic and intellectual life of the city and soon went sightseeing. Of the buildings, the most interesting to Elise was the *Glypotek*, a musem of ancient sculpture where she discovered statues created by Christian Rauch, along with great works of sculpture from ancient Egypt and Greece. In the Old *Pinakothek* (art museum), she viewed for the first time the works of such artists as Altdorfer, Dürer, Muelich, Rembrandt, Rubens, Titian, Van Dyck, Murillo, and El Greco. Then, in the New *Pinakothek,* she first became acquainted with the modern French Impressionists and the German Expressionists, as well as finding paintings done by Academy Director Wilhem von Kaulbach. She visited the *Altes Rathaus* (Old Town Hall), built in the fourteenth century; also, to her delight, on the boulevard Maximilianstrasse, she discovered a colossal sculpture of King Maximilian I executed by Christian Rauch.

Eventually, after six weeks of Elise's continued harassment by visits and letters, Herr von Kaulbach surrendered and told her that she might attend classes, contingent, however, upon the understanding that she was being accepted *on trial*; that she must be properly escorted to and from the Academy building; and that she must be in no way disturbing to the other students.

To all these restrictions, Elise joyfully agreed; she also promised herself that once she was in the class, she would stay no matter what might be required of her. That she was the first female ever admitted to an all-male German art academy, as well as the first to study sculpture, was unimportant to her. Her primary interest was to obtain the training necessary to become a sculptor.

Elise, dutifully accompanied by an official from the Academy, attended her first class on November 12, 1852.[5] She marched stiffly into the classroom and settled into her designated place without looking left or right, acutely conscious that every young man was watching her expectantly and would have some comment on how she behaved. The most straight-laced, virginal, Puritanical old maid could not have conducted herself more properly than did Elise. After continuing this sort of performance for several weeks, the students, without too many remarks, accepted her.

The courses offered at the Academy were exactly what Elise needed: the history of art, mythology in art, and the great works of the old masters; drawing, copying lines and designs of art in the museums and making anatomical drawings from male and female skeletons, and occasionally from live models; and sculpture, learning every detail of the craft as well as copying great statues in the museums. For the course in sculpture, Max Widnmann, a thorough and exacting taskmaster, was Elise's teacher.[6] She was very much at home in the all-male environment of the clutter, clay, and marble dust; in fact, she was already more adept than many of the students in assembling armatures or modeling in clay. She asked no favors, even when it meant moving heavy marble, and skirts or not, could climb a ladder as well as any of them.

"What's she trying to prove?" one of the students asked his classmate, "That she's the best man in the Academy?"

Elise not only earned the students' respect but also their envy, as she proved herself more capable in modeling and sculpting than they were. In other areas such as drawing and design, she realized her weakness and decided to continue lessons with Berdellé for his additional assistance. This time as a student, Elise returned to the museums to copy meticulously the styling and costuming of the great statues and to better analyze the artists' techniques. Eagerly absorbing this excellent training, Elise felt that now she was a part of a great artistic lineage.

One morning when Elise was ready for class, her Academy escort failed to arrive. Because Frau Dietrich was busy in the bakery and the Academy was only a short distance away, Elise started there alone. Word was quickly passed that "the *Fräulein*" was on her way to class unattended. Because Elise had appeared so smug and self-righteous toward her fellow-classmates, they could not resist the opportunity to tease her.

"Well, if it isn't Her Royal Highness without her body-guard," a *Jüngling* taunted. "Make way before she steps on you."

"So how about a roll in the hay, Fräulein Ney?" Much laughter.

Elise recalled how, with a haughty stare, she had subdued the *Mädchen* who had ridiculed her dress; so she applied the same withering look to the students. One of the young men stepped back in mock alarm when Elise glared at him. "Wow!" he exclaimed, "I feel like I've just been stuck in the face with a saber. Watch out, this *Fräulein* is dangerous." They bowed in mockery as she continued to walk primly to class.[7] Elise resented the students' derision, she proved that she could take care of herself outside as well as inside the classroom. Perhaps the students thought her a prude, but that was not important.

She had been too dedicated to her studies to think about having fun until one day in January when she unexpectedly became aware of gaiety and festivities all around her — in the shops, in the homes, and in the decorated streets. She asked Frau Dietrich what was happening. Frau Dietrich explained that Munich was celebrating Carnival, or Twelfth Night after Christmas, which lasted until the beginning of Lent. No other Carnival in Germany was as famous as this one in Munich, especially *Fasching,* the last three days of Carnival, which was seventy-two hours of continuous gaiety. On the stroke of midnight, the beginning of Lent, this fun was over and the burial procession for the Prince of Carnival began, after which everyone started his fasting and denials for Lent.

Elise, as any nineteen-year-old might be, was intrigued with the prospect of Carnival. She had been so strict with herself for fear that she might do something detrimental to remaining in the Academy that she had made few friends and had allowed herself almost no social life. In fact, the only young person with whom she felt friendly was a student who was also studying under Berdellé, Johanna Kapp.

Johanna was an enigma to Elise, who had never known anyone in her twenties as knowledgeable and sophisticated as Johanna, a *Fräulein* who was as individualistic as Elise. Tall and very blond, with delicate white skin and large expressive grey eyes, she often made fluttering gestures with her hands and dramatized her appearance by wearing all-white clothes topped with an exotic shawl. With her whiteness and gestures, she appeared to be a wistful mime or some illusory character. Although Elise was beguiled by Johanna, they had not become intimate friends; however, Elise reasoned that Johanna appeared to be the sort of person who would be interested in the make-believe of Carnival. In this conjecture she was correct. Johanna insisted that Elise join her and her friends for merry-making.

The following afternoon, when Elise arrived at Berdellé's studio for a lesson, she found Johanna and Friedrich Kaulbach also there. Elise knew that Friedrich Kaulbach, a nephew of the Academy Director, was a well-known portrait painter and that he was married. Friedrich Kaulbach was a tall, bearded, handsome man, and from his expression when they were introduced, Elise could discern that he was interested in her when he congratulated her on being accepted into his uncle's all-male Art Academy.

Elise realized that if she were to continue the same role of aloofness with Friedrich Kaulbach that she had assumed with the Academy students, she would appear disinterested. But Kaulbach was different, and some day he might be useful to her; so she smiled at him.

He responded by asking her, "Are you by any chance related to the famous Marshal Ney?"

Elise decided that it would be difficult to explain her actual relationship as a distant cousin; so to impress him, she exaggerated: "*Ach ja*, I'm his grandniece."

Not being able to resist the opportunity of appearing im-

portant before Berdellé and Johanna as well as Kaulbach, Elise
said that as a child she had studied under her father, a sculptor
in München. (She felt her father would not object to this exag-
geration.) She told Kaulbach that since she had only recently
come to Munich, she knew very little about the city. "Johanna
has been telling me about Carnival—especially about *Fasching*
—and has asked me to celebrate it with her."

Kaulbach pulled a stool closer to where Elise was seated at
the drawing table and said, "I'm sure you'll find it fascinating.
I would enjoy experiencing *Fasching* through the eyes of someone who had never seen it before. May I accompany you and
Johanna?"

Elise was not prepared for this unexpected development,
but Johanna always welcomed another attractive man. "We'd
be delighted," Johanna told him. "Wouldn't we, Elise?" Elise
reacted with mixed emotions, but as Johanna seemed so cas-
ual, why shouldn't she accept Kaulbach's friendship? Johanna
explained that there were parties and masked balls every night
and that she planned to attend as many as possible. Elise
would be welcome to join them, but Elise was far too serious
about her studies to attend the festivities every night. She did
want to participate in *Fasching*, however, and was curious as
to whether or not Friedrich Kaulbach would join them.

On the last two days and nights of *Fasching*, the restau-
rants and *Rathskellers* stayed open until five in the morning
with an abundance of food, beer, wine, champagne, music, and
dancing. In the midst of the merriment Elise appeared a striking figure: wearing a white Grecian–styled gown and cape that
she had designed, emerging as a red–haired goddess. Friedrich
Kaulbach, true to his word, joined their party, and, needless to
say, found Elise quite attractive. They danced in the streets
around the *Marienplatz*, had dinner at the *Café Luitpold*, show-
ered each other with confetti and serpentine, and drank much
wine.

As the night progressed, so did the gaiety: in the tradition
of Carnival, conventions were set aside, and the young men
took advantage of the chance to steal an unexpected kiss or
two. Kaulbach did not miss this opportunity to kiss Elise's
cheek. Elise, excited by the fun and strangeness of the jovial-
ity around her, accepted his kisses in the spirit of carnival.

The next day, the last day of *Fasching*, parties continued

in the streets throughout the day. And for a climax of the fun, Elise, Johanna, Kaulbach and other friends hired an open carriage, filled it with bags of confetti, and drove along the Maximilianstrasse to the *Marienplatz*, throwing confetti and shouting greetings to the other noisy passengers in passing carriages and to the crowds in the streets. Their group continued their revelry into the dinner hour at the *Augustiner Restaurant* in Schwabing, dining, drinking and dancing. This was the first time that Elise had drunk so much wine and felt such a happy abandonment; she enjoyed the smell of the perfume, the flush of the wine, and the warmth of Kaulbach's arm solicitiously enclosing her waist.

At five minutes before midnight all the merrymaking stopped, the lights in the restaurant were lowered, and the carousers attempted to sober themselves by going out into the cold night air to view the funeral procession winding through the streets on the stroke of twelve. Men in black robes with flaming torches preceded a black bier bearing a gorgeously dressed, recumbent effigy of the King of Carnival, carried on the shoulders of eight men completely covered with black cowls and robes that enveloped them from head to foot, with only their eyes visible through small holes. These figures were followed by a band playing a mournful dirge. After the musicians, a crowd of maskers walked slowly, swaying in tempo with the sorrowful music. The lights went out as the gloomy procession filed into the great hall of the *Frauenkirche*. All the once gaily lighted places were dark. It seemed to Elise as though the entire city, including herself, slowly went home to wait the *Katzenjammer* (hangover) of the grey dawn of Ash Wednesday.[8]

Elise made a number of acquaintances during the Carnival and soon was accepted into the artistic society of Munich. The information was repeated and enlarged upon that she was the grandniece of Marshal Ney, the daughter of a Münster sculptor, and the best friend of Johanna Kapp, whose father was the prominent philosopher and intellectual leader, Hofrath Christian Kapp of the University of Heidelberg.

On the last day of the Academy's winter half-season, March 31, 1853, Elise received a certificate which read:

> Fraulein Elise Ney, of Münster, in Westphalia has
> proved herself capable of becoming a regular student in the
> Royal Bavarian Academy of Fine Arts. She has promised by a
> handshake to obey the rules, to be diligent, to conduct herself
> according to the highest moral standards, and to respect the
> directors and professors. She has been accepted as a (female)
> student, with sculpture as her special field, and is entitled to
> all the privileges granted by the laws.
> In recognition of these facts, this matriculation certificate
> to which the Great Seal has been affixed is hereby issued.[9]

This acceptance certificate Elise joyfully welcomed (even
though it contained the word "female" in parenthesis), for it
represented another step toward her goal of learning sculpture
under Rauch.

After receiving this diploma and after the fun of Carnival,
Elise and Johanna became closer friends because each had
much to learn from the other. Johanna was older and had absorbed some of the intellectually stimulating ideas of the circle
usually assembled around her father. From observing Johanna
in art classes, Elise recognized that she had talent as an artist,
but possessed none of Elise's strength and ambition.

"My drawings and writings are for myself," she informed
Elise. "Why should I care what anyone else thinks of them —
except Ludwig Feuerbach. I have now and always will have a
passionate love for the great philosopher.[10] I intend to spend
the rest of my life trying to understand and to interpret his
thoughts and writings."

"Does Feuerbach love you?" Elise queried.

Johanna continued, "That's not important. What *is* important is that my entire life is obsessed by thoughts of him. I
know that he is old enough to be my father and is married, but
it doesn't matter. Just knowing him and reading what he writes
and thinks is all the nourishment I need in this life."

"Aren't you interested in other men?" Elise asked incredu-
lously.

Johanna shrugged her shoulders, "Of course, and when
they fall in love with me, I don't really mean to break their
hearts; yet I know I'll never be able to love any man but Feuerbach. He doesn't believe in immortality, and yet . . . deep inside
I know our souls will be together someday . . . perhaps on another plane of consciousness."

All of Johanna's revealing confidences fascinated Elise,

whose provincial life in Münster had not prepared her for someone so urbane as Johanna. As their friendship deepened, Johanna, who seemed to sense that she was drifting through life unable to direct her emotions except for her unattainable fixation upon Feuerbach, began to look to Elise for stability and guidance.

When they discussed Carnival, Johanna told Elise that, second to Carnival, another Munich festival she enjoyed was the *Oktoberfest,* sixteen days of beer drinking and partying which had been celebrated since 1810 when King Ludwig I ordered the holiday to announce his engagement to Maria Theresa of Austria. To provide the most beer and entertainment, every brewery in Munich tried to outperform the other.

Elise commented, "I love Munich. There is always something to experience and enjoy, but I haven't been away from my art studies for a year, and I would enjoy a change."

When Johanna heard Elise's remark, she knew that the month of September was a vacation period for the Academy; so she asked Elise to come with her for a visit to her family in Heidelberg.[11] Such a prospect pleased and excited Elise; however, she realized that she would have to obtain permission from her parents.

In her letters to her family, Elise had been careful to write only what she wanted her parents to know, such as her success at the Academy, her visits to the museums and cathedrals, and her friendship with Johanna Kapp, stressing that Johanna's father was a prominent philosopher at the University of Heidelberg. She knew that her parents' world was so far removed from the intellectual and artistic world that she had discovered in Munich that they would have no knowledge of Christian Kapp's liberal and heretical ideas. When the Neys received Elise's request to visit the Kapp family in Heidelberg, Herr Ney gladly gave his permission. Now he could brag to his neighbors about Elise's success at the Academy and about her invitation to visit in the home of a distinguished professor of the University of Heidelberg.

With permission granted, Elise and Johanna set out for Heidelberg, the historic old university city, which Elise was most eager to visit.

3

Edmund and Heidelberg

... Us who were strong in love!
Bliss was it in the dawn to be alive,
But to the young was very Heaven!

William Wordsworth

When Elise and Johanna arrived in Heidelberg, the dignified, courteous Herr Doctor Hofrath Christian Kapp welcomed
Elise to his family home, a villa with elegant gardens known as
"Waldhorn Estate," situated across the Neckar River in the
suburb of Neuenheim. Dr. Kapp had retired from his professor-
ship at the University of Heidelberg and spent his days working in his gardens and presiding over a clique of liberal thinkers from all parts of Germany who considered his hospitable
home their meeting place. Professor Kapp and his associates
were continuing the University's centuries–old liberal tradition: founded in 1386 and Protestant since the Thirty Years'
War, the University served as a hub for propagating liberal
ideas in politics and religion.

The ancient town of Heidelberg, as Elise observed, was
dominated by the red walls of an old *Schloss* rising three hun-

dred feet from the surrounding wooded mountainside. Elise
and Johanna visited this popular tourist attraction and walked
through the grounds of the University of Heidelberg where
they stopped for a beer at the *Roten Ochsen* (Red Oxen) Tav-
ern, a student *Rathskeller* since 1703, before walking across
the bridge toward the Waldhorn Villa. As they strolled along
the path known as the *Philosophenweg* (Philosopher's Walk),
they observed a young man ahead of them. Elise, with the dis-
cerning anatomical eyes of a student of drawing, appreciated
his well–proportioned body and graceful carriage. He wore the
traditional student's jacket and his blond hair almost reached
his shoulders. When he came to the gate of a house beside the
road, he paused, turned, and looked directly at Elise. When she
saw his handsome face, and as her gaze met his penetrating
blue eyes, she felt a spark travel between her heart and his.

Instinctively she knew that he felt the same attraction for
her. As she and Johanna continued past him, she could feel his
eyes following her, obviously admiring the radiant, hazel-eyed,
auburn–haired beauty.

"What a *gutaussehend* (handsome) young man!" Elise exclaimed and Johanna agreed.

That evening after dinner, Elise and Johanna joined the
discussion group in the drawing room. Elise was not particularly interested in the political talk and had let her mind wan-
der to sculpture at which time this same handsome student entered the room. He smiled in recognition and immediately
came and sat on the sofa beside her.

"I'm Edmund Montgomery, a student at the University of
Heidelberg," he said.

Flattered by his attention, Elise replied, "I'm Elise Ney, a
student at the Bavarian Art Academy in Munich and guest of
Johanna Kapp."

Edmund told her that he often came to the gatherings at
Dr. Kapp's home and how fortunate he was to have come on this
particular evening. Neither of the two young people heard the
discussion of politics because they were too interested in becoming acquainted with each other. Elise explained that she was
visiting the Kapps during the vacation time of the Art Academy, and Edmund said that the University was also closed for
vacation; so they must spend as much time as possible together.
The next day he promised that they would explore the town and
the surrounding mountainside.

After Edmund left, Elise spent the night in a dream reverie filled completely with visions of Edmund Montgomery. September 1853 was the time and romantic Heidelberg was the place where the two had found each other.[1] Eagerly Elise greeted him when he arrived the following morning to show her the environs of the interesting old university town.

As they roamed through the ruins of the antiquated castle, Edmund explained the structure's contrasting styles of architecture as each new ruler added an additional wing or tower. The first destruction of the castle had occurred in 1679 when Louis XIV of France devastated Heidelberg, but the sturdily built castle, though badly damaged, survived. Then in 1693, a disasterous fire ravaged the town, but once again, the old castle walls, some as much as twenty feet thick, remained. After the fire, the town was rebuilt; however, renovation of the castle proved too expensive for the depleted township, and the castle was left as it now stood.

After Elise had carefully scrutinized the sculptures of the ancient rulers of Bavaria around and in the castle, they climbed to the top of the tower for a spectacular view of the town below, the Neckar Valley, the distant Rhine Plain, and the Palatinate Mountains. Then Edmund lead her down the narrow winding stairs from the tower into the depths of an enormous wine cellar to behold the *Grosses Fass* (great vat), the largest winecast in the world — twenty-four feet tall with a capacity for a quarter of a million bottles of wine.[2]

Besides exploring the castle and the University, the two hiked in the surrounding wooded mountains. Elise was amazed by Edmund's knowledge of rocks, birds, and flowers as well as history and art. They gathered grapes and berries for an impromptu picnic on the mountainside. While they were sitting together on the grass, Edmund suggested: "Let me recite a few lines from a poem, 'Prelude,' by the English poet, William Wordsworth:

> Bliss was it in that dawn to be alive,
> But to be young was very Heaven! O times,
> In which the meager, stale, forbidding ways
> Of custom, law, and statue took at once
> The attraction of a country in romance![3]

Wordsworth was referring to the French Revolution, but he could be speaking to us too."

Elise concurred: "I especially do not want 'the meager, stale, forbidding ways of custom, law, and statue' to dominate my life." The liberal ideas of the Kapps and now of Edward were beginning to awaken a sympathy in Elise's mind.

During these days that she and Edmund spent together, they told each other about their lives. Elise recounted her upbringing in Catholic Münster, her ambition to be a sculptor, the opposition of her parents that she had to overcome before being allowed to study art in Munich, and the further obstacles she had to surmount before being admitted to the Bavarian Art Academy. In Edmund she found a sympathetic, understanding listener. "What was your life like before you came to study in Heidelberg?" she asked.

Edmund told her that he was born March 19, 1835 (which meant that he was eighteen), in Edinburgh, Scotland, and that his father was a judge.[4] When Elise realized that she was two years older than he, she was appalled, and told him that her birthday was January 26, 1835, so that he would think that she too was eighteen.

Edmund said that when he was four years old, he and his mother, who was separated from his father, went to Paris until he was nine; then they moved to Frankfurt-am-Main. His mother, a strict Scottish Presbyterian, did not allow him to attend the *Gymnasium* (boys' school), but hired a tutor for him. He had no opportunity to grow up in the same manner as other boys, with interests in sports and other activities, and so he withdrew into books; however, he was interested in politics, and his mother was sympathetic toward the German liberals' opposition to absolute monarchy, as the Scots were opposed to their British rulers.

In 1848 there were uprisings against the monarchies in France, in Berlin, and also in Frankfurt, which inspired him with a zeal for freedom. In a confrontation in the streets of Frankfurt, although he did not participate in any fighting, with the bravado of a thirteen-year-old he had helped to erect street barricades against the monarchists; however, the small revolt was suppressed, and he later became disillusioned by the entire affair. For a short time afterwards, the boys in his neighborhood looked upon him as a hero, but not for long.

"Why not?" Elise asked, fascinated by what he was telling her.

"Because despite intense religious instruction, I could not accept the strict doctrines of the Presbyterian Church as my mother did completely. I refused to be confirmed in the church that was my mother's life, and the boys whom I had thought were my friends no longer considered me a hero, and now called me an 'atheist' who would be damned in hell."[5]

Elise sympathized with Edmund's rebellion, for she had gone through her own period of revolt against her parents and the customs of the town. Edmund told her that he had become very despondent and disenchanted with life and the world. He had read all of the works of Arthur Schopenhauer, who lived in Frankfurt, and accepted his pessimistic attitude that life was an evil to be cured only by overcoming the will to live. He had even had thoughts of suicide.

"You are not to think such thoughts now that you know that I care for you," Elise reassured him as he sat beside her in their mountain hide-away.

Impulsively he took her hand and looked intently into her eyes. "Elise, since I've met you my whole life has changed. Before I was discouraged: my life had no real purpose; I really didn't care whether or not I ever finished medical school. Now, with you, life seems wonderfully worth living."

Although Elise did not want to end their fulfilling talk together, she observed that it was twilight, and she should return to the Kapps' home before dinnertime. Unwillingly they walked back to the Waldhorn Estate. Although they spent as many moments with each other as possible, time was running out for the two to be together. In the afternoons, when they were not hiking in the mountains or strolling in the town, Elise and Edmund joined with Johanna and her brother Max and their friends in the Kapps' garden for tea or wine. In the evenings they attended the group in the drawing room where Edmund sometimes offered his opinions, which Elise could recognize as brilliant, on the ideas discussed.

On the evening before Elise was to return to Munich, she and Edmund listened to the assembled company for a short time before going into the coolness of the night to the fragrant garden, where they sat beside each other on a bench almost hidden by shrubbery.

Edmund put his arms around her. "Don't leave me Elise, *meine Liebchen.* We love each other. Our love is a *Seelenbund* (union of souls) forever."

With her head on his shoulder, Elise responded, "Edmund, I'll love you always. You're my 'best friend.' Our love is an ideal love, a special understanding above what ordinary people call love." They kissed, softly at first but their kisses became more intense as their passion for each other grew. Neither felt the restraint of the rigid morality of the day, and they allowed their attraction and natural instincts to bring them together in a mutual experience of love.

The next day Elise regretfully kissed Edmund *"Auf Wiedersehen."* Then she and Johanna left Heidelberg to return to Munich. Every day she and Edmund wrote to each other of their love and of the happenings in their daily lives.[6] From his letters, Elise discovered that Edmund had set a goal for himself: he wanted to learn about the human body, biology, philosophy, and through scientific methods, to find the explanation for the origin and nature of life. He wrote to Elise, "Our whole-being-consuming love has enabled me to bring into clearer focus my purpose in life. My wish is that we'll both be free to pursue our ambitions, yet always be held together by our love."

From Edmund's letters, Elise found renewed inspiration for her studies at the Academy. Because she had completed her course in drawing and design, she could devote more time to sculpture. For a class project, Elise used a tombstone on which she sculpted a guardian angel with flying birds in the foreground. This work so impressed her instructor, Max Widnmann, that he asked if the monument could remain in his studio as an example for the other students.[7]

Edmund wrote that he was more interested in the intellectual circle centered around Christian Kapp than he was in his courses at the University. In this group, he was accepted as a participant rather than merely a student observer. In his daily letters Edmund included his interpretations of the rights of man, of rebellions against enslaving governmental and religious authorities as well as his feelings against "the meager, stale, forbidding ways of custom, law, and statute."

Elise's fertile mind eagerly absorbed Edmund's ideas on personal freedom and rebellion against the restrictions of man-made morality. After hearing Edmund's arguments against organized religion, as well as reading them in his letters, Elise confessed that she, too, had become an atheist — or at least an agnostic. They agreed that their love should not be

inhibited by conforming to conventional patterns, and that together they would fight all forms of tyranny and live a truly
free, ideal life.

To commemorate Elise's twenty-first birthday (although
Edmund thought it was her nineteenth), January 26, 1854, Edmund sent her a manuscript which he had assembled for the occasion. When she opened the package, she discovered greetings
of love in nine different languages, none of which she could
translate, because, other than her native German, she understood only some French and English. She was amazed at Edmund's knowledge of languages and wrote that if he intended for
her to read his verses, he would have to send translations. When
Elise received the package of romantic poems which Edmund
had translated from Hebrew, Sanskirt, Greek, Latin, Italian,
Spanish, and Portuguese,[8] she was touched by this tribute to
their love.

Their daily correspondence continued. In June, Elise wrote
about meeting the great Christian Rauch, who stopped a few
days in Munich on his way from a visit in Italy to Berlin. The
Wilhelm von Kaulbachs feted Rauch with a dinner in his honor,
and after the formal party, they invited the Academy students
to meet Rauch for an informal entertainment at an artists'
Rathskeller. Elise was among hundreds of students who attended, but her primary concern was not in fun and beer drinking, but rather in the opportunity to meet Rauch. When he arrived in the *Rathskeller,* the students immediately formed a
line to be introduced to him, with Elise among them. At this
time Rauch was seventy-seven years old, but appeared to be
much younger. He was healthy and mentally alert, with clear
blue eyes and flowing white hair.[9]

Elise was gratified that the wide-awake and kindly old
man to whom she was introduced did not disappoint her expec-
tations of the master sculptor of Germany. "So you're Fräulein Ney, whom the sculptor Max Widnmann has praised to
me," he said to her. "Once Goethe sent me a young student
sculptress, years ago, named Angelika Facius, not as pretty as
you. I've just come from Rome, where I met another young
sculptress from America, who is working with the sculptor
John Gibson — a Miss Harriet Hosmer. She seemed quite talented, but neither is she as pretty as you, *Fräulein.*"

Elise was immediately jealous of the praise that her

chosen teacher directed toward another woman sculptor. So many students were waiting in line, however, that Elise did not linger for any further conversation. After this encounter with Rauch, she was more determined than ever to study with him and to show him how much better sculptor she could be than Harriet Hosmer.

After this meeting with Rauch, Elise wrote to Edmund for advice and guidance. What should she do, she asked in her letter, to persuade Rauch to accept her as his student? Elise had now become so much a part of Edmund's life that whatever she wanted, he wanted for her. He suggested that she obtain a certificate from the Academy, stating what work she had completed, along with letters of recommendation from Widnmann and Kaulbach. Acting on Edmund's suggestion, Elise used all her wiles to acquire a certificate from the Art Academy, dated July 29, 1854, to the effect that she had successfully completed two years work, showed great talent and industry, that her conduct satisifed the highest moral standards, and, furthermore, that she would be recommended for a scholarship in any art academy she might wish to attend.[10] With encouragement from Edmund, she obtained other letters of recommendation to the Berlin Art Academy, where Rauch taught. Finally, she achieved the objective that she had set for herself — a scholarship to the Berlin Art Academy.

Even after being granted this scholarship, Elise was not certain how her parents would feel about Berlin. They had understood that when she agreed to study art in Munich, that her ultimate purpose was to study in Berlin under Rauch, and they also knew that she must have worked very hard and behaved herself in a ladylike manner to be awarded this scholarship. Surely now they would have no objection to her studying in Berlin. She wrote to Bishop Müller telling him of her scholarship and hoping that now he would support her effort to obtain her parents' consent.

Upon receiving Elise's letter, the Bishop was happy for her success. When the Neys asked his opinion, he advised, "Your daughter has proven herself a good artist and a good Catholic. Why not allow her to go to Berlin? Surely such a virtuous Catholic maiden as Fräulein Ney can withstand a den of Protestant lions."

After talking with the Bishop, the Neys agreed that Elise

could study in Berlin, especially since Adam Ney's business was prospering — so much so that the family had moved into a larger house. Now that he was able to provide sufficient financial support for Elise after she had been awarded a scholarship for study with Germany's most prestigious sculptor, he was happy that he could do so. This achievement of his daughter he could announce to the citizens of Münster with fatherly pride.

Good news for Elise was coming all at once. Edmund wrote that he had decided to enter the University of Berlin, after he had completed the last half of the academic year in Heidelberg, so that they could begin their life together.

Study With Rauch

Freedom in love is *morality.*
                                    Rahel

Feeling like Marshal Ney leading his troops to battle, Elise advanced upon Berlin, capital city of Prussia with a population of almost a million, second only to London among the cities of Europe. Immediately she saw and felt the difference between this militaristic, business-like city and the easy going *gemüt-lichkeit* of Munich. Berlin was handsome with wide tree-lined boulevards, an impressive palace and government buildings, and streets filled with statues and monuments depicting military heroes, rulers, mythological warriors, and victorious battles. From the railroad depot, she hired a carriage to the Berlin Art Academy where she enrolled with no difficulty and procured nearby lodgings. Afterwards she walked along Unter den Linden, under the lime trees, to find Rauch's renowned equestrian statue of Frederick the Great standing near the Brandenburg Gate, where it had commanded attention since it was unveiled in 1851 as the climax of Rauch's work of twenty years.

In awe Elise stared at the gigantic sculpture of the King
proudly mounted on a fine horse, dressed in military uniform
with a cloak and three-cornered hat, as if he were reviewing
the crowd continuously passing below. Carved on the four
sides of the base of the statue, life-sized figures formed an un-
interrupted line of warriors and statesmen, some on horseback,
all appearing to be alive, moving as an escort to the soldier,
poet, and philosopher, King Frederick the Great.[1] Just beyond
the King's monument was another memorial, the symbol of
Berlin, which also impressed Elise, the massive seventy by two
hundred foot Grecian-styled Brandenburg Gate, surmounted
by a statue of the Goddess of Victory driving a four horse cha-
riot (the *Quadriga* by Schadow).

When classes began, Elise discovered that Rauch's studio
was not in the Academy building, but in his own atelier known
as *das Lagerhaus* (the wool house), a large structure built in
the 1300s as a residence for the electors of Brandenburg. In
years long past it had once been used for storing wool, thus its
name.[2] Now it presented a drab, dirty appearance and contained artists' studios and army and government offices.
Eager to be accepted as Rauch's pupil, Elise wasted no time
visiting his studio and asking him to include her as his student. Rauch asked to see sketches of her work.[3] When she
brought some of her drawings done at the Bavarian Art Academy, Rauch scrutinized the sketches and also Elise.

"The work is good, *Fräulein*," he said. "If your ability mea-
sures up to your looks, you might become a sculptress; however, if I accept you, I will expect nothing but hard work and
your best effort."

After being accepted, once again Elise found herself in an
all-male academy, but this time, as a student of Rauch, she
had gained a certain prestige. During her lessons, Elise demonstrated how she had learned to carve drapery like the dress of
the gravestone figures chiseled by her father, but Rauch was
indifferent and told her that it was not the man-made cover-
ings that were important, but rather the God-made body.
Rauch explained to Elise that he considered himself a creative
artist who modeled from life, and described his style as that of
classic naturalism.

To study sculpture in detail, Elise went to the Pergamum
Museum, where she meticulously copied the figures of Greek

nudes for the purpose of capturing the human features. She discovered that modeling a person's portrait, penetrating and producing in clay his inner character, was the sort of sculpture she enjoyed and in which she excelled. Rauch commended her ability to understand a complete individual and to shape his features and personality into a marble likeness, a capacity that should enable her to produce worthwhile art. Of course she must understand that sculpture is expensive. To be able to charge substantial commissions, the person whom she modeled should be royalty or wealthy, and, with luck, she could receive governmental appropriations for statues commemorating people or events. Aside from ideals and artistic achievements, a sculptor must earn a living.[4]

In her hero worship of her teacher, Elise had deliberately placed him on a pedestal, like one of his own statues. When he moved about the dusty studio in his dark artist's smock, she followed his every word and movement with obvious admiration. Such an environment filled her with enthusiasm and creative ideas. Here she conceived portraying the frustrations and remorse of Shakespeare's Lady Macbeth. But with so many assignments and hours of instruction, she had to leave this conception in the back of her mind. Subconsciously she imitated Rauch's style, which fortunately was suited to her talents.

Ever loyal to her teacher, whenever she heard Rauch's personal life criticized by other students because he had never married the mother of his two daughters, she immediately defended his domestic affairs by saying that he loved his children and their mother and whether or not they were "legally" married was no one's concern. Rauch's household situation reinforced Elise's determination not to be restricted by marriage — even to someone she loved.

In spite of this resolve, Edmund was constantly in her thoughts and their letters continued: Elise wrote of her days working and learning under Rauch's tutorage and her gratitude for this opportunity to become one of his disciples. Edmund encouraged her efforts in her art studies and approved of her tolerance of Rauch's family arrangement. As for his own work, he wrote that he was able to study, analyze, and devise his own research independently from courses offered by the University of Heidelberg and was impatiently waiting until the semester ended so they could actually be together instead of having to commune by post.

While Elise was waiting for Edmund to join her, Johanna
Kapp, for a pleasant surprise, arrived in Berlin and introduced
Elise to persons she knew through her father, who were important in the artistic and intellectual circles of the city. The first
evening salon that they visited was in the home of Karl August Varnhagen von Ence, husband of the deceased Rahel, a
philosopher of Jewish background who espoused free love and
the feminist movement and gained much of her reputation for
wit and insight at the congeries that she had presided over in
this same house.

Johanna had previously told Elise that Rahel died in 1833,
twenty-two years ago, the year that Elise was born; yet Varnhagen acted as if it were only yesterday. Although Rahel had
been eighteen years older than he, her age apparently made little difference in their relationship.[5]

Upon arrival, Elise and Johanna were greeted by Ludmilla
Assig, Varnhagen's niece, who acted as his hostess and introduced Elise to the seventy-year-old Varnhagen, who still
wrote literary criticisms and reminiscences of Rahel and other
famous persons whom he had known. He told Elise that he understood that she was studying with Christian Rauch, which
was a rare privilege, for Rauch was a great artist. He welcomed
Elise to their evenings-at-home, but regretted that she could
not have been there when his wife, Rahel, reigned over the gatherings. Elise agreed and asked to read some of Rahel's philosophy and sayings. Obviously pleased, Varnhagen had Ludmilla
bring Elise a copy of a book of Rahel's reflections that they
were editing.

Elise soon attached Varnhagen as a friend and sponsor.
Ludmilla, thirty and unmarried, became Elise's friend and confident as well; the two often conversed about Rahel. One of
Rahel's statements especially impressed Elise: "Freedom in
love *is* morality."

"I understand that Rahel's name was originally Rachel,
which she shortened to Rahel," Elise observed. "I'll drop the
'h' from Elisabeth and be known professionally as Elisabet
Ney."

"Good," Ludmilla agreed. "I'll now call you Elisabet."

In a letter to Edmund, Elisabet wrote about her new friends
Varnhagen and Ludmilla, about Rahel's philosophy, and also
about her new professional name. The next letter she received

from Edmund was addressed "Miss Elisabet Ney." He wrote
that he liked "Elisabet" better than "Elise" and "Miss" better
than *Fräulein*. From now on whenever he mentioned her, he
would refer to her as Miss Elisabet Ney, Sculptor.

Elisabet continued her visits to the evening salons and
was impressed with the prominent persons whom she met in
Varnhagen's entourage. Eighty–six–year–old Alexander von
Humbolt, a famous world traveler and naturalist, whom Edmund respected, and whom Elisabet thought might advance
her career, became another of Elisabet's easy conquests. The
old man was flattered to be sought out by such an attractive
young woman for private conversation.

Within this circle, Ludmilla had resigned herself to remaining unmarried, yet she enjoyed matchmaking and invited
eligible young bachelors to the soirées to meet Elisabet and Johanna without realizing that Johanna was still fantasizing
about Ludwig Feuerbach, or how sincerely Elisabet was in love
with Edmund Montgomery.

One of the invited eligible bachelors, Hans von Bülow,
Elisabet was delighted to know, not only because he was attractive, but also because he was a talented musician and pro-
tégé of Franz Liszt.[6] Johanna told her that Liszt's two daughters by his mistress Countess Marie d'Agoult were staying
with Hans's mother, Frau Franziska von Bülow, so that Hans
could teach them the piano and Frau von Bülow could introduce them into society.

"I'm afraid we have too much competition from Liszt's
daughters for the attention of Hans von Bülow," Elisabet
laughingly remarked to Johanna, who was also aware of Ludmilla's schemes. "With two of his patron's daughters available, you know he feels obligated to marry one of them."

Another of Ludmilla's invited eligibles was Gottfried Keller, author and poet, who had fallen in love with Johanna and,
having been rejected, was now in love with Betty Tendering
for whom he had written a poem, "La Bella Trovata." Keller
acknowledged his introduction to Elisabet by gallantly kissing
her hand. To Elisabet he was almost comic, much shorter than
she, slightly bald, wearing thick–lensed glasses half–way
down his nose above his straggly goatee; yet she found herself
listening, in spite of herself, to his resonant voice as he read his
own and others' poetry and related amusing stories and antec-

dotes, usually satirizing himself. From his attentions, Elisabet
sensed he would willingly change the dedication of his "La
Bella Trovota," to her.

Elisabet was not interested in Keller's avowals of love.
With a haughty look, she said, "Herr Keller, you're a talented
writer and interesting person, but I have a 'best friend' whom I
love dearly, and for me he is the only one."[7]

In her letter to Edmund about meeting an interesting
author, Gottfried Keller, she did not elaborate; however, she
wrote so enthusiastically about salons, literary circles, concerts, opera, and theater that Edmund replied that he would be
coming to Berlin as soon as possible, because "Miss Ney"
seemed to be enjoying life too much without him.

Elisabet's social activities were interrupted in February
1855 by a letter from her father asking her to come to Münster
for a visit to see their new home, and also hinting that Bishop
Müller might give her a commission for a statue for the dio-
cesan museum. Because her studies with Rauch were going
well, she did not want to leave, but she decided to go, nevertheless, when she realized that Edmund would be coming to Berlin in a couple of months and she would not want to leave soon
after he arrived.

In Münster her parents' lives were much the same except
that they had moved to a larger house at Bohlweg No. 34 on the
corner of Puisalle.[8] Her brother Fritz was teaching in the Mauritz School. On a visit to Bishop Müller, she enthusiastically
told him about her studies with Rauch and other experiences
which she thought would interest him, but she carefully con-
cealed the fact of her waywardness from the Catholic faith and
of her friendship with Protestants, Jews, and free-thinkers.
She did not mention Edmund Montgomery to the Bishop nor
to her family, and during her stay, she skillfully played the role
expected of her. While she was with her family, she modeled a
relief medallion of the head of her father, which captured his
pride of being a Ney, and a head of her mother, which portrayed her submissive womanliness.

As a result of this visit, Bishop Müller did give her a commission for a marble statue of Saint Sebastian — her first commission with a substantial recompense.[9] Her career had begun.
After this commission there would be others. Although she
knew she had deliberately deceived her family and Bishop Mül-

ler into thinking she was the same innocent *Fräulein* as she had been before leaving Münster, her conscience was untroubled.

With happy anticipation she returned to Berlin knowing that her "best friend" would soon be with her. When in April of 1855 Edmund arrived, looking handsome and intelligent, she fell in love all over again. For Elisabet, the joy of being with her lover, in addition to a successful beginning for her career, was a time of real happiness. Edmund told her, "Besides being with you, *meine Liebchen,* which I want more than anything else in the world, I have another reason for enrolling in the University of Berlin. I'll be able to work under the direction of Professor Johannes Müller, an authority on physiology, who is conducting scientific investigations into the physiology of the nervous system, a subject which interests me very much."[10]

With Elisabet's assistance, Edmund obtained lodging in a boarding house convenient to her and to the University. They spent as much time together as Elisabet's busy schedule would allow. She wanted Edmund to enter into the group of friends that she found congenial at Varnhagen's; however, Edmund cared little for such gatherings. Other than the work done by Professor Müller, Edmund was not inspired by the routine academic courses offered by Berlin University.[11] It appeared to him that a degree was more a mark of mediocrity than of merit.[12] He could learn more by setting up his own experiments and doing his own research.

Even though Elisabet's work kept them from being together as much as they wanted, their love for each other was intense. The ideal love. Both agreed that their love must have no restrictions, no bonds, no jealousy, with each free to live his own life and follow his own goals in a union of true love. Never had Elisabet been so happy as when she was in the company of Edmund.

Upon returning from her work at the Academy one evening, Elisabet rushed into Edmund's room, telling him excitedly: "I'm so happy! Rauch has asked me to execute a design for a tombstone to be shown at the next biennial exhibition of the Academy. Already I can visualize it: a woman sitting in melancholy beside the bier of her beloved. I'll have a whole year to work on it; it must be as good as Rauch expects it to be.

Now if I could only do a bust of someone important to exhibit
with the grave piece, it could be a real accomplishment. What
famous person could I persuade to sit for me? Do you think
Humbolt might agree? I've met him several times at Varnhagen's—or better yet, perhaps he could persuade King Friedrich
Wilhelm to pose for me."

Edmund laughed. "Humbolt, *ja*, but why would you want
to waste your talents on that senile old Friedrich IV, even if he
is a King?" Elisabet knew that Edmund did not share her ven-
eration of royalty; yet she was undaunted by his remark and
began forming her strategy to snare some famous person as a
model. Unsuccessfully she tried to persuade Edmund to accompany her to Varnhagen's home, explaining that she should
attend these gatherings in her efforts to secure an important
person to portray — perhaps even to find a sponsor; however,
true to the pact they had made with each other, Edmund did
not object to Elisabet going alone, or with Johanna.

On one such evening Ludmilla invited Elisabet to join her
and Varnhagen for a musical recital at the home of the Bülows.
Delighted to be included, Elisabet was curious to meet Liszt's
daughters, Blandine and Cosima.[13] Elisabet thought Blandine
was pretty, with too sweet a smile; Cosima, plain and quiet.

During the evening Hans von Bülow brilliantly played a
series of Liszt's compositions. Afterwards Elisabet complimented his performance and asked his opinion of the controversial new music of Richard Wagner. He told her that he
thought Wagner was a great composer. He and Liszt had
brought a whole new concept to music. Others might disagree,
but Bülow said that he was willing to let history be the judge.

During the evening Elisabet made an opportunity to talk
with Cosima, four years younger than she, who seemed pleased
by Elisabet's attention. After their conversation, Cosima invited her for a return visit to the Bülows' musical soirées,
which she eagerly accepted.

Later when Elisabet told Edmund about the evening at
the Bülows, she chatted about the rumored love affairs of both
Liszt and Wagner. "I understand that Liszt's present love is
Princess Carolyne von Sayn–Wittengentstein, who left her husband in Russia to live with him in Weimar.[14] As for Richard
Wagner, he has had so many marriages and mistresses that
it's hard to count them.[15] Men like Rauch and Liszt and Wag-

ner are too famous to make a pretense of 'morality.' They have greatness. Speaking of greatness, I've noticed that both Blandine and Cosima would like to marry the attractive, up-and-coming Hans von Bülow. If that does happen, would it make one of them legitimate?" Elisabet laughed.

"On whom do you place your bet?" Edmund asked.

"On Cosima. She's quiet, not too attractive, but obviously she's the sort who will get what she wants."

Elisabet was also ready to pursue what she wanted and worked even harder on her new project at the studio as well as her social activities; so she had less time to spend with Edmund. In contrast to Elisabet, Edmund was not challenged by his studies at the University. He also disliked the cold Berlin winter. One evening Edmund confronted her, "Elisabet, I do not like this austere city of Berlin with its freezing weather. Ever since I was a boy, I've had a tendency toward coughs, colds, and lung congestion, which this cold climate exacerbates."

Edmund's frequent coughs and colds concerned Elisabet; she also sensed his mood of discontent and unhappiness. "I wish I weren't so busy at the studio right now so I could have more time to look after you."

Edmund replied, "You seem to have plenty of time for the evening salons and musicals." His reproach was unexpected.

"But Edmund, my very best friend, don't you remember that I explained to you that it was necessary for me to attend these social functions; the persons I meet there can give me commissions. Even Rauch admitted that he could have never become known as a sculptor if it hadn't been for royal patronage. Men like Varnhagen and Humbolt have influence in important circles."

"Even in the Court of King Friedrich?" Edmund asked with a hint of sarcasm.

Was Edmund jealous of her preoccupation with her work and other activities? "You haven't forgotten our promise to each other — no jealousies and complete freedom to follow our careers — have you, Edmund?"

"Of course not," he reassured her. "Of course I want you to be free to pursue your career in whatever way you feel is best. I suppose I love you so much that I was hoping we'd have more time together. Perhaps I've been attending universities for so long that I've become bored. Even my own experiments

are frustrating. I understand that Professor Herman von Helmholtz, a former student of Müller's, will be giving a series of
lectures on 'The Physiology of Senses' at the University of
Bonn.[16] They might be stimulating. What do you think of my
going to Bonn?''

The suggestion surprised her. Now that he was in Berlin,
Elisabet had expected him to stay; yet she realized that she
must be as true to their pledge as she expected him to be. "If
you feel that going to Bonn will be helpful to your career, then
you should attend the lectures. You know how much I'll miss
you, but our love will be as strong as ever."

She sensed that Edmund was hesitating to make a decision to leave her; however, it was also obvious that he was not
pleased with their present relationship. He said, "My own beloved, you know I love you more than anything in my life, including my work and ambition; yet I feel frustrated by the little time that we have to spend together. Perhaps it would be
best if we were separated for a time. I want you to have a successful career. I, too, believe that our love is strong enough to
hold us together even though our paths may sometimes part.
For the present, it would be better that I attend the lectures at
Bonn University."

In January of 1856 Edmund left Berlin for Bonn. With a
sad heart, Elisabet said *"Auf Wiedersehen"* once again to her
"best friend."

Deaths in Berlin

Therefore over the inevitable
Thou shouldst not grieve.

Bhagavad Gita

From Edmund's first letters from Bonn, Elisabet learned that he had not found the academic interest nor the peace of mind for which he was searching. In an effort to cheer his discouragements, Elisabet wrote how she loved and believed in her "best friend." Slowly as he became more interested in Helmholtz's lectures and in his own experiments, his letters regained a more positive attitude, becoming more like his letters from Heidelberg.

Although Elisabet felt a void left by Edmund's absence, she engrossed herself in her assignment of carving the gravestone figure of a grieving woman, a work which was progressing even to Rauch's satisfaction. Because the time for the Academy's exhibition was near and Elisabet still had no suitable candidate to pose for a bust, she mentioned to Varnhagen the possibility of asking Humbolt to pose. Varnhagen replied that Humbolt was not in Berlin at present and suggested a friend,

Hermann Weiss, an author and professor whom he thought would consent to sit for her. In fact Herr Weiss felt complimented to have his countenance molded and placed on exhibition and even agreed to a wax face mask to assist Elisabet's workmanship. In this life-sized bust Elisabet captured in realistic detail Weiss's strong facial expression. When Rauch made a final inspection of the two pieces of sculpture, he approved and complimented her on the way that she had worked tirelessly the past year, and how that she was able to finish her assignments on time for the Exhibition. He told her that her gravestone relief merited executing in marble.

Rauch's praise delighted Elisabet, who displayed her work at the Berlin Art Academy's Exhibition of September 1, 1856. But it was not until the December issue of the *Kunsblatt,* an art journal, that she read a critique of her sculpture. She happily sent the report to Edmund:

> We must approach the bust of Fräulein Ney with gallantry, not because it is the work of a woman, but because it is a work of merit. The head which we have before us is the portrait of Professor Hermann Weiss. It is a face whose lines the artist had only to follow in order to gain interest. She has captured the nuances without giving too much detail. She has put as much reality into the portrait as the medium of sculpture would permit. The piece shows that Fräulein Ney possesses to a high degree a rare feeling for art. Another work by her in the Exposition is a relief for a gravestone — a kneeling figure who is placing a wreath on a bier of a loved one. It shows depth of conception and reveals in the workmanship the careful instruction of Rauch, the master.[1]

To celebrate the successful Exhibition, the Academy hosted a party in the artists' favorite *Rathskeller* where Elisabet was seated in a place of honor at Rauch's table. The dancing and beer drinking lasted until four in the morning, which was almost unusual in staid Berlin. In a newspaper account of the Academy's social events, Elisabet was mentioned as "the beautiful and gifted Fräulein Ney."[2]

After having completed her works for the Exhibition, Elisabet turned her attention to the four-foot statue of *Saint Sebastian* that Bishop Müller had commissioned to be reproduced in marble. In this statue Elisabet wanted to create a lasting work of art to repay the Bishop in some way for his belief in her, because she realized that without his help in persuading her parents, she would not now be studying with Christian Rauch.

Once the *Saint Sebastian* statue was well underway, Elisabet's restless energy required another project. Whose bust should she model . . . ? Of course, Varnhagen, another man to whom she was grateful for giving her encouragement and for introducing her to the important persons in his circle of friends. When she asked him, he was agreeably pleased; so she set up the necessary equipment in his home to reproduce her friend's likeness.

During this period Elisabet continued her visits to the Bülow's home and her friendship with Cosima, who by this time had become engaged to Hans, as Elisabet had predicted that she would. "It makes me very happy to be marrying a man like Hans, who I'm sure will be as famous a musician as my father some day," Cosima said to Elisabet. "Then I'll be known as the daughter of Franz Liszt and the wife of Hans von Bülow."

It was obvious to Elisabet that Cosima was a strong character who would be pushing Hans in his career, while Hans appeared more easygoing. Elisabet sympathized with him, realizing that his life with Cosima could be difficult. When the wedding date was finally set for August 18, 1857, Cosima asked Elisabet to be one of the attendants. Having accepted Cosima's invitation, Elisabet said nothing of her real sentiments about marriage. If Cosima intended to have a career by marrying a famous man, that was her prerogative, but Elisabet intended a career of her own devising.

The wedding of a daughter of Franz Liszt was a social event in Berlin, even though Liszt had planned a small private affair. So many reporters and curious onlookers gathered that the police were forced to form a cordon to hold back the throng outside the Catholic *Hedwigskirche*.[3] For the ceremony Cosima dressed in a richly embroidered traditional wedding gown; Blandine, the maid-of-honor, Elisabet, and the other bridesmaids wore dresses of blue lace, a color especially becoming to the auburn-haired Elisabet, who moved down the aisle like a royal princess, making a more striking appearance than the bride. Liszt, as father of the bride, enjoyed himself; however, Cosima's mother, Countess d'Agoult, did not attend, nor did Liszt's current mistress, Princess Wittgenstein.

Among the wedding guests whom Elisabet was pleased to see again was Herr Wilhelm von Kaulbach, the Bavarian Art Academy Director and friend of Liszt's,[4] who congratulated Elisabet and said that even Rauch had praised her work, which indicated that she had talent as well as beauty. His Academy was proud of her.

Happily Elisabet wrote to Edmund about the wedding and her meeting with Herr von Kaulbach. With Edmund's usual dislike of such a display of bourgeois respectability, he was unimpressed by her descriptions of the wedding, especially when it concerned such an ethical compromiser as Franz Liszt. Edmund wrote, "But I'm not surprised that Wilhelm von Kaulbach gives himself credit for recognizing your talent. His talent, on the contrary, seems to be in forgetting his past behavior toward your efforts to join his Academy."

In a later letter Edmund wrote that his studies with Helmholtz lead him to read Immanuel Kant's *Critique of Pure Reason,* which ignited his interest in philosophy. Although he had now completed five years of medical studies required in German medical schools for a degree of Doctor of Medicine, he wrote that he still had further examinations and an internship.[5]

After the excitement of the wedding, Elisabet returned to a normal routine of work. Three months later, on December 3, 1857, Elisabet was busy chiseling marble when Varnhagen appeared in the doorway, walked directly to her, took her chisel, and held her hand. "Fräulein Elisabet . . . ," he began solemnly. From the concerned look on his face, Elisabet sensed that something sorrowful had occurred. "I wanted to be the one to tell you that I received news from Dresden that Rauch died suddenly today."

Elisabet was stunned. "*Nein,* it cannot be true! When he left for Dresden, he was in good health, good spirits. How can I continue without him? I loved him as if he were my father."

Grief and a feeling of helplessness in the absence of Rauch's understanding guidance overflowed in her letters to Edmund. Now she needed Edmund's love and support more than ever. Edmund tried to help her to attain calmness and understanding. Having studied the philosophies of leading German thinkers such as Kant, Hegel, Fischer, and especially Schopenhauer, he could be more abstract and objective in his thinking about death than Elisabet. This was her first experience with the death of someone for whom she deeply cared. Edmund wrote that she must try to understand that death is as much a part of life as birth. "You will keep Rauch alive in your heart. He will always live in his masterpieces of sculpture."

Edmund's advice influenced Elisabet's decision to set up her own studio in the old *Lagerhaus* and to become known as a professional artist: Elisabet Ney, Sculptor. In an effort to console Elisabet, Ernest Rietschel, Rauch's friend in Dresden, sent her a bust of Rauch, that he had modeled, which she kept thereafter in an honored spot in her studio.

At this time, Edmund, like Elisabet, felt that he had reached a critical juncture in his own career. In November of 1857 he transferred to the University of Würtzburg for advanced medical courses. "Finally I've attained my goal," he wrote. "On February 18, 1858, I received my diploma as a Doctor of Medicine from the University of Würtzburg. I've also been accepted for an internship at a hospital in Prague. My next letter will be from there."[6]

She was very proud of her "best friend," now *Doctor* Edmund Montgomery, Elisabet wrote in reply. Edmund's success inspired her to work harder than ever so that he could be proud of her also. With renewed vitality, she returned to her sculpture, but again, she had no commission. Once more she turned to Varnhagen, who had anticipated Elisabet's need to stay busy and had already suggested to his friend, the philologist and story-teller Jakob Grimm, who with his brother Wilhelm had written *Grimm's Fairy Tales,* that he should sit for a bust portrait by Fräulein Elisabet Ney. Pleased that such a well-known person agreed to pose, Elisabet immediately began work, deciding to complete the bust in time for the fall Exhibition of the Academy, so that it could be entered along with her *Saint Sebastian, Martyr.*

During this difficult period for Elisabet, Varnhagen and Ludmilla proved valuable friends. They made her feel that their home was her home. They also wanted to help her professionally — especially now that she had her own studio. Other friends, including Hans and Cosima, frequently invited her to their homes. Cosima commissioned Elisabet to execute a medallion of herself, which proved to be an accurate likeness, but which nevertheless revealed a detachment and unhappiness in

her face.[7] On an evening of a duet performance of Liszt and Bülow, Liszt remarked to Elisabet that he considered her medallion an excellent portrait of Cosima, which gratified Elisabet.

With encouragement from friends and with work to do,
Elisabet was achieving a sort of inner stability when, on October 10, 1858, Varnhagen died. This unexpected catastrophe for
Elisabet was like reinjuring an old wound that was beginning
to heal. Without realizing it, she had transferred her emotional
ties from Rauch to Varnhagen. Now that Varnhagen was gone,
she not only felt grief but also a numbness and loneliness, and
Ludmilla, after her uncle's death, decided to close the house
and to live in Italy to write her memoirs of Varnhagen and his
wife Rahel.[8]

Six months after the death of Varnhagen, Alexander von
Humbolt died, leaving Elisabet, within a little over a year,
with the loss of her three revered friends and benefactors. As
for her other friends, Hans and Cosima had left Berlin for Paris
where Hans gave a series of concerts; Johanna Kapp had wandered back and forth between Berlin and Heidelberg, but little
was left of their once strong friendship. Johanna had become
even more distraught, still swearing undying love for Feuerbach, writing poems and painting pictures, only to destroy
them. Sometimes Elisabet visited the Dunckers, whose home
had become a focus for political liberals; however, she had only
a perfunctory interest in the discussions. Only Edmund's sympathetic letters full of consolation, love, and genuine concern
kept her from a deep melancholy.

Even though Elisabet was not particularly interested in
the political discussions, one evening in August 1859, when
she was feeling especially lonely, she visited the Dunckers' liberal group. Her looks and charm so impressed one of the
guests, a rising young diplomat, Gerhard Hoppe, that he fell in
love with her, and wrote long poems and allegories of his admiration and devotion. In Hoppe Elisabet discovered a sympathetic listener and to her their relationship was a satisfying
friendship, but Hoppe wanted to believe that her revelations of
her difficulties might mean that she was ready to forego her
ambitions and to consider marrying him.

After a year of courtship, Elisabet realized that the time
had come to terminate the affair. She told him that she was
dedicated to her art as a sculptor and for that reason could not

consider marriage. When he persisted, Elisabet told him that she had pledged her love to a young doctor. This confession wounded Hoppe's ego; so to bolster his self-esteem, he wrote a poem to her accusing her of misleading him and of betraying their friendship.[9]

While this affair with Hoppe was transpiring, Elisabet's "best friend" completed his medical internship in Vienna, having gone there from Prague. In that summer of 1859 he wrote that he had met a prominent British surgeon, Dr. John Simon, who was with St. Thomas's Hospital in London and who might obtain a position for him in that medical center.[10] Such news that Edmund's career was progressing successfully delighted Elisabet, even though hers seemed to be at a stalemate.

Her spirits improved somewhat when the Bülows returned from Paris and again invited her to their home. From her intimacy with the family, Elisabet grew to recognize Cosima's dark mood when she was displeased and her "gloomy silence" (as Richard Wagner was to describe it). Hans, a sensitive, outgoing person, was upset and impatient whenever Cosima displayed this sullenness. Elisabet sensed problems in the Bülow household, yet again felt more empathy with Hans than with Cosima.

With the passage of time and with her involvment in her work, Elisabet's sadness grew less acute. A letter that she received from Edmund pleased and displeased her: first, he was coming to Berlin and, second, his friend Dr. Simon had secured a position for him as resident physician in the German Hospital in London.[11] Although Elisabet was overjoyed at the prospect of seeing Edmund, his being in London, so far from Berlin, would make their being together even more difficult. After she was reunited with Edmund when he arrived in Berlin, Elisabet's aching sorrow over the deaths of her friends almost disappeared in their mutually satisfying deep love for each other.

"My grief would have been easier to bear if only you had been with me when my dear Rauch, Varnhagen, and then Humbolt died, all in such a short time," she said as she lay in his arms. "My heart is comforted just to be with you."

Edmund kissed her. "You know you're my life, *Liebchen.* Nothing matters to me as much as you. I don't have to go to London, although it's the opportunity I've been hoping for.

Now that I'm licensed to practice medicine anywhere in Germany, we could go to Munich, or wherever you like. I could practice medicine; you could have your studio and sculpture. We could be married and share an ideal life together. What do you think of the proposition?''

Elisabet was tempted: she knew that she loved Edmund and wanted to be with him; yet she realized that Edmund did not really want to practice medicine. She knew that, like herself, he wanted to follow his inner ambition. To pursue this objective, he must have time for study and research. In the position that he had been offered with the German Hospital, he would not only have research facilities, but also Dr. Simon's sponsorship and assistance. She decided *nein.* She must not hamper his career. She also had not yet achieved the fame as an artist that she had promised herself. To be true to their vow, each must be free to pursue his own goals.

Reluctantly Elisabet said, "Marriage is out of the question. We've pledged ourselves to keep our love above such conventionality, no bonds except our love.''

As for her future at the moment, Elisabet unburdened her problems to Edmund, how her commissions had almost stopped since she no longer had the support of Rauch and Varnhagen. "To be frank, *meine Leibchen*," Edmund said, "people here in Berlin think of you as a gifted student of the master Rauch. But if they intend to commission an expensive work of sculpture, they'll turn to Rauch's successor Ernst Rietschel in Dresden, or to any other well-established sculptor, not to a student who has yet to prove herself other than by being a female and beautiful. What you need is to model someone who is either very famous or who would provide a shock element, such as an important person who had previously refused to pose.''

Then Edmund outlined an idea. In his youthful days in Frankfurt, when he had been depressed, he studied the philosophy of Schopenhauer. He knew of the old man's reputation as an unsociable misogynist, of how the stout, heavy-set, white-haired Schopenhauer walked his dog about the streets of Frankfurt, scowling and swinging a stick at any child who ventured too close. Although Schopenhauer was one of the best known philosophers in Europe, no bust of him had been made. If Elisabet could accomplish a likeness of this crusty, famous (and infamous) old man, such a triumph would give credence to her ability as a sculptor as well as to advertise her name and background as a student of Rauch.

"Schopenhauer could also use some publicity," Edmund observed, "because the third edition of his book, *The World as Will and Idea*, is soon to be issued.[12] Your statue could promote his book as well as his colossal ego."

Elisabet excitedly agreed with Edmund's selection of Schopenhauer. "I'll do it! I know I can do it! I'll write and ask for the opportunity of creating his portrait for posterity."

"No letter," Edmund vetoed. "Schopenhauer would never reply to such a letter, especially from a 'female.' The only way you'll succeed is to personally confront and charm the ill-tempered old crank into agreement. I'm well aware of your ability to cajole older men."

Elisabet, too, was aware of her successful acquisition of older gentlemen admirers. With this in mind, they planned her strategy. Because Edmund knew the city of Frankfurt, he directed her to a boarding house on the residential avenue of Schöne Aussicht, paralleling the River Main, and near Schopenhauer's apartment. Even though Edmund knew that his mother was living in Frankfurt, he did not mention this to Elisabet because he had no reason for them to meet.

With a purpose and a challenge once again, Elisabet's usual sparkle and energy returned. Impatiently she waited to depart for Frankfurt. Before leaving, Edmund briefed her as to Schopenhauer's life and philosophy. When Edmund accompanied her to the train for Frankfurt, he was encouraged to see his Elisabet behaving like her normal self, her eyes sparkling with determination. Unhappily in October of 1859, they parted once again: Edmund, age twenty-four, to begin his life's work as a physician and scientist in London, pursuing his scientific search for the explanation of the origin and meaning of life; Elisabet, age twenty-six, to launch her career as a woman sculptor in a man's domain.

Schopenhauer and King George V

*When you meet the Ney; you'll feel like tearing
yourself to pieces for her. She's incomparable!*

Arthur Schopenhauer

Following Edmund's instructions when she arrived in
Frankfurt, Elisabet rented a room at a small hotel on Schöne
Aussicht, near Schopenhauer's apartment, where she could observe the seventy-one-year-old philosopher's daily habits. Although Edmund had briefed her on Schopenhauer's background and philosophy, Elisabet was more interested in the
old man's fame and reputation than in his theories, more interested in discovering a weakness in his gruff defenses. His life
was regulated by the clock, she quickly discerned: she noted
that each day at the same time he walked with his dog for two
hours; so she planned her strategic assault for a time when she
knew that he would be at home.

Carefully groomed and wearing a becoming white lace
dress, she pounded the knocker on Schopenhauer's door, which
was opened by a plain looking peasant *Haushälterin* (housekeeper). "I'm Fräulein Elisabet Ney, a sculptor from Berlin

who has come to model a bust of Dr. Schopenhauer," Elisabet announced and presented her engraved card: Fräulein Elisabet Ney, *Bildhauer* (sculptor), das Lagerhaus, Berlin. When he received the card, Schopenhauer was amazed. *"Nein! Nein!"* he roared, *"Bildhauer!* There's no such thing as a *female sculptor*. Tell her to leave. I will not see her."

The *Haushälterin* dutifully reported his message to Elisabet, who had expected such a reply, and to the woman's astonishment, stepped inside the doorway. "Tell Herr Dr. Schopenhauer that I'm already inside and that I expect to see him."

Such impudence aroused Schopenhauer's ire and also his curiosity. "What does this female sculptor look like? She must be an audacious hussy."

"Nein, Herr Doctor," the *Haushälterin* said. "She's young and pretty and dressed in white lace."[1]

With this description, Schopenhauer's curiosity overcame his temper. "Well, I'll see her and be rid of this brazen intruder." In spite of his prejudiced conception of women,.Elisabet's youth and attractiveness surprised and even impressed the Herr Doctor. Within a short time she was sitting beside him on the couch in his comfortable, masculine study making friends with his poodle, Atma, "which means 'soul' in Sanskrit," Schopenhauer informed her. "Why did you come all the way from Berlin thinking that I would pose for you? Now why should I allow some unknown *Fräulein* to make a bust of me?"

Having handled crotchety, pompous old men before, Elisabet replied, "Because, Herr Dr. Schopenhauer, I consider you to be one of the greatest men alive today; your fine features should be preserved for posterity; a marble bust is immortal."

"And what makes you think that you are capable of creating such an immortal statue?"

"Because I have talent and have studied with the great sculptor Rauch," Elisabet stated frankly. "Dr. Schopenhauer, I'll make a bargain with you. I'll model your bust in clay. If you are pleased with it, I'll cast it in plaster, then marble, but if you are not pleased, I'll destroy it and you'll owe me nothing."[2]

Such a proposition amazed yet intrigued Schopenhauer, who agreed to pose if Elisabet promised not to waste too much of his time, for he was proof-reading the third edition of *The World as Will and Idea,* to be published as soon as he finished his editing. Elisabet agreed and suggested that after reading the new edition of his book, people would be interested in seeing his statue. It would also be an advertisement for the book. Elisabet told him that his statue would be displayed at the Art Academy Exhibition in Berlin and in Vienna, also in Frankfurt.

"And also in Leipzig," Schopenhauer added enthusiastically. "My book's published in Leipzig."

Because they were both anxious to begin the project, Schopenhauer allowed Elisabet to set up her paraphernalia— stool, clay, armature, measuring devices, tools, sketch pad and pencils—in a room next to his study. When Elisabet began work the following morning, Schopenhauer's bachelor existence had not prepared him for her competence in proceeding with the work of modeling. Dressed in her dark artist's smock with clay on her hands, and a smudge on her face, she confronted him on a no-nonsense basis, telling him to strip to the waist so that she could observe and model his shoulders. Stubbornly he refused to have a mask made of his face, even though Elisabet explained that without it her work would be slower. All during the time that Elisabet was observing, studying, measuring, building an armature, and modeling the clay, he was asking personal questions. "Are you related to Napoleon's Marshal Ney?"

"*Ja*, I'm his grandniece."

Schopenhauer asked why she had left home to study in Berlin. How old was she? Did she live all alone? Did she have a lover?

Elisabet answered that she was twenty-four [actually she was twenty-six] and had left home because she wanted to study sculpture with the best teacher available, Christian Rauch in Berlin. But she had no intention of allowing Schopenhauer to probe into her personal affairs. "*Nein,* Herr Doctor, I have no lover. My only love is my art," a statement which Schopenhauer found hard to believe.

The old man was growing tired. "You must stop now, *Fräulein.* I've given you my morning and now is the time when I eat my lunch. If you'll wash your hands, and also your face, I'll have the restaurant send lunch for you, too."

In the study where they ate lunch, a portrait of Johann Wolfgang Goethe hung on the wall, as well as pictures of all the dogs that Schopenhauer had owned. Elisabet asked if he had known Goethe.

Schopenhauer replied that he had known him for many years. They had met when Schopenhauer was a young man in Weimar, and later they both had taught at the University of Dresden. Goethe was one of the few persons, along with Immanuel Kant, whom Schopenhauer said that he could admire and respect. Goethe was born in Frankfurt, where he conceived some of his finest works, and where he died in 1832, a year before Schopenhauer moved there twenty-six years ago.[3]

On another occasion of lunching in the study, Elisabet inquired about the gold-plated statue of the Buddha, sitting in lotus position, wearing his serene, eternal smile. "I'm glad you admire my Buddha, *Fräulein*. I've studied Buddhist philosophy for many years. In fact, I'm one of the first European philosophers to introduce the conceptions of this Oriental religion to the shallow-minded thinkers of our Western Civilization."[4]

During their conversations on philosophy and art, while Elisabet busily modeled his features, Schopenhauer became enamored with the young "female sculptor." "It's hard to believe you, *Fräulein*," he said as he stared almost rudely into her face. "I'm looking for a sign of a moustache. You are too capable and talented to be a woman."[5] He behaved toward Elisabet like a spoiled child — possessive and demanding. Elisabet humored him because she realized that he was writing to his friends and correspondents, many in places of influence and importance, praising her as a fine artist.

To one of his correspondents, Friedrich Arnold Brockhaus, Schopenhauer wrote: "The sculptress Ney (grandniece of the Marshal) has come from Berlin to make my bust and has been at work on it for eight days. I'm tossed between sculpture and proof-reading."

In another letter to Brockhaus, he said: "The bust will be exhibited in Berlin and Vienna. The Ney herself will see about the exhibit in Liepzig. I beg you to devote to it the flourish of your many publicity trumpts. When you meet the Ney, you'll feel like tearing yourself to pieces for her. She's incomparable!"

In further correspondence to Adam von Doss, a state official in Munich, he stated: "The Ney is twenty-four, very beautiful and indescribably *liebenswürdig*. Day after day she works in a room adjoining my study. At noon she has her lunch sent down from a restaurant on a floor above me, and when I come in, she and I have coffee together. Often we take walks along the Main, over stick and stone. We are wholly sympathetic."[6]

When acquaintances came to call, they were astounded to hear Schopenhauer (the unrelenting woman-hater) praising his newly found sculptress friend. He even remarked to Baron Robert von Hornstein that having Fräulein Ney with him all day almost made him feel like a married man.[7]

Schopenhauer was equally pleased with the clay bust that Elisabet completed which captured his broad forehead with deep wrinkles, furrowed brow, receding hairline and sideburns, sardonic mouth and face revealing his virility and character. When this clay model was placed on display in the Frankfurt Art League gallery, the egocentric old grumbler went every day to admire his likeness. Knowing that it would please the old man, Elisabet also modeled his poodle, Atma.[8]

During this time that she was modeling Schopenhauer, Elisabet's letters to Edmund bubbled with enthusiasm: because Edmund felt that he was the instigator of this successful venture, her mood uplifted his spirits. Through Dr. Simon's influence, Edmund was designated a resident physician in the German Hospital in London; however, because he had acquired his medical degree in Germany, he was restricted in his medical practice in England to German immigrants until he could pass the necessary British requirements.

Edmund wrote that Dr. Simon, a prominent physician in London as well as director of the British Board of Health and Sanitation, had become his close personal friend, confidant, and sponsor.[9] He had told Dr. Simon of his love for her, Miss Elisabet Ney, Sculptor, a circumstance which was of great interest to Dr. Simon, who was an admirer and patron of the arts. Edmund also wrote that Dr. Simon had many friends who could be useful to Elisabet if she should come to London.

From London, he sent an article about Christian Rauch in a Paris journal, which stated: "Rauch's last pupil, Fräulein Elisabet Ney, was mentioned as being his most talented."[10] Now that she had finished the bust of Schopenhauer, she wrote to Edmund that she was ready for another challenge, someone like Queen Victoria and the Royal Family. "Could Dr. Simon arrange for me to model the Queen?" Elisabet asked in a letter.

"Such a commission would be *most* unlikely," Edmund answered, "for Elisabet Ney, Sculptor, is unknown in English Royal Circles, as is Schopenhauer. But Dr. Simon could introduce you to Tom Taylor, art critic and dramatist, and to John Ruskin, well-known writer and critic."[11] Edmund's remark that she was not known in the British Court circles caused Elisabet to begin thinking of some way that she could become known. Surely she had a friend who could be of assistance. But who?

Then she remembered Friedrich Kaulbach, who had been interested in her in Munich. According to reports, Kaulbach's wife had died and he was now court painter to His Majesty, King George V of Hannover, who, as Elisabet knew from her studies of royal lineage, was a first cousin of Queen Victoria. Elisabet reasoned that if she could receive a commission to sculpt a bust of King George V, such a work might attract the attention of his cousin, the English Queen.

With this scheme in mind, Elisabet immediately wrote to Kaulbach, informing him about her latest achievements, stating that she had just completed a bust of Schopenhauer and asking if he would use his influence with His Majesty King George V to give her a commission to execute a bust of himself.[12]

Elisabet's manipulations resulted in a summons from King George V of Hannover to come to his Court for the purpose of sculpting a large bust. When Elisabet showed the letter to Schopenhauer, he was immediately jealous. He chided, "You have a lover at court who influenced the King. Who is he?"

Elisabet smiled and denied Schopenhauer's insinuation, but Schopenhauer did not believe her; yet he enjoyed her flattery. "Does that mean that you'll leave me? What about my bust being cut in marble?"

Elisabet explained that although she must leave soon for Hannover, she would send his clay bust to her Lagerhaus studio in Berlin and would personally oversee its being reproduced in marble. Still, Schopenhauer was petulant, "So you're leaving and taking my statue, too. I see that you're just like all women — unreliable."[13]

To soothe his annoyance, Elisabet promised to return with his countenance perpetuated in marble for future generations to gaze upon. As soon as she had made arrangements for the bust to be shipped to her studio in Lagerhaus, Elisabet left Frankfurt for Hannover where Kaulbach met her. He told her that he had recommended her to the King as an excellent sculptress. That she had studied with Rauch impressed the King, especially because Rauch had sculpted busts of his mother and father. Kaulbach said that he convinced King George that he needed a bust of himself for the Palace, and that he also needed a designated Royal Sculptor, such as Kaulbach's title of Royal Painter to His Majesty's Court, which gave him certain privileges. He further told His Majesty that Elisabet was not only a talented artist, but also an attractive and intelligent person who would be an asset to his court.

Without knowing how much of Kaulbach's statement about his influence with the King was true, Elisabet realized that without his suggestions and recommendation, she would never have received the commission from King George. "I'm grateful to you, Herr Kaulbach. You're a real friend. Tell me, what is the King like? I need to know all I can about him."

Kaulbach explained, "You know, of course that the King is blind and also a little eccentric."

This fact surprised Elisabet. "*Nein*, I didn't know that he was blind. So many Germany Royal Families have a streak of madness; does he also?"

"*Ach nein, nein.*" Kaulbach reassured her that the King was actually a kind man, who believed that as the reigning head of the House of Guelph, he ruled by divine right, and he expected everyone to act accordingly. Actually, Hannover was a small duchy, ruled in the eighteenth century by the King of England, who was of Guelph descent. If the English right of ascension had forbidden a woman to become the ruler, George, instead of Queen Victoria, would have become the King of England. When Victoria was crowned in 1837, her uncle Ernest Augustus, Duke of Cumberland, ascended the throne of Hannover; upon his death, his son George V succeeded him.[14]

Kaulbach invited Elisabet to dinner, and during the meal over candlelight and wine, he told her that the King was moralistic and strict in the observance of the niceties of etiquette and that his blindness cast a gloom over the Court, with few parties and little entertainment. "We'll have to make our own fun," he suggested. "We have a good theater, and the violinist Joseph Joachim, Concert Master of the Royal Orchestra, is a talented artist."

Kaulbach was a sophisticated, good-looking man, Elisabet observed, who was attractive to women, including herself. Obviously he expected to receive some of her time and attention. She asked him about his life since she last saw him. He said that his wife had died a few years before and that now he was free of entanglements. Elisabet apprehended that Kaulbach intended to make her his next conquest, but felt capable of foiling his advances while retaining him as a friend.

The following day his Majesty King George V, his wife Queen Marie, his two children, and members of the Court received Elisabet. The King, a tall, heavy-set man with a drooping moustache, which gave his face a sad appearance, had been blind since he was fourteen and was now forty; yet he carried himself with the erectness of a sighted person. Queen Marie, an unprepossessing woman, looked as though she spent her life anticipating her husband's desires. Curtsying before Their Majesties, Elisabet expressed her gratitude for being selected to execute a likeness of His Royal Highness and hoped that her artistic efforts would please him.

The King granted Elisabet a studio in the palace where she could work and was patient and agreeable when he posed. The sessions seemed routine to Elisabet, except when he looked toward her with sightless eyes, or when he ran his sensitive fingers over the model, seeing it through his touch. After several sittings, he seemed pleased. Elisabet told him that he could see very well with his fingers and had an appreciation of beauty.

Before Elisabet had completed the bust of the King, the festivities of Christmas began. At this time Elisabet received a gift which aroused much interest in the Court — a copy of Arthur Schopenhauer's newly released third edition of *The World as Will and Idea,* inscribed: "To my artistic and most highly esteemed young friend, Elisabet Ney, I present, according to her wish, this copy of a most serious book. Frankfurt-am-M., 4 Dec. 1859. Arthur Schopenhauer."[15]

Whenever Elisabet was not occupied with modeling the King, Kaulbach occupied her time. He escorted her to concerts, to the theater, and to a special violin recital of Joseph Joachim, after which the three celebrated *Weihnachten* (Christmas) together with a midnight supper, complete with holiday music, wine, good food, and light-hearted conversation.

During the King's final sitting, Elisabet told him how much she had enjoyed the music of the Royal Orchestra and especially the violin of Joseph Joachim. "Then I suggest that you model his bust," the King ordered.

The King's proposal was agreeable to Joachim and to Elisabet, who soon began work on the bust. Kaulbach came often to observe Elisabet as she went about forming Joachim's clay image, and the King appeared from time to time to inspect the progress of the sculpture through his sense of touch. He commented to Kaulbach: "This Fräulein Ney is preserving our likenesses, but who is recording her looks for posterity? As Court Painter, Herr Kaulbach, I suggest that you do it."[16]

Elisabet knew that to be painted by Friedrich Kaulbach was an honor coveted by the ladies of the Court, because his reputation as an artist was greater than that of being Court Painter for the King of Hannover. As for Kaulbach, it was the opportunity that he had desired ever since Elisabet came to the Court. He had wanted to paint her ever since the first time he saw her in Munich, but here she was under the command of the King, so he had hesitated to ask whether he might put her beauty on canvas. Kaulbach painted Elisabet standing beside the newly completed bust of the blind monarch, holding a chisel in her hand, with the other elbow resting on the pedestal supporting the King's bust.[17]

As Elisabet was able to capture the essence of a person's character in her sculpture, so Kaulbach was able to project Elisabet's individuality as she appeared to him, standing confidently straight and tall with a slightly self-satisfied smile, looking as though she had proudly completed a work which she felt was worthy of her talent. To accent her glowing face, penetrating hazel eyes, and auburn curls, he painted her wearing a dark dress against the dark background of the King's sombre statue. The completed portrait stood approximately six and one-half by three and three-fourths feet, an arresting life-size image.

As they admired the painting, Kaulbach pulled Elisabet to him and kissed her passionately. "Elisabet, *meine Liebe,* I'm sure you know that I've fallen in love with you. You're so beautiful and talented. Do you have any love for me? Could you love me?"

He pulled her gently to the sofa where she stayed in his arms while telling him that she was very fond of him and respected and admired him as an artist; yet her feelings were not the sort of love that he was asking. "You could learn to love me," Kaulbach persisted. "We're both artists. We could be married; we could have a joint studio—painter and sculptor."[18] When Elisabet did not respond, he asked, "Is there someone else?"

"To be frank, Friedrich, my dear friend, *ja*, it's true, my love is pledged to a young Doctor, now in London."

Although hurt and disappointed, Kaulbach was not surprised. "I suspected that you had a lover; yet you can't blame me for trying to change your feelings. I know that you care something for me and that we enjoy being together. Why can't we make love? Your Doctor need never know." Elisabet was tempted, but she had an overwhelming feeling that Edmund was beside her. She felt suffocated. Wresting herself away from Kaulbach, she ran out of the studio in tears.

Kaulbach, a man experienced in romantic affairs, accepted his defeat. *L'Artiste* was the title that he gave to Elisabet's portrait, which he hung in the Hannover Museum beside another Elisabeth, the Empress of Austria. Art critics agreed that *L'Artiste* was Friedrich Kaulbach's masterpiece. Elisabet expressed appreciation to him not only for her beautiful likeness but also for his influence in her behalf with King George. Kaulbach kissed her hand and wished her much happiness with her doctor. Gallant and attractive, he would not be long without female companionship. Elisabet had heard gossip that a certain young lady whom Kaulbach had previously courted was hurt because he had painted Elisabet's portrait and not hers. Elisabet hoped that he would now return his affection to the lady.

When Elisabet formally presented the completed large marble bust of King George V to the Royal Family, it was well-received; Queen Marie rewarded Elisabet with a bracelet as a gift of appreciation. The King's bust was placed in the Hannover Museum, which also housed *L'Artiste*.

Because of her work in Hannover, it was not until the summer of 1860 that Elisabet completed Joachim's likeness and returned to Berlin. Her sculpture had so preoccupied her that she had not found time to write to Schopenhauer. In a letter to Herr von Doss, Schopenhauer bitterly complained that he had heard nothing from Elisabet Ney since she had left Frankfurt

— not even a "thank you" for his autographed, inscribed book
which he had sent her as a Christmas gift. Elisabet's apparent
neglect caused him to be jealous as well as suspicious, although he knew nothing of Kaulbach. He continued writing his
grievances:

> The Ney thinks it is so important to be in a Royal Court
> that she forgets about her friends — and her promises. She
> promised she would have my plaster bust cut in marble —
> said she was taking it to Münster where her father would
> cast it in marble and offer it for sale. She told me she would
> be *all alone* in Berlin working with her sculpture; yet I have
> heard nothing. She is probably too busy with some lover to
> do what she promised me.

Schopenhauer wrote other, even more disgruntled, letters
to "The Ney." These letters and accusations were becoming an
annoyance to Elisabet, especially since he demanded so much
attention and had not as yet paid her so much as a pfennig for
all her work. Finally, on March 2, 1860, she wrote to Schopenhauer explaining why she had been delayed in executing his
clay bust into plaster (excerpted here):

> And is your bust still here? How can you ask? It has
> never left my side. Now don't scold me any more; don't call
> me faithless again. I simply could not bring myself to part
> with it, which is why it has not been cast. I dared not trust
> such an important task to anyone save myself, and I have
> had to wait because I have been so crowded with work. Fort-
> night after fortnight has passed without time for me to at-
> tend to the matter.
>   Please be charitable about this delay. Can I help it if
> Schopenhauer has become my individual pride? You told me
> my friendship came to you at the most beautiful and spirit-
> ual time of your life, and meant much — consider my attitude
> toward you in the same light.
>   Your precious gift (*The World as Will and Idea*) has
> meant more to me than I can put into words. It seems to me
> that I would have to invent new words to express my sense
> of your greatness to its fullest meaning. I have a presenti-
> ment that the future will make something infinitely more of
> it than I am able to say.[19]

Elisabet concluded the letter with a promise that she
would have his plaster bust ready as soon as possible. In an at-

tempt to pacify his feelings, Elisabet enclosed a photograph of herself standing beside the bust.[20]

Schopenhauer proudly showed the photograph to his friends and told David Asher, "She and I make a very pleasing picture." After three months, Schopenhauer's bust arrived with the explanation that it was not sent sooner because the plaster had not dried sufficiently. The clay bust, the first model, had pleased the old man. But when he saw the inscription on the base of this plaster mold, he was indignant. "Art. Schopenhauer," it read. "How could she do a thing like that?" he stormed to everyone in hearing distance. "How could she abbreviate my name? My father gave me the name of Arthur because it is the same in German, French, and English. I'll not abide this indignity." Immediately he wrote to Elisabet of his piqued feelings.

After several more letters full of recriminations and complaints, Elisabet answered and explained that his first name had to be shortened to fit the space available on the base of the bust, but to please him, she would try to find a workman able to change it.[21] The best she could do, however, was to add another letter, "Arth," which was of small satisfaction to Schopenhauer; however, his feelings were soothed somewhat when Elisabet wrote to him that she would enter his bust in the Exhibition of the Berlin Academy in September. She flattered him as usual in this letter:

> How often I am thankful, even if I do not write you so, for the place of honor in the world which your portrait has brought to me. I am very proud of this work — the more so since you yourself gave me permission to make it. The memory of that first day when I called upon you and was almost thrown out of your house is a bit of queer drama, the like of which I shall never find again should I seek the world over. And consider what came of the visit! The greatest friendship — the greatest fulfillment! *Tempora mutantur!*

In this letter Elisabet also commented upon his inference that it was an *affaire de coeur* that kept her so long at King George's Court:

> You refuse to accept any other explanation for my extended sojourn there.
> My brain, being a woman's, is probably too small to form

abstract masculine philosophical judgments, but experience has taught me, too, that large–brained men are capable of understanding an aesthetic friendship, and are always prone to turn such an intimacy into an affair of the heart. This is not true in my case, at least . . . .

When an effort is made to force upon a woman's aesthetic existence the elements of nature called primitive, is it any wonder that the hothouse plant becomes a trifle nauseated with the ways of men and the world? And I ask whether this condition may not be as deemed an illness with as much right as a toothache or a headache, for instance.[22]

To placate Schopenhauer's complaints, she promised to come again to Frankfurt to visit him. But on September 21, 1860, Schopenhauer, who was apparently recovering from an earlier hemorrhage of the lungs, was sitting on the sofa in his study, where he had often conversed with Elisabet, reading his mail, which contained letters praising his bust that was on exhibit in Berlin, when, suddenly, he collapsed and died.[23]

His death saddened Elisabet, for she had grown fond of the irascible old man with his almost childlike affection for her. She found satisfaction in remembering what he had often told her: "When I'm in your presence, I'm always happier."

Berlin and Münster

These rigid spirits are the first to fall.
The strongest iron, hardened in the fire,
Most often ends in scraps and shatterings.

Sophocles

With confidence Elisabet began work again in her Lagerhaus studio. Her sculptures of Schopenhauer, Joachim, and
King George V proved her ability as a professional artist. Now
she had earned the right to be respected as a sculptor and to follow the manner of life best suited to her needs: she bobbed her
long auburn hair, and since skirts were cumbersome when she
climbed over clay pots and up and down ladders, she adopted
full breeches to wear in the studio, modestly covering the calves
of her legs with leggings; furthermore, she went alone whenever
and wherever she pleased. In gatherings of arttists and other acquaintances, she endeared herself by openly expressing her
opinions, usually liberal, on controversial subjects.

At one of these get-togethers a friend asked Elisabet if she
had heard that Friedrich Kaulbach had announced his engagement to the daughter of a prominent Hannover official. Elisa-

bet had not heard, but she was not surprised. Gossip quickly spread in Berlin's art circles that Friedrich Kaulbach had an affair with Elisabet Ney shortly before announcing his engagement to someone else.[1] Elisabet's fellow–artists were glad to repeat the rumor because many were envious of her rapid success and resented the fact that she blatantly flaunted accepted respectabilities. But Elisabet ignored her denigrators, for she knew the goal that she intended to achieve and how she intended to achieve it.

Since the completion of Schopenhauer's bust, Elisabet had received no commissions. As a result, her letters to Edmund betrayed her disheartenment. Edmund replied that his first reaction to her unhappiness was to come to her in Berlin, but he hoped that she would understand that he had committed himself and felt an obligation to Dr. Simon, as well as to others who were backing him, to continue his work in London. He tried to lift her spirits by writing encouraging letters telling her to ignore whatever unkind and envious persons might say about her, to believe in her own talent, and to continue her work as a sculptor, knowing that she had his love, encouragement, and support.

In the summer of 1861, a year and a half since she had completed her bust of Joseph Joachim in Hannover, Elisabet received a letter from her father telling her that a new Westphalian provincial parliament building was under construction in Münster with plans for eight sandstone statues of local heroes. The old fourteenth–century *Rathaus,* the *Friedenssaal,* would become a museum. Herr Ney suggested that Elisabet come to Münster and make a bid for the execution of these statues. In the hope that this project might offer an opportunity to continue her work in sculpture, she followed her father's suggestion, came to Münster, submitted her proposals, and was awarded a commission for four of the statues: Count Englebert III von der Mark, ancestor of Prussian Royalty, fourteenth century; Walter von Plattenbert, General of the German Order of Livland, sixteenth century; Justus Moser, lawyer, and Franz von Fürstenberg, founder of Maximilian Friedrich University, both eighteenth century.[2]

Herr Ney was proud when his daughter received this recognition as a sculptor in her native township. She was regarded as a celebrity for having studied with the famous sculp-

tor, Christian Rauch, having modeled busts of the King of
Hannover, Joseph Joachim, and Arthur Schopenhauer (although the noted philosopher was considered a heretic in Münster), and also having been portrayed by Friedrich Kaulbach.
Most of the townspeople had seen Elisabet's *Saint Sebastian,
Martyr,* which Bishop Müller had commissioned for the Dioce-
san Museum. Herr Ney admitted to his daughter that he realized that she had real talent when he chiseled into marble her
plaster bust of Schopenhauer. But, as usual, neither Elisabet's
mother nor brother could understand her ambition and eccentricities; in fact, Frau Ney was embarrassed by her daughter's
notoriety.

To research the lives and times of her four Münster heroes,
Elisabet obtained information concerning their personalities,
pictures, descriptions, biographical material and the manner of
dress of their era. When she began her sculpture, neighbors
and friends often dropped by the atelier to watch her. They
were shocked by her short hair, her short artist's smock, and
her breeches. They also knew that she had not been attending
Mass and had expressed some alarmingly liberal political opinions. But she was accepted because she was the daughter of
Adam Ney and still found favor with Bishop Müller, who felt
that the creator of *Saint Sebastian, Martyr,* although she had
temporarily strayed from the church, was a person with the
God-given gift of creativity and would someday return to her
faith and use her capabilities for the Lord and the Church.

Elisabet, who had admirers as well as critics, was the major focus of attention in Münster for more than a year. One admirer, a German poet, Eli Marcus, who at the age of seventy,
wrote that he remembered when he was a boy in Münster at
the time Elisabet Ney was there:

> I asked my mother who this beautiful woman was, and
> she said it was the sculptress Elisabet Ney. She was gowned
> in black velvet which left her noble white throat free, her only
> ornament a silver filigree collar four inches wide and of such
> a fragile lovliness that it appeared made of silver lace. Her
> hair was cut á *la Titian,* short and curly. Her profile was no-
> ble; she looked more like a handsome youth than a woman.
> Her manner was free and proud, but easy, and I recall with
> what grace she moved — like a young empress or queen. It is
> now well over sixty years since that day, but the impression
> which Elisabet made on that boy (myself) has never dimmed.[3]

On a pleasant fall day when Elisabet was modeling under a rose arbor in her family's garden, a friend, Valentin Müller, brought Hermann Hüffer, a professor of history at the University of Bonn, with him to call on her. Hüffer told Elisabet that he had wanted to meet her ever since he had seen her portrait, *L'Artiste,* at an art exhibition in Cologne. He also considered *Saint Sebastian* and the bust of Schopenhauer to be remarkable works of art and felt that Münster should feel honored to have her sculpt the statues of its heroes. Hüffer told her that as a child he had lived in Münster, but had not been fortunate enough to know her. From the smitten look on his face, Elisabet knew that she had acquired another admirer. Hüffer carefully documented the two weeks of their friendship in his *Lebenseriennerungen* (Reminiscenses), wherein he related his infatuation.[4]

Soon after his first meeting, Hüffer visited Elisabet again, this time at her studio, where he approved her finishing details to the statues. Hüffer contrived musical evenings at his mother's home, garden parties, or walks in the countryside to be with Elisabet. Hüffer's shyness amused her, especially on one occasion when he became so anxious to tell of his affection that he became tongue-tied, and seeing a forget-me-not flower, picked it and handed it to Elisabet, reciting from Goethe:

> You grant me the greatest joy, Tasso!
> Without a word I say to you my thoughts.[5]

Hüffer's naïvete reminded Elisabet of her friend Gottfried Keller, who also enjoyed reciting poetry. For Elisabet, Hüffer had none of the sophisticated charm of Friedrick Kaulbach, nor the intellectual sincerity of Edmund; yet he was congenial, and Elisabet encouraged his friendship.

After working for over a year, Elisabet completed her four statues, and on September 22, 1861, they were placed in the assembly hall. Elisabet, as well as Hüffer, was upset by the poor lighting and overall gloomy appearance of the hall, which provided an atmosphere that detracted from a proper appreciation of the statues. This situation prompted Hüffer to write to the *Cologne Zietung* praising the artistry of the statues and condemning the parsimony of the committee which had commissioned the statues for not providing them with adequate illumination.

When it became necessary for Hüffer to return to Bonn, Elisabet told him that she would always value their friendship. She also told him that when she left Münster, she would go to Heidelberg where she had a commission and from there to London to execute another commission and to visit a young doctor whom she had known for a long time. She planned to travel the Rhine by boat from Heidelberg on her way to England and would stop in Bonn to visit him.

When Hüffer asked if the Englishman were her lover, she answered, "I call him my 'best friend.' "

Before he left Münster, Hüffer, along with other of Elisabet's friends, suggested to the officials that the statue of Fürstenberg, considered the best of the four statues, be executed in marble and placed in the *Domplatz*. In anticipation of this proposal, Elisabet made two models of this statue to submit for the committee's preference and even prepared sketches of scenes from Fürstenberg's life to depict in relief around the base of the statue; yet after allowing her to spend her time and effort, a committee spokesman announced that no funds were available for the project.

Furious, Elisabet confronted the committee members with an imperious countenance and accused them of being unfair and misleading when they allowed her to spend months completing the models when they had no money to pay her. To add to her indignation, because of their stinginess, as she told them, the four statues were cast in impermanent sandstone and placed in such a poorly lighted room that their effectiveness was lost. She informed the members of the committee that they had only to look around them at the many statues in their ancient town which had survived for hundreds of years to realize that their miserliness had denied her art its deserved recognition by future generations of Münster.[6]

As a result of this controversy, Elisabet was dissilusioned with the entire project; her father agreed, although her mother and brother were chagrined by Elisabet's attitude.

"What a pity that I must leave this hallowed ground of Münster to return to the wicked world outside," Elisabet said to her father, who came into her studio with a carefully wrapped box. Elisabet knew. It was the Napoleonic lace. Gently she kissed his forehead. *"Danke schön, Vati, Danke schön.* I'll try to be worthy of this gift."

Upon her return to Berlin, Elisabet called upon the Bülows, where Cosima, in a despondent frame of mind, greeted her with the news that her sister Blandine had died in the past year and that she and Hans had another little daughter. But not even this new child, nor the fact that Hans was now Court Pianist to King Wilhelm, seemed to lift her spirits. "Did you know that Hans was also promoting the music of Richard Wagner to warrant recognition for his musical genius?" she asked Elisabet. "We think Wagner is the greatest musician of our generation, even including my father." When Cosima mentioned Wagner's name, Elisabet noted the first trace of animation in her face.

While visiting the Bülows, Elisabet met Baron George von Werthern, a distinguished, successful foreign diplomat engaged to Hans's cousin Gertrude von Bülow. Elisabet knew that the Baron was an intimate friend of King Wilhelm and also of one of the King's most influential advisers, Count Otto von Bismarck. The Baron commented to Elisabet that he knew that she had modeled busts of the King of Hannover, Joachim, and Schopenhauer, and had studied with Christian Rauch, and he offered her a commission for his portrait bust.[7]

Elisabet accepted readily, for not only did she have immediate need for such a commission, but also this portraiture might be an opportunity to meet the Prussian King Wilhelm. During the time that Elisabet modeled Werthen's bust, her lively conversation and attractiveness charmed the Baron. After she had completed the sculpture to his satisfaction, he remarked that he hoped to see her again.

"And I have a feeling you will, Baron," Elisabet predicted.

Now that this commission was finished, Elisabet looked to her next assignment, a bust of her friend Dr. Christian Kapp in Heidelberg. By the time Elisabet arrived there, two years had passed since she had seen Johanna, who greeted her warmly, yet seemed vague and distraught as though she were living in her own imaginary world. While Johanna's behavior was distressing, Elisabet's primary purpose was to create a bust of Herr Dr. Kapp, a project that occupied most of her time.

Being in Heidelberg again filled Elisabet with a nostalgic longing to see Edmund, for it was at the Kapp's Waldon Estate where they met and fell in love; where they had walked and talked, explored the romantic old city and had grown to know each other; where they promised each other to have an ideal life together. "I've been thinking about my 'best friend,' Edmund Montgomery, ever since I arrived in your home, Herr Kapp," Elisabet said as she worked on the clay model of his bust.

Herr Dr. Kapp said that his family had grown fond of Edmund when he came so often to their gatherings and asked what Edmund was doing. Elisabet explained that Edmund was a Doctor of Medicine in a hospital in London. Dr. Kapp told her that Edmund was by far the most intelligent young student who had joined in their discussions. It was hard to believe that Edmund had been so young at the time.

During the conversation, Johanna came in the room. "Edmund, Edmund," she said softly. "*Ja*, . . . I remember Edmund . . . Elise, you were in love with him, *ja?*" With this remark Johanna wafted out of the room without so much as glancing at her father or the bust Elisabet was modeling. Dr. Kapp sadly shook his head and told Elisabet how heartbreaking it was to see Johanna in her present condition. Elisabet could only sympathize.

In speaking of Edmund, Elisabet realized that some time had elapsed since she had heard from him, which was unusual. Perhaps she had changed her address so often lately that his letter had missed her. That evening she must write to tell him of the changes in the Kapp household. A few days later she received a letter from Edmund explaining that the reason he had not written was that he had been ill. Perhaps, he suggested, if she could come to London and sculpt the bust of the playwright, Tom Taylor, which had been commissioned, her presence would help his recovery.

Edmund's illness was disquieting news for Elisabet. Both Herr Kapp and Johanna were concerned to learn of Edmund's ill health and urged Elisabet to go to London as soon as possible. She sent a cable that she would be with him as quickly as she could make arrangements. After putting the finishing touches on the bust of Herr Kapp, she wrote to Hermann Hüffer that she had no time to see him in Bonn, but asked him if he could board her boat at Linz and travel to Cologne with her on her journey to London. Because she was worried and upset about Edmund, she felt a need for Hüffer's friendship and consolation.

According to Hüffer's account in his *Lebenserinnerungen,* on February 14, 1863, he joined Elisabet on her Rhine steamer. She confided her worries that her "best friend's" physical condition might be more serious than he had told her. Hüffer accepted his role as friend and consoler and realized how sincerely Elisabet was in love with Dr. Edmund Montgomery. She was glad that he accompanied her on the Rhine steamer trip and to the railroad depot in Cologne. After thanking him for his kindness, she continued her journey to London that night.

8

Edmund in London

...That it is only through one's works that one ought to become known.

Edmund Montgomery

After Edmund's sad farewell to Elisabet, who had departed for Frankfurt in October of 1859 to confront Schopenhauer, he left Berlin by train for Bremen, where he boarded a steamship to continue his journey to London. While relaxing in a deck chair, and gazing into the North Sea before him, he thought of Elisabet and the possibility of a long separation from her and of his future in London. Although his friend and benefactor Dr. Simon assured him that the proposed position in St. Thomas's Hospital would allow opportunities for research, he wondered whether or not he could continue his experiments to explain scientifically the origin, organization, and development of life.

In his reverie, he recalled his mother, a tall, beautiful, and intelligent, yet impetuous and quick-tempered woman, with whom he conversed only in French. He remembered how he had not been allowed to attend school with other boys, but had

had his own tutor; how he had acquired books rather than boys as his companions.[1]

He had encountered other families with fathers and asked his mother, "Do I have a *Père*?"

"*Mai oui*," had been her answer.

"Then where is he?" he had asked. "Why doesn't he come to see us?"

Evading his questions, his mother had told him that his father lived in Scotland and that because he was a barrister, his work required him to live there. As Edmund had grown older, he had suspected the true answer, but had not wanted to confront it.

Such thoughts brought him the painful recollection of an incident when he had joined some boys at play in the park. One of them had said, "We don't want you to play with us because you think you're too good for the *Gymnasium*. You have your own tutor and wear fancy clothes, but we know about you — you're a bastard."

Hurt and humiliated, he had not replied and had left for his home where the *Buben* (boys) would not see his tears. So they were the fine fellows, he had thought; so they were the ones who had called themselves his friends. Filled with resentment, he had asked his mother the truth about his father. Expecting such an eventuality, she had gone to her desk, brought him a key and a leather box, told him to unlock the box, and to read for himself.

He had opened the box and had found a photograph of a handsome man with the accompanying description:

> This is a copy of a portrait of Duncan McNeil, Solicitor General for Scotland, Member of Parliament from Argyll-shire, Ordinary Lord of the Session, and Lord Justice-General and President of the Court of Session. Born on the Island of Oransay, August 1793; educated at St. Andrews University, with honors in mathematics, awarded M.D. degree; studied law in Edinburgh; admitted to the Scottish bar in 1861. The original of this portrait hangs in the National Portrait Gallery in Edinburgh next to a portrait of his father, John McNeil, Baron of Colonsay.[2]

Another paper had been a legal document, an acknowledged claim by Isabella Davidson Montgomery for support and to some "other person connected with her," against the es-

tate of Duncan McNeil.[3] Edmund's mother told him that she
wanted him to have these legal papers if anything should happen to her.

"Then I am a bastard!" he cried.

"You could never understand," she had sobbed. "I'll not
try to explain. I was very young; your father was over forty, an
important barrister; to him, we had a love affair; to me, he was
my love, my life. Son, you are too young to understand."

"*Mais non.*" he had said, "I do not understand."

While the steamship churned through the water, Edmund
sat motionless in his deck chair and allowed himself to remember his most intense moments of depression with the knowledge of his illegitimacy, and how he had thought of suicide. His
mother, however, had filled her life with support of liberal leaders in Germany, whom she compared to the patriots of Scotland, and with her absorption with her Scottish Presbyterian
religion.[4] Upon her insistence, Edmund had attended the En-
glish-speaking Presbyterian Church in Frankfurt, but the
more he had studied the set doctrines and beliefs of the church,
the more determined he had become not to accept them. To be
confirmed also would mean to reveal his birth and background.
When he asked his mother about his father's religion, she had
said that he did not belong to any church, although he was a
moral man. She had explained that she had received forgiveness for her sins, had been saved by the grace of her Lord and
Savior Jesus Christ, and had said, "My son, if you'll accept
Jesus, you can also be saved."

Resolutely he had refused to accept the church's doctrine
and had spent anguished hours pondering his destiny. He had
thought: I'll go my own way, even if it is to hell. Although he
had been only sixteen, he had absorbed and agreed with the
pessimistic philosophy of Schopenhauer,[5] the contemplation of
which returned his thoughts to Elisabet. That she would succeed in winning over the old cynic, he was positive. Because of
her, he was inspired to continue his search, through science, for
the answer to the why and wherefore of life; because of their
love, he felt the strength and courage to succeed.

As he shook himself from his daydreaming, his ship approached the estuary of the Thames and would soon dock in
London. Although Edmund was accepted as a Scotsman, his
life and education in Germany resulted in a manner of expres-

sion and thinking that was essentially German; he was coming to London as a stranger. He recalled that Dr. Simon had told him that his English had a German accent.

Upon disembarking, he hired a hansom cab, with the driver seated outside on a perch behind and above the passengers, for the first trip that he could remember through the teeming streets of London filled with carriages and horse-drawn omnibuses, for his ride to the hospital to meet Dr. Simon.[6]

During the time in 1859, when Edmund had been interning in Prague and Vienna, he had become acquainted with vacationing Dr. and Lady Jane Simon. Dr. Simon was alert to discover intelligent young doctors who might be persuaded to intern in St. Thomas's Hospital. Dr. Simon was interested in scientific research as well as in the practice of medicine, and he appreciated Edmund's similar inquisitiveness. The friendship which developed prompted Dr. Simon to obtain the appointment for Edmund at St. Thomas's.[7]

Dr. Simon welcomed Edmund, who was eager to see the hospital and to learn what his duties would be. While touring the hospital, Dr. Simon explained that although the hospital had adequate facilities for Edmund's experiments, the salary was not adequate for his needs. Because Edmund was not yet licensed to practice medicine in England, Dr. Simon found a position where Edmund was allowed to practice as a resident physician in the German Hospital, which treated German immigrants; the two positions should pay enough to meet his expenses.

These arrangements pleased Edmund, especially because Dr. Simon encouraged his research project. Later, again through Dr. Simon's recommendations, Edmund obtained a residency in Bermondsey Dispensary, a charity clinic serving the slum area of London. Soon Edmund was spending hours in the laboratory making microscopic examinations of various types of cells and performing innumerable experiments, which he carefully analyzed in copious notes. At St. Thomas's Hospital he was the Curator of the Hospital's museum and Demonstrator of Morbid Anatomy, which was not the most cheerful of jobs, Edmund concluded.

Always a student, Edmund studied the scientific books and journals available. Of special interest to him was the recent work by Charles Darwin entitled, *The Origin of Species,* the thesis of which was that biological species originated through evolution and natural selection. Although Edmund did not completely agree with Darwin, he recognized the meticulous care and thoroughness of this research. Darwin had confined his evolutionary hypothesis only to the organic realm, wherein Edmund agreed with him that the evolutionary principle was operative through the universe; however, Edmund carried Darwin's thesis a step further than Darwin was willing to go, proposing that animate forms have evolved from inanimate.[8] At scientific meetings, Edmund discussed his ideas with Darwin.

The Bermondsey Infirmary, where Edmund was resident physician, was located in one of the worst slum areas of London, where the most wretched of the poor were treated. "The cruelty and impoverishment in this district shouldn't be tolerated in a nation that considers itself to be civilized," Edmund complained to Dr. Simon, who, among his other positions, was head of the British Board of Health and Sanitation.

Dr. Simon agreed, but explained that as always, his department was not allocated sufficient funds to deal adequately with that cesspool of a slum. He was glad that Edmund was interested in the fate of the poor slum-dwellers, because many doctors objected to treating such a bedraggled lot.

Because of his resentment against the poverty and inequality that he saw daily and read about in the popular novels of Charles Dickens, Edmund sought the company of similar thinking liberals, one of whom, Karl Blind, a German liberal from Baden-Baden, had been forced to flee his country during the political upheavals in 1848-49 and to settle in London, the only place allowing him to immigrate.

Herr Blind's step-daughter, Mathilde, a precocious young writer, recently returned from a trip on the continent, told Edmund that in France there could soon be a revolt against Louis Napoleon, and in Italy she recognized discontent against the Monarchy and the Papacy. She spoke of a freedom fighter, Giuseppe Garibaldi, who had defeated the French in Sicily, Palermo, and Naples, and had aroused such fanatic devotion that Italy's King Victor Emmanuel wanted him out of the country.[9] Mathilde gave Edmund a copy of *Mémories de Garibaldi,* written by Garibaldi's friend Alexander Dumas, and also gave him

078446

Howard County Library
Big Spring, Texas

a book of sonnets that she had written, inscribed to E. M. from
M. B., 1859.[10]

While living in London, Edmund thought of his father, a
member of the House of Lords. Often in reading the *London
Times,* he searched for some notice of Lord Duncan McNeil
(Lord Colonsay), or news from Argyllshire in Scotland. An article attracted his notice. It stated that Queen Victoria would be
attending a session of Parliament where a subject on the agen-
da was consideration of a dispute over a Scottish claim to be
presented by Lord Colonsay, Chief Advocate of Scotland.
Within himself Edmund debated whether or not to attend the
session. Did he want to see his father? Should he make himself
known? Finally his curiosity overcame his reticence, and he
went to the House of Lords.

Because the Queen was expected, the gallery was crowded;
however, Edmund found standing room. The chamber, where
the Peers of England sat on long leather-upholstered benches
rather than on chairs with desks, was elaborately decorated in
rococo style with rich filigree and carvings over almost every
foot of the walls and the balcony. Light from the stained glass
windows illumined the statues of all the Kings and Queens of
England since the Norman Conquest in 1066 and also the statuary around the walls of the Barons who had forced the Magna
Carta from King John in 1215.

Upon the approach of the Queen, everyone rose, including
the formally dressed Lords and the black-robed, white-wigged
Jurists. Preceded by her colorful guards, Queen Victoria,
short, fat, and not too attractive, entered wearing voluminous
skirts, which made her look even rounder, but her regal manner
and bejeweled Royal Crown left no mistake, as she was seated
under the gilded canopy of the Royal Throne, that she was the
ruler of England.

As Edmund searched the faces of the Lords in the Chamber, he saw a tall man dressed in his robe and white wig, rise to
address the assembled law-makers and recognized him immediately from his photograph as Lord Duncan McNeil, his father. According to the document that Edmund had seen, the
year 1793 was his father's birthdate, which would place his
present age at sixty-nine, but his appearance and vigor were
that of a younger man; his speech concerning the rightfulness
of the Scottish claim was forceful and to the point. With pride

and resentment, Edmund watched as his father, a titled jurist, a leader in his country, addressed the Assembly. After seeing his father, Edmund knew that he could never make himself known; he had no desire to risk any further humiliation. Too discontented to stay longer, he rushed outside to waste the remainder of the afternoon wandering beside the Thames, feeling unhappy and frustrated, wondering what his life might have been.

This experience renewed his determination to excel, with the result that he was recommended for membership in the Royal College of Physicians in London. The following notice from the Annals of the College and from the minutes of the Censor's Board of December 19, 1862, states: "Dr. Edmund Montgomery produced the diploma of a Doctor of Medicine of the University of Würtzburg, dated February 18, 1858, together with the certificates of medical studies and clinical attendance at St. Thomas's Hospital. He was examined in Latin, French, Anatomy, Physiology, and in Pathology and Therapeutics. He was admitted a member of this College on 22nd of December, 1862."[11]

Dr. Simon, as a "fellow and member of the College," sponsored Edmund and testified regarding his moral character and conduct, and as a consequence, Dr. Edmund Montgomery's name was added as a member of the Royal College of Physicians. He was also licensed to practice medicine in England; however, Edmund's continuing preparation of a scientific paper, entitled "On the Formation of 'So-Called' Cells in Animal Bodies," a minutely detailed and illustrated presentation containing his observations and conclusions concerning his experiments, left him no time for the practice of medicine.

While performing a dissection during the first week in February 1863, Edmund suffered an accidental knife wound.[12] Blood poisoning developed and he became dangerously ill. Dr. Simon attended him medically, and after Edmund's release from the hospital, Lady Simon insisted that he stay under their care in their home. As soon as he had sufficiently recovered, he experienced a longing to see Elisabet and wrote to her about being ill and received her reply that she would be with him as soon as possible.

Because of his lack of physical activities during his developing years, Edmund had never experienced robust health.

Since he had been in London, his physical constitution was strained by working at the equivalent of two jobs, one in the laboratory at St. Thomas's, and the other at the German Hospital and the Bermondsey Dispensary, where he was constantly exposed to contagious and communicable diseases, and where his lungs were further weakened by London's cold, damp weather.

Because of the care he received from the Simons, Edmund felt well enough to meet Elisabet's ship when it docked at the pier in London on February 15, 1863. "*Meine* Elisabet, *meine Liebchen,*" he said as he hugged and kissed her. "For over three years I've longed for you. We mustn't be separated again — ever." As happy as Edmund was to see her, that is how happy Elisabet was to see him. But she was concerned about his coughing, loss of weight, and slight fever every day.

"Now that I'm with you, 'my dearest friend,' I'll take care of you. You'll see how being together will lift your spirits," Elisabet reassured him.

When Elisabet met Dr. and Lady Simon, she expressed her gratitude for their kindness and care for Edmund. The Simons told her that they considered Edmund as a son, and they were sure that her presence would be more effective than medicine. Dr. Simon told Elisabet that he hoped she would enjoy her first visit to London. He also understood that she had a commission to model a bust of the playwright Tom Taylor.

Elisabet said, "And I have a feeling that you, Dr. Simon, were influential in my obtaining it. I'm grateful to you for an opportunity to create a work of sculpture in London."

To watch his Elisabet charm the Simons gave Edmund a feeling of gladness, which only increased when the reunited lovers spent the evening at Elisabet's hotel. They had much to share with each other during the time that they were apart. For hours they talked and discovered that their desire for each other was as strong as when they first met. They were fulfilled in the passion of their love.

Edmund wanted to spend the days quietly together, but Elisabet was eager to begin work on the bust of Tom Taylor, and wanted to know about the playwright. Edmund explained that Tom Taylor was a dramatist, barrister, and art critic as well as secretary to the Board of Health, where Dr. Simon knew him.

When they visited Mr. Taylor, they found him to be an amiable subject, but communication between them seemed a major difficulty. Elisabet's English was far from perfect, and although Taylor's grandparents had come from Frankfurt, he spoke little German and neither he nor Elisabet was fluent in French. "So I'm to be the interpreter," Edmund surmised. "But let me warn you, Mr. Taylor, that Miss Ney will probably understand what you say, even if she says she doesn't."

To ease the communication difficulties, Edmund attended the sittings. "And also to chaperon," he reminded them. The modeling of the bust went well and when it was completed, Taylor was pleased and promised Elisabet that he would use what influence he had to have the plaster model entered in the Royal Academy Exhibition the next year.

Because Elisabet was with him, Edmund's health improved; yet he was still too weak to follow a full schedule at the Hospital. But because there was always a possibility of Edmund's developing consumption (about which the medical profession knew little in the way of treatment except to recommend a mild climate), Dr. Simon cautioned him not to over-exert. Although Edmund regretted not being strong enough to continue his working schedule, he gave up his job at the hospital and retained only his position as Curator of the Hospital Museum.

Elisabet's obvious enjoyment of this London visit pleased Edmund. Dr. and Lady Simon entertained her and treated her as a recognized sculptor and introduced her to such eminent persons as the art critic John Ruskin and Lady Simon's friend Thomas Woolner, who represented sculpture in the Pre-Raphaelite Brotherhood in London.[13] "Surely some of these people could introduce me to Queen Victoria," Elisabet speculated to Edmund, who discouraged this idea.

"Elisabet, you and I know of your competence and reputation as an artist, but somehow I feel that such knowledge has yet to reach Her Majesty."

These pleasant days in London ended in April of 1863, when Edmund suffered a relapse with a diagnosis of consumption.[14] Although Dr. Simon explained to Edmund that his disease was in the first stages, and with special care in a warm climate could be arrested, his experience in its treatment was that, even with a subsiding of the disease, the patient must always live prudently and always be aware of the possibility of a recurrence. Because Edmund knew that Dr. Simon was sincerely interested in his future, he asked his advice as to the best course to follow.

Knowing that Edmund and Elisabet had been in love for ten years, Dr. Simon suggested that they marry and go to Madeira, a Portugese island approximately 350 miles from the west coast of Africa in the North Atlantic, where the climate was perfect for a consumptive. For that reason, many of Europe's rich and important persons had moved there, or at least spent their winters there; so he felt sure that Edmund could acquire enough patients to earn a livelihood in the practice of medicine and that Miss Ney could obtain commissions from wealthy patrons.

Edmund welcomed this advice because he wanted to marry Elisabet, but he knew how she felt about her career, and remembered how they had promised that their love was to be above social conventionalities; yet he also knew the hurt of illegitimacy.

After Edmund's conversation with Dr. Simon, he told Elisabet about Dr. Simon's advice concerning Madeira, when she came to visit him in the hospital. "I've heard of Madeira," she said. "Princess Elisabeth of Austria vacationed there. I understand that it's warm and beautiful, *meine Liebchen*. You should go."

"Sit beside me, Elisabet," Edmund said, "I've loved you since the day we met in Heidelberg and I want you to marry me. You've insisted on first achieving success in your career, that we have no ties but our love, but now you are successful. Marry me. We'll go to Madeira, where Dr. Simon assures me that my health will improve to the extent that I'll be able to practice medicine and you can set up a studio. Because so many wealthy persons come to the island, you should have no trouble receiving commissions."

"I'll go," Elisabet agreed, "But why marriage? We've talked of this before. Why shackle our love with such a tradition-bound ritual?"

Edmund did not answer immediately, then said, "Elisabet, I've never told you, although you've probably surmised, but my mother and father were not married. I've felt the cruelty of ostracism because of it, and I would not want a child of mine to have such an experience."

"I have no intention of having children." replied Elisabet, "especially at age twenty-eight [actually thirty]. You know how much I love you and you also know that I'm dedicated to my career; I see no reason for marriage."

Edmund pleaded, "If you love me, you will follow Dr. Simon's advice, marry me and we'll go to Madeira together."

Elisabet hesitated, "My 'best friend' give me time to think. I'll answer you tomorrow." Gently kissing his cheek, she left the hospital room. When she returned the next day, she made the following proposals: "Edmund, I do love you enough to marry you if you'll agree that, first, I retain my name, Elisabet Ney. For a woman to change her name to her husband's is a subtle form of slavery. For years I've worked to have my name recognized; also, I'm proud of my Ney heritage. Second, you must agree that our marriage will be kept our private knowledge. I need to settle my affairs. And, further, I've received a commission from the University of Berlin to sculpt a bust of the celebrated chemist Dr. Eilhardt Mitscherlich, which I want to execute as soon as possible because he's very old, and I know how quickly old men can die; also, I need to close my studio in the Lagerhaus, and after that I have unfinished business in Münster. If you'll agree to these conditions, as soon as I finish my tasks in Germany, I'll return to London; then we can be married and leave for Madeira."

With reluctance Edmund agreed to her conditions. "*Meine Leibchen*, I realize that you've earned the right to keep your identity. I promise that in public I'll refer to you as 'Miss Ney' or 'Elisabet Ney,' never as 'Mrs. Montgomery' or 'my wife.' And I agree to wait until you return from Germany for us to begin the rest of our lives together."[15]

When Elisabet returned to London from Germany on September 10, 1863, Edmund was glad that she noted the improvement in his physical condition. In telling him of her activities while she was away, she related that she had successfully completed the marble bust of Mitscherlich, which was awarded a place of honor in the Hall of Science in Berlin University. "And, Edmund, Dr. Mitscherlich died on August 28, only two weeks after I completed the sculpture. I rushed this work more than I would normally. It's well that I did. When I went to Münster, I was able to arrange a better placement for my statues in the parliament building and to collect some money still owed me. My friend Hermann Hüffer, whom I've told you about, was very helpful to me in dealing with those block-headed, ignoramus Münster officials."

"Did you tell your family about our plans to marry?" Edmund asked.

"*Nein*, I did not. I told them that I plan to spend the winter in Madeira to enjoy the mild climate and the possibility of obtaining commissions from the wealthy persons who live and vacation there. When do we leave, *mein Leibst*? I'm eager to see Madeira."

Edmund, even more intent than Elisabet to marry and to depart for Madeira, realized that he should consult with Dr. Simon and the other doctors who were treating him as to when he could travel. Because he showed such improvement with his set routine of treatment, the consensus of the medical advice was that he should continue the same regime as long as possible, at least until cold weather. Dr. Simon felt that the drastic changes of marriage, moving to a strange place, finding living quarters, with all the necessary adjustments, could possibly cause a setback in his recovery.

When Elisabet heard these recommendations, she suggested, "Why shouldn't I go to Madeira before Edmund, find living accommodations, a studio, and whatever else is necessary? We can be married in Madeira."

With both Edmund and Dr. Simon in agreement with her offer, Elisabet left London in the middle of September for Madeira.[16]

9

Marriage in Madeira

... Then in the marriage union, the independence of the husband and wife will be equal, their dependence mutual, and their obligations reciprocal.

Lucretia Mott

After Elisabet left Edmund and the dreary climate of England to sail south toward Africa, she welcomed the warmth and brilliance of the sun and the first glimpse of the green volcanic island of Madeira, called the "Rock Garden of the Atlantic," rising six thousand feet up from the ocean. When her ship docked in Funchal, a port guarded by an ancient fortress, sunlight broke over the headland to the east and flooded the harbor with golden light. Dozens of small fishing boats, filled with men and women selling embroidery work, wickerware, and brightly colored faïence (Italian–style pottery), and with small boys who dived for coins, surrounded the ship. As Elisabet watched the scene, a native girl festooned her with a boa of colorful orchids, bougainvillaea, camellias, hibiscus, and other tropical flowers.

This little port, the capital, with clean, sandy beaches, narrow tree-lined streets, and white stone houses with flowering gardens terraced on the surrounding green mountains, was built on such rugged terrain that travel by carriage, or even horseback, was difficult. When Elisabet came ashore, to transport her to her hotel up the steep narrow cobblestone street, the natives seated her in a contraption made of a strip of yard-wide canvas strung from the shoulders of two strong men. Later, when she related to Edmund this novel and relaxing means of travel, she said that she felt like a truncated half-moon with her head and feet greeting the public. She knew that she looked ridiculous, but so did everyone else who rode in a hammock.

As soon as possible Elisabet began her search for a suitable dwelling where she and Edmund could live. Her choice was a vine-covered villa, known as *Formosa* (beautiful), situated on a mountainside with sunshine, fresh sea breezes, and a splendid view of the ocean. With remodeling, she could convert it into living quarters, with a studio for her, and a study and laboratory for Edmund. She hung a hammock between two trees in the villa's blossoming garden to rest and admire the lush tropical setting. She was surprised to learn that supplies must be brought up the steep mountainside on sleighs drawn by oxen, which considerably slowed the construction time.

As soon as Edmund received word from Elisabet, two weeks later, that she had purchased a studio-villa, that the country was beautiful and the weather like springtime, he boarded a ship in London bound for Madeira and arrived after a week's restful voyage. His spirits were lifted by the sight of Elisabet waiting to welcome him and by the warmth and beauty of the country. Although he approved of Elisabet's purchase of the villa, he decided that until the renovations were completed, he could rest and be more comfortable at a hotel on Avenida Arriga. That evening, with a bottle of mellow Madeira wine, they toasted Edmund's swift recovery and their future together.

The day following Edmund's arrival, November 7, 1863, ten years after they first met, Edmund insisted that they go to the British Consulate in Funchal to be married. The Consul legally performed the marriage and their recorded license certificate read:

Edmund Montgomery, age: twenty-eight; condition:
bachelor; occupation: Doctor of Medicine; place of residence:
Funchal, Madeira; father's name and occupation: Duncan
Montgomery, Advocate.

Elisabet Ney, age: twenty-eight; condition: spinister; occupation: none given; place of residence: Funchal, Madeira;
father's name and occupation: Johann Adam Ney, land proprietor.

Witnesses: two members of the staff of the British Consulate.[1]

After this very brief ceremony, the newly-weds, Dr. Montgomery and his bride, Miss Ney, returned to the hotel. This
event had not gone unnoticed by the European community.
Because Funchal was a self-contained village, isolated even
from the rest of the island by mountains, the European residents, mostly Englishmen and a few Germans, had little to do
for entertainment except to visit the English and Portugese
clubs, to listen to a daily band concert and to exchange all the
gossip they could unearth. Miss Ney and Dr. Montgomery
added a new spark of interest to the latter pastime. Word was
quickly to spread that the newly arrived couple were an unusual pair.

As usual Elisabet and Edmund paid little notice to the
wagging tongues around them. They enjoyed each other, the
quiet beauty of the island, and the native customs such as the
Christmas feast of an ox barbequed over an open pit and served
with vegetables, tropical fruits, and much wine. Then on New
Year's Eve, a special holiday to Elisabet and Edmund, they
watched the display of spectacular fireworks.

In their peaceful and secluded privacy, Edmund's health
improved, but Elisabet's restless energy was too contained.
When she discovered that Lady Marian Alford and her son,
Lord Brownlow, a consumptive, were in Funchal, she obtained
an introduction. Elisabet knew that Lady Alford, a well-
known patron of the arts, had paid generous commissions for
sculpture by John Gibson in Rome and to his protegee Harriet
Hosmer. Although Lady Alford may have had misgivings
about the unconventionality of Miss Ney and the Doctor, life
in Funchal was dull; so she welcomed news from England and
the continent, especially the interesting anecdotes that Elisabet told about persons in royal and artistic circles.

Lady Alford's son, Lord Brownlow, a frail young man in

his twenties, liked Edmund immediately and asked him to be his physician. Because Edmund was also a victim of consumption, he was in an excellent position to understand, to prescribe, and to supervise treatment, and the young Lord's health improved under Edmund's care. Soon Lady Alford commissioned Elisabet to sculpt a statuette of Lord Brownlow and a miniature bust of herself.[2]

Elisabet was pleased to have this work to do, and that night she dreamed of two angels — two children smiling and holding out their arms to her, disappearing into a cloud — only to reappear again, beckoning for her to follow as they drifted away. A few days after this dream, when Elisabet was being carried through the town in the customary hammock, she saw two cherubic little boys, approximately three and four years of age, playing in their garden. Impulsively she knocked on the door of the house where the children were playing outside and requested of the surprised German mother, Frau Elisabeth Lewald, permission to sculpt the two little brothers.

After Frau Lewald agreed, Elisabet spent many happy hours creating the first idealistic work she had done since modeling in her father's studio. The two little boys, Karl and Theodore,[3] were so natural and unaffected that Elisabet loved them both and modeled one with his arm around his brother, apparently leading him onward; the other child carried a torch in his upraised arm. Both children looked upward with concentrated attention.

In later years, Elisabet wrote the following description of this statue:

> It represents two children with heads uplifted and eyes directed upward, moving toward a height. Both say "upward" in every line of their figures. It is a work of intense youthful conviction and conveys unmistakably the fixed ideas of the artist's life. Studied in the light of her then and ever afterward, it is a declaration of independence for all who chafe at convention; for women as well as for men; for herself in particular just as a human being, irrespective of any thought of her sex.[4]

The statue pleased Edmund as much as Elisabet and he suggested that the boys appeared like spirits or sprites, two genii, especially since Elisabet dreamt of them as spirits. The statue became *Lés Génies Frères,* but Elisabet usually referred to it as *Die Brüder Genii.*

When Lady Alford saw the *Genii* statue, she agreed that it was lovely and told Elisabet that it was the sort of work that she should create rather than portraits. She said that her friend Harriet Hosmer specialized in abstract sculpture and that several American sculptresses had studios in Rome. The American author Nathaniel Hawthorne had called them "The White Marmoreal Flock" and had used Harriet Hosmer as his example when he wrote his book *The Marble Faun.*

Bristling at these cutting remarks, Elisabet could not refrain from asking, "I suppose you've heard of my teacher, the famous Christian Rauch?"

Lady Alford had heard of Rauch, but in her opinion he could not compare with John Gibson.[5]

When Elisabet completed the statuette and minature bust, Lady Alford was pleased with the statue of her son, but seemed puzzled by her own likeness. Instinctively Elisabet had portrayed a conceited, garrulous, unattractive woman in the image of Lady Alford, much as she had done in the medallion of Cosima von Bülow. In any event, Lady Alford was not flattered by the art work. Instead of paying Elisabet a sum reasonably expected, she presented her with an elaborately embroidered ball gown. Although Lady Alford was oblivious to the fact, her treatment only increased Elisabet's determination to become such an excellent sculptor that even the likes of Lady Alford would recognize her talent.

To accomplish this goal, Elisabet decided to create what was in her heart. After years of separation, she and Edmund were finally together with ample time to enjoy each other. Amid the beautiful scenery of *Formosa,* with its relaxed atmosphere, Elisabet was inspired to model a bust of her "best friend," as well as a self-portrait. She became so interested in creating Edmund's likeness, however, that she neglected to complete the details of her own. Her bust of Edmund revealed his strength of character in his well-defined, handsome features; it also captured a touch of wistfulness in his eyes and mouth. The result was an artistic tribute to her love.

The days passed quickly with Elisabet enjoying her modeling and with Edmund engaging in some medical practice as well as in his ever-consuming scientific research. From Lon-

don, Elisabet received news that her bust of Tom Taylor had
been entered in the Royal Academy Exhibition in the spring of
1864, and that the bronze statuette of Lord Brownlow was
shown in the Berlin Art Academy Exhibition in September.[6]

After a happy and productive year for Elisabet and for Edmund, whose health continued to improve, Lord Brownlow became restless and bored and decided to visit his mother's estate in Menton on the French Riviera and asked Edmund to accompany him as his physician. Being concerned over her son's
physical condition, Lady Alford humored his wishes. Because
he was aware that the young man was growing weaker and
would require his medical attention, Edmund agreed to accompany Lord Brownlow and Lady Alford to Menton.[7]

Although Elisabet enjoyed Madeira, she realized that future commissions might be difficult to obtain and that life on
the island without her "best friend" would be frustrating; yet
she could not imagine herself living as a guest of Lady Alford.
Because she wanted the sculptures of Edmund and *Die Brüder
Genii* carved into marble, she decided that while Edmund was
on the Riviera, she would go to Munich to accomplish this. Before she left Funchal, Elisabet told Lady Alford, "When I've
finished my work in Munich, I intend to open my own studio in
Rome. I also have reason to believe that I'll model a bust of
His Holiness Pope Pius IX."[8] Actually she knew of no one who
could intercede to the Pope for her except perhaps Bishop
Müller, but she was no longer sure of his feelings about her; yet
she felt impelled to impress Lady Alford that Elisabet Ney
was as important an artist as Harriet Hosmer.

After the two statues were cut in marble, Elisabet left
Munich for Rome and early in 1865 opened her studio in the
section of the city where most of the artists' studios were located. In Rome, however, she had no circle of artistic friends
such as she had known in Berlin, and having been a student of
Rauch did not have the same prestige in Italy as that of being
a disciple of John Gibson.

Still thinking of gaining prestige by creating a portrait of
the Pope, Elisabet was drawn to Vatican City, where she understood that His Holiness would appear that day to bless the
multitudes crowding into St. Peter's Square. Upon entering
St. Peter's Cathedral, the greatest citadel of Christendom,
Elisabet was overpowered by the magnificence inside: the

scent and haze from the incense was so thick that she could only vaguely perceive the gold, jewels, and gilded shrines and chapels. The Cathedral appeared to her more like a city with marble streets and a golden sky than a sanctuary containing forty-four altars, 748 columns, 400 statues, as well as a confessional for every prominent language in the world. With her knowledge of art, the masterpieces of Michelangelo, Raphael, Reni, Domenichino, Canova, and so many others; the statuary on the tombs of 132 Popes; the sepulchre of Saint Peter, with its grand golden High Altar appearing as a pearl within the gigantic dome above; and the glorifying art of Michelangelo that filled the dome,[9] thrilled and excited her.

In all this grandeur, Elisabet felt insignificant. When she heard the cries, "Viva Pio Nono. Viva Pio Nono," she hurried out to push through the crowds just as His Holiness Pope Pius IX appeared on the balcony overlooking the Square. When he was elected Pope in 1846, Elisabet remembered that she had been a girl in Münster and had listened to the nuns, who told her about him. The Holy Father, a calm, handsome man of seventy-three, dressed completely in white, raised his arms upward, with full Papal gesture, to outline the sign of the Cross for his apostolic benediction to the throng, of cheering people below him.

After witnessing the awe and reverence that the populace demonstrated for their spiritual and temporal ruler, Elisabet realized that she had small possibility of ever being granted a sitting from His Holiness. Discouraged, she returned to her studio and wrote about her experience to Edmund in Menton. As always he was concerned whenever Elisabet was downhearted and unhappy. As he had done in the past, he made a suggestion that she model someone who was famous, but also accessible, such as Giuseppe Garibaldi, the freedom fighter of Italy. Because such a person appealed to her, she wrote to Edmund for more information and said that she would try to persuade Garibaldi to become her next subject.

10

Garibaldi and *Prometheus*

Here I wait a fresh call to arms.
Giuseppe Garibaldi

When Edmund received Elisabet's letter for more information about Garibaldi, he wrote that he had first learned of the
General's accomplishments from friends in London and had
read his biography by Alexander Dumas. According to Edmund, Garibaldi was regarded as a rebel and a heretic by the
Catholics and Monarchists, but acclaimed as a charismatic
emancipator by the poor and underprivileged. The latter supported his fight for freedom and made up his volunteer red-
shirted army. Money for Garibaldi's battles for freedom and
unification of Italy came from liberal sympathizers all over Europe.[1] He had led a successful revolt in Sicily and had captured
Palermo, Naples, and Volturno in Italy. Edmund further wrote
that he understood that at the present time Garibaldi was apparently in retirement at his retreat on the island of Caprera.

After following Edmund's advice about obtaining letters
of introduction as well as writing personally to Garibaldi, Elisabet remembered that her friend Ludmilla Assing,[2] now living

in Florence and a known supporter of the movement to unify Italy, would surely know Garibaldi and would recommend her, which Ludmilla was glad to do.

A few weeks after Garibaldi received these letters, he sent Elisabet an invitation to visit Caprera and perhaps to model his likeness. Caprera, as Elisabet discovered, was a three-by-four mile island off the north coast of Sardinia, purchased by Garibaldi in 1856 for his home. Whenever he was not at sea or engaged in a military campaign, he lived there with his family, friends, and supporters. She also learned that the only means of reaching the island was by a once-a-month steamer from Genoa to the nearby island of La Maddaleno.

Because Elisabet was convinced that she could persuade Garibaldi to sit for her, after making the many necessary arrangements, in May of 1865, she departed from Genoa for La Maddaleno. To record this sojourn, she kept a diary, written in her individual style of German-English, entitled "My Time With General Garibaldi."[3] In Maddaleno she was met at the Dearty Inn by a red-shirted secretary sent by Garibaldi. She sent her card to Garibaldi by the secretary, with the message that she would arrive at Caprera in the late afternoon. To her dismay, she found that to reach the small island of Caprera, she must hire a bark or a dingy and sail or be rowed across the choppy water to Caprera's rocky shore, then walk a quarter of a mile up a rugged path to the main house.

It was seven in the evening before Elisabet finally arrived; however, a servant, also wearing a red shirt, was waiting at the dock to escort her. Even in the semi-darkness, Elisabet could discern that the main house was large and comfortable and the smell of the fresh sea breeze and flowers reminded her of Madeira.

Garibaldi was not in evidence, however, when the servant knocked on the door of Garibaldi's room, Garibaldi answered by ringing a handbell. At this signal, the man ushered Elisabet into Garibaldi's bedroom.

Regarding this introduction, Elisabet wrote in her journal that everything was different from what she had expected. Garibaldi was sitting in bed wearing a red shirt with a spotted woolen poncho thrown over his legs. He greeted her cordially and told the servant to bring another chair because, as she noticed, his trousers were on the one beside his bed. When he asked if she spoke French because he was not fluent in German, she replied that she knew only a little French and English. Elisabet told the General, "Now I have crossed Portugal, Spain and France to come here and to ask you to sit for me. I know I will do well your bust; what answer will you give me?"

Garibaldi said that he had decided to sit for her when he heard that she had arrived in Maddaleno. "What time will you begin?"

"Tomorrow at once, very early," was her reply. When Garibaldi asked how long she would stay in Maddaleno, she said, "Only for doing your bust."

When she started to leave, Garibaldi asked if she were afraid of the sea so late in the evening. She replied, "Nein, I am an old sailor; so I have no fear."

He motioned for her to come to him, reached up and pulled her head down to kiss her gently on the forehead as a guarantee that she was really welcome. Elisabet wrote: "I went then, silent; bearing with me a immens [immense] weight of feeling and thought. A grand satisfaction entered with me, but undescribable was the motion of my soul at the same time. How will I fulfill my test? which I see so immens, but so clear! . . .

"Scarcely I slept the night; most early I wished to start. Seven I arrived at Caprera with the necessary things, which I brought from Genoa."[4]

In the daylight Elisabet could see the handsome white stone house with its adjoining buildings outlined against the granite cliff. The style of the house was that of the South American farmhouses that Garibaldi had seen as a youth, with spacious rooms, tall windows, and a flat roof. Surrounding the buildings were gardens of grapevines and fig, chestnut, and orange trees. Fields of corn and grain as well as potatoes and beans were framed by flowering shrubs and trees. Beyond lay the domain of farm animals hedged by a stone fence.[5]

Because Elisabet did not want to disturb Garibaldi any more than was necessary, she explained that he did not need to pose that day, for she must set up her materials in a room where she could work. Graciously telling her that she had the freedom of the house and to ask for anything that she needed, he changed his cap[6] for what Elisabet termed a "calebreses" (Calabrian) hat, a high-topped, black felt with ostrich feathers in the hatband, a style adopted by Garibaldi and his troops along with their red shirts, and walked toward the fields. In her diary, Elisabet described the fifty-eight-year old Garibaldi:

> I followed with my eyes his walking through the court:
> The red shirt and grey trowsers: over his right shoulder a
> "poncho" of white wollen stoff rare with coloured spots & a
> fine red border round it; his right hand a stik for making his
> steps more safe it seems. He's walking light; it is the walk of
> a strong but elegant figure; his shoulders are brought (broad)
> & the whole torso exceedingly well built.[7]

Garibaldi returned for his dinner at noon; Elisabet's place was on his right at a table filled with his red-shirted supporters. Elisabet could not understand the lively Italian conversation. "Once Garibaldi rose, very animated his voice, but spoke Italian, so I could only observe how grand and brilliant his features were. That was the spirit I have to reproduce in the bust," Elisabet noted in her diary.

When the sittings began, Garibaldi tended to become melancholy when forced to sit quietly for a length of time. This was not the mood that Elisabet wanted to create; so she began work on a statuette until such time as she could find him with an expression more in keeping with his personality. Another problem for her was the round trip by boat and the walk up the rough path to the house, which were becoming more and more wearing. After an illness forced her to spend a day in bed, she finally asked one of Garibaldi's sons, who had been escorting her to and from the house, if she could possibly stay in the main house. The boy asked his father, who readily agreed that it would be no problem because sometimes as many as sixty people stayed at Caprera, as the young man explained.

For lodgings in the main house, the secretary assigned Elisabet a room next to one of Garibaldi's daughters, her husband and three children, one of whom was named "Lincoln" for Garibaldi's friend President Abraham Lincoln. During the weekend, Garibaldi entertained many visitors and had no time for sittings.

On Monday morning of the second week of her stay, Elisabet rose at five o'clock, as was Garibaldi's custom, and found him working in his vineyard. When he saw her, he stopped his work and motioned for her to sit beside him on a low stone wall. In her journal Elisabet commented that whenever they had a long or important conversation that she "must be sharp listening what he say in French, as well as I must think how much to put that together [with] what I wish to reply."

As they talked together, Garibaldi told her that he was interested in her as a strong and beautiful woman and a good artist; sometimes he woke up at night and thought about her. When Elisabet said that she also felt sympathy for him, he sighed and said his heart was true, but that he was a man with many weaknesses. "So deep, so truthful was his sound in saying this, that all at once I saw developed the ernest of battling he undertakes with himself & the true mourning when ever he failed," Elisabet wrote. They left the vineyard and Garibaldi filled a sack with grain and started to feed his ducks, who came to greet him as though he were an expected friend. Then he went to a parcel of land known as "The Dessert," where he grazed cattle, sheep, wild goats, and game. Here, too, the cattle, and also a small donkey, came to him to be fed and petted. "This is Pio Nono,"[8] he informed Elisabet, who was startled by the impiety and asked if he believed in any religion.

"I am a Christian," Garibaldi stated. "Christ was a man of the people. It's the Pope who is anti-Christ, the Papacy which has enslaved its believers."[9]

When they returned to the house, the General was in a more amiable mood to pose for modeling. After supper with family and followers, Elisabet often took a walk to enjoy the ambience of the place, the rugged scenery, sea air, and friendliness, because Garibaldi retired immediately after the meal and no modeling could be done. This evening, however, he asked to accompany her on her stroll. As they walked, he talked about his triumphs and disappointments in his battles in Italy and Sicily, his life in South America and the United States, his trip to England, and his dreams for the future of a united Italy. In reply, Elisabet wrote: ". . . I tried to raise the hope & to console him, showing him how he shared the fate of all those who had been living grand & good, but earned ingratitude. I told him that seeing him thus on this island remind me to the old chained Prometheus. — This all did quicken him & he was pleased with last comparason."[10]

As they walked back to the main house, Elisabet said, "General, my 'best friend' Dr. Edmund Montgomery feels the same as I about you and your cause of freedom. Inform us if we can ever be of assistance." Pleased, Garibaldi told her that he would remember that offer.

After two weeks, the plaster models of the bust and statuette were completed. In the portrait Elisabet had captured Garibaldi's strong features as well as his look of gentleness. Of all the men whom Elisabet had modeled, Garibaldi was the only one who reminded her of her esteemed "great-uncle" Marshal Ney. Garibaldi was not only gratified with the bust, but also to be compared with Marshal Ney. To execute the plaster model into marble, Elisabet explained that it was necessary to take the statue to her studio in Rome.

After Elisabet had completed packing her equipment to leave Caprera, Garibaldi, with a servant to carry the bundles, accompanied her down the path from his house to the water. When the boat arrived for Elisabet, Garibaldi put his hands on her shoulders and again kissed her forehead.

Looking back upon Caprera on her return journey to Genoa and Rome, Elisabet felt that she had acquired another friend, another hero. Now she would have much work to do until Edmund could join her. By the time Edmund arrived in Rome, she had Garibaldi's bust in marble and his statuette in bronze. In their happy reunion, Edmund explained that Lord Brownlow's health had improved, at least temporarily, to the extent that he could leave him in the care of another physician. Lady Alford had been so kind in her recommendations, however, that he had more patients than he could conscientiously treat because of his own insecure health. Many of Lady Alford's friends in Menton were his patients, actually he preferred treating his poor patients in the slums rather than the idle, wealthy busybodies.

Some of Edmund's patients followed him to Rome; one, Mrs. Mary Jane Forbes,[11] a widowed Englishwoman, seemed to place an especially high opinion on his medical capabilities. By limiting his practice, Edmund had time to work on a paper which he was asked to prepare for a December meeting of the Royal Society in London regarding his research on the formation of cells, which he had performed while at St. Thomas's Hospital.

Meanwhile Elisabet, under the sponsorship of Joseph Joachim, had submitted her work of the bronze statuette of Garibaldi to the Royal Academy Exhibition in London and

was ready for another subject. Lady Macbeth? She had first
conceived of creating such a statue while studying with Rauch;
she made some preliminary models, but this effort did not have
the necessary inspiration. Once when she related to Edmund
her experiences with Garibaldi, she casually mentioned that
Garibaldi reminded her of Prometheus of the Greek myth.
"Then why not a statue of Prometheus?" he suggested.
"Sometimes I feel like Prometheus myself, with my life and
work fettered by prejudice and ignorance."

As Elisabet began her preliminary work on this statue, she
remarked to Edmund, "When I think of the story of Prometheus, who braved the wrath of Zeus to steal fire from heaven to
bring enlightenment to mankind, and who, because of this act
of love for man, was chained to a mountain and tortured daily
for ten thousand years, I want to create a memorial to all brave
souls who have endured scorn and condemnation in their efforts to better their fellowmen. I'll represent Prometheus as
still bound — just before his deliverance — strong and contem-
plative, in spite of all the injustice he suffered, still believing in
a better future for mankind."

While Elisabet and Edmund were occupied with their individual endeavors, political unrest in Europe, caused by Prussia's determination to unify and to dominate Germany, culmi-
nated in April of 1866 in what became known as the Seven
Weeks' War between Prussia and Austria. Italy allied with
Prussia because King Victor Emmanuel saw an opportunity,
with Prussian dominance over Austria, of freeing the Venetian
provinces from the rule of the Austro–Hungarian Empire.[12]
When Elisabet and Edmund, newly inspired with ideas of freedom from their preoccupation with the myth of Prometheus,
learned that Garibaldi would be leading troops against the
Austrians, they sent a message, through friends, offering their
services to this cause.

Gratefully accepting their assistance, Garibaldi informed
them, also by a messenger, that they would be useful as secret
agents in the Austrian Tyrol, especially since they were from
Rome, which was under French control and officially neutral.
After agreeing to accept this responsibility, with the assistance of Garibaldi's sympathizers, Elisabet and Edmund hurriedly left Rome and were assigned a post in the ruined Castle
Kropfsberg, located in the Alps on the River Inn twenty-five

miles from Innsbruck, Austria, a short distance from the Bavarian border.[13]

Before leaving Rome, Elisabet packed her modeling equipment, a plaster copy of Garibaldi's statuette, and her unfinished *Prometheus*; Edmund brought his notes and the materials necessary for the paper he was writing. Upon their arrival at the Castle, they discovered that only one wing of the old *Schloss* was inhabitable. Under such circumstances, Elisabet realized that housekeeping would be difficult and advertised in Innsbruck for a domestic worker.

One of the applicants was Fräulein Crecentia Simath, the daughter of an Innsbruck bookbinder, thirty-two years old, only a year younger than Elisabet, who employed her. "Cenci" (her sobriquet) proved to be not only an efficient housekeeper, but also an intelligent and trustworthy friend. When Elisabet and Edmund received reports from Garibaldi's followers concerning movement of troops in the Tyrol, Cenci was entrusted to deliver this information to the designated person. Even though Cenci was an Austrian, she was obviously sympathetic toward Garibaldi's mission.[14]

When Cenci returned from one assignment, she brought news that during the fighting in the Tyrol, Garibaldi was wounded and was forced to conduct his campaign from a carriage. In spite of this setback, Garibaldi's operations were going well. On the other fronts, however, the Italians were defeated, but their allies, the Prussians, overwhelmed the Austrians on July the third at Königgrätz (Sadowa). Eventually Bismarck granted King Victor Emmanuel the province of Venetia to be reunited with Italy. On August 23, 1866, a Treaty of Peace was signed at Prague with Prussia and Italy victorious over Austria, Bavaria, Saxony, and Hannover.[15]

With the war concluded, Garibaldi no longer needed the services of Elisabet and Edmund; however, they loved the beauty of the Austrian Alps and remained in the Castle until the weather became too cold for Edmund's health. While still in the Castle, Elisabet completed the plaster model of *Prometheus Bound.* The face was a blend of the features of Garibaldi and of Edmund, and the body a beautifully carved Adonis. During this period Edmund also completed his paper entitled "On the Formation of 'So-Called' Cells in Animal Bodies," in which his views differed from the two generally accepted, yet opposing, explanations of the vital phenomena — the "vitalistic" and the "mechanistic" theories. The hypothesis that Edmund offered was that the vital phenomena (life) was a continuity of development from the inanimate to the animate through the means of gradual chemical elaboration. This monograph Edmund sent to Dr. Simon in London for Dr. Simon to read to the next meeting of the Royal Society.[16]

When the weather forced Elisabet and Edmund to return to Rome, Cenci accompanied them. Already she was indispensable: she relieved Elisabet of worry about household chores and spoiled and mothered "Herr Doctor." Later Edmund received Dr. Simon's report that his monograph was not well received and was considered too materialistic by the conservative authority and adviser of the Society, and for that reason was not published in the Society's Journal; however, a comprehensive abstract was published in the Society's "Proceedings." "I know I'm right in my findings," Edmund said. "In fact, I feel so strongly about my convictions that I'm going to London and publish the paper at my own expense."

Because Elisabet understood that Edmund's theory, defined after years of careful research, meant as much to him as her sculpture did to her, she agreed that he should publish his paper in London. But it was not until the summer of 1867 that he was able to publish "On the Formation of 'So-Called' Cells in Animal Bodies." To conduct further experiments to prove his conclusions, he had set up a laboratory in London's Zoological Gardens, encouraged by his friend Dr. Simon and the English naturalist Richard Owen, and continued his research.

In meetings with other scientists, Dr. Montgomery again encountered Charles Darwin. The two discussed Darwin's hypothesis of pangenesis, that the living organism is merely a combination of individual cells in which the fundamental properties of life are inherent and that the activities of the organism are the result of the interaction of various autonomous elements. Edmund disagreed with Darwin and explained the conclusions that he had drawn from his own research.[17]

Meanwhile in Rome, Elisabet had finished *Prometheus* and wanted to copy it in marble, but because it was an idealistic work rather than one done for a commission, she and Edmund did not possess sufficient funds for the marble. While waiting for another commission, Elisabet worked in her studio

1

and studied in the museums. She was glad that Prussia and Garibaldi's army had triumphed and believed that Bismarck was attempting to unify Germany in much the same way that Garibaldi was fighting to unite Italy. When she learned, however, that Prussia had taken over control of the Duchy of Hannover and that Bismarck had sent the unfortunate, blind King George V to Vienna in exile, she was saddened by the news, for the King had been very kind to her.

During this period without a project, she remembered that her friend Baron von Werthen, whose bust she had modeled, was now in favor with both Bismarck and King Wilhelm; she also knew that Garibaldi was allied with Bismarck during the Seven Weeks' War. Perhaps if she wrote to the Baron and told him about modeling Garibaldi, he might obtain a commission for her to model Bismarck, or perhaps, even the King.

What Elisabet did not know was that Garibaldi had already recommended her to Bismarck, not only as a competent artist, but also as an intelligence agent.[18] Although Elisabet did not know the persons responsible, nor their reasons for sponsoring her, she was delighted to receive an order from His Majesty King Wilhelm I of Prussia to come to Berlin, in February 1867, to model a portrait bust of Count Otto von Bismarck.

Berlin and Munich

When I am a famous sculptor, the great persons
of the world will come to me for a portrait.

Elisabet Ney

In response to His Majesty's order, Elisabet returned to
Berlin to sculpt a portrait of Count von Bismarck. The Prime
Minister was courteous but busy and instructed his aide to
make an appointment for his sitting. When Count von Bismarck arrived in Elisabet's studio, she maintained her usual
composure and worked as quickly as possible on the clay
model. During one of the sittings, when Elisabet was concentrating intensely on her work, she looked up in amazement to
see His Majesty, King Wilhelm, standing beside her. "Your
Majesty," gasped Elisabet, "I had not expected you. I'm deeply honored. Do you approve of my progress on the portrait?"

The King commended her work, and as soon as the session
was completed, he left the studio with Bismarck. The Berlin
newspaper *Dioskuren,* on February 14, 1867, reported: "Last
week His Majesty, the King honored the studio of the Sculptress Fräulein Ney on Munzstrasse with a visit. He inspected

the model of a bust of Minister-President Count von Bismarck on which she is working, and expressed a great satisfaction with her progress.[1]

At another sitting, the Count asked Elisabet if, other than modeling the bust of Garibaldi, were there any other services that she and Dr. Montgomery had performed for him. Elisabet hesitated, but remembered that Garibaldi and Bismarck had been allies against Austria. "*Ja*, while in the Austrian Tyrol, we supplied Garibaldi with information."

Bismarck seemed satisfied with her answer, but soon he became restless and informed Elisabet that he was too preoccupied with other matters to give her any more time. Although he was pleased with the bust so far, she would have to complete the statue from portraits and photographs.

When the bust was finished, Elisabet exhibited a plaster model at the Eicher gallery in Berlin and also sent a copy to be shown at the International Art Exposition to be held in Paris later in 1867. She also submitted *Die Brüder Genii* under the title of *Les Génies Frères*, the busts of Dr. Montgomery, Garibaldi, the miniature of Lady Alford, and the bronze statuette of Lord Brownlow as a memorial to the young Lord, who had died at Menton a week before.[2]

During the summer, Elisabet made a trip to the Exhibition in Paris to see how well her works were displayed. On this first visit to Paris, Elisabet felt the gaiety and excitement of riding in a carriage along the Champ-Élysées. At the *Arc de Triumphe*, in the apex of a circle of boulevards extending outwards in all directions, she stopped and examined this monumental arch built to glorify the victories of Napoleon I.

She rode across a bridge over the swiftly flowing Seine to view the Tuileries, the residence of Emperor Napoleon III and Empress Eugénie.[3] What an attainment if she could model portraits of the Emperor and Empress! If only she had a friend who could recommend her, surely the Emperor would receive a relative of Marshal Ney.

After sightseeing, Elisabet found the International Exhibition, housed in a series of adjoining buildings on the Champ-de-Mars. When she made an inspection, she was pleased with the lighting and placement of her entries and found that, as she had requested, her bust of Bismarck was placed on one side of the entrance of the German exhibit and Garibaldi's on the other.[4] While viewing her own and other art works, Elisabet encountered her friend Hermann Hüffer, who was pleasantly surprised to see her and wanted to observe her sculpture that was on display.

When Elisabet pointed out her works, the statue of *Die Brüder Genii* most impressed him and he asked what the two children represented. "Whatever you see in them — life and death, hope, faith — the future," she suggested.

When Hüffer saw the bust of Dr. Montgomery, he realized that this was the "best friend" whom Elisabet had to visit the last time he saw her. Elisabet admitted that he was the person. As they strolled through the gallery, they found themselves standing beneath the portrait, *L'Artiste.* Hüffer told her that she was as lovely now as she had been when the picture was painted, while he had grown duller leading the existence of a teacher and writer of history.[5]

"But I'm many years older now," Elisabet said, "and I hope many years wiser. I've modeled many great persons and expect to sculpt many more. I hope that before I leave Paris that I'll be presented to the Emperor and Empress as the great-niece of Marshal Ney." Such a possibility was only a wish, but in any event, she realized that Hüffer was sufficiently impressed.

Elisabet and Hüffer toured the Palace of Versailles and also saw the Dome of the Invalides, Napoleon Bonaparte's massive tomb. They visited the Luxembourg Gardens where Marshal Ney met his fate, and Elisabet related that Napoleon had called Ney "the bravest of the brave" and had named him Duke of Elchingen and Prince of Moskowa. She recalled to Hüffer that after Napoleon's abdication, Marshal Ney changed sides to King Louis XIII, but on Napoleon's return from Elba, Ney again joined forces with him. After Napoleon's defeat at Waterloo, where Marshal Ney had commanded the Old Guard, Ney was tried for treason by the House of Peers and ordered executed in the Luxembourg Gardens.[6] With sadness Elisabet retraced the events of the Marshal's career, and again felt proud to be his descendant. Although she enjoyed Hüffer's companionship, she continued her almost daily letters to Edmund about her stay in Paris and about meeting another old acquaintance, Joseph Joachim, the violinist, who had concert engagements at the Academy of Music. After one of his recitals, when she went backstage to congratulate him, he invited her to join his friends for a later supper. During the evening, Joachim asked her if she would accept a commission in Hannover to model the bust of his beautiful young wife Amalie, which Elisabet agreed to gladly.

Now that the Prussians had overthrown and exiled the unfortunate King George V, Elisabet asked Joachim about the political situation in Hannover. Joachim told her that he had faith that Bismarck, under King Wilhelm, would unify Germany into a great nation. In Hannover, Joachim said that Elisabet would find his wife very domesticated, with two little sons and another child expected, although they had been married only four years. Before her marriage, his wife was Amalie Weiss, a gifted singer, who gave up her career to marry him.

Frau Joachim, the first woman for whom Elisabet had modeled a life-sized bust, was warm and friendly, and her two small boys reminded Elisabet of her marble *Genii*. In her statue of Amalie Joachim, Elisabet created a portrait of loving young motherhood. Joachim liked the bust and told Elisabet that he would adorn it with flowers and place it where he could admire it as he practiced his violin. Elisabet suggested that Amalie's portrait, together with the one of him, should be entered as a pair in the Royal Academy Exhibition in London next year.[7]

With a feeling of accomplishment, Elisabet returned to Berlin from Paris and Hannover and was ready for another assignment, which soon arrived in the form of a summons to come to Munich from her friend Baron von Werthern, recently appointed, at Bismarck's suggestion, as Prussian Ambassador to Bavaria. Filled with joy to return to Munich, her favorite city, she visited the Baron's office. He told her that Bismarck liked his portrait so much that he had recommended her as a sculptor to the Bavarian King Ludwig II.

Because Ludwig II considered himself a patron of the arts like his grandfather, Ludwig I, Bismarck further suggested that His Majesty should sponsor Fräulein Ney, who would be a talented addition to the artistic and cultural life of the city, adding that there was a possibility that King Ludwig might be persuaded to sit for her.

Such a possibility was an unexpected bonus for Elisabet. "I'm grateful to you, Baron von Werthern, and to Count von

Bismarck. It means very much to me to have this opportunity to work in Munich, especially with encouragement from you and Count von Bismarck. I hope that I'll never disappoint your faith in me," Elisabet said, innocently, to the Prussian Ambassador.

With great excitement, Elisabet wrote to Edmund in London that through the influence of Baron von Werthern she was given a commission for a statue of Iris and another of Mercury for the exterior decoration of a new college of engineering edifice, *the Polytechnikum,* and for busts of the chemists Justus von Liebig and Friedrich Wöhler to be placed inside of the building, as well as for a bust of King Ludwig.[8] As soon as possible, she wrote, he must join her in Munich. During this period, Elisabet accepted the situation as it appeared on the surface; she looked upon Bismarck as a liberator, and her feelings about him corresponded to her feelings about Garibaldi. She was eager to be of service toward the goal of the freedom and unification of Germany.

Soon Elisabet found herself looked up to and envied by the other artists in Munich, even by her old friends and teachers — Widnmann, Berdellé, and Julius Zumbusch, who had already completed a bust of King Ludwig, and by Johanna Kapp, now in Munich, but drifting into a state of near mental illness. Because it had been thirteen years since Elisabet had lived in Munich, she wanted to learn all she could about what had taken place in the interim — especially anything concerning the young King Ludwig, who had become King on March 10, 1864, at the age of nineteen, upon the premature death of his father, Maximilian II.[9]

In her conversations with the *Müncheners,* Elisabet soon discovered that another item of gossip, besides the eccentricities of the King, was the Bülows: Cosima was reported to be having an affair with the fifty-five-year-old composer Wagner. He had divorced his wife, had been forced to leave Munich, and was living at Tribschen, near Lucerne, Switzerland where Cosima and her two daughters, rumored to be fathered by Wagner, had joined him. To further complicate the situation, Cosima was again pregnant.[10]

From her friends, Elisabet also heard that King Ludwig was infatuated with Wagner and his music and had spent such vast sums from the treasury to subsidize Wagner's expensive tastes that public pressure had forced the King to send Wagner from Munich.[11] As for Cosima's behavior, Elisabet's condemnation was acrimonious. (Elisabet was oblivious to the gossip also circulating that the unmarried Fräulein Ney was openly living with a British doctor.) When reports of Elisabet's outspoken disapproval reached Cosima's ears, she retaliated by giving a commission to Elisabet's rival, Julius Zumbusch, for the execution of a bust of her father, Franz Liszt.

In her letters to Edmund, Elisabet repeated these happenings in Munich as well as her feeling of bitterness toward Cosima. "Poor Hans," Elisabet wrote, "he was so loving and trusting. Cosima, the perfect wife, even encouraged his homage to Wagner. When I attended the opera where Hans conducted, ironically Wagner's *Lohengrin,* I went backstage after the performance to congratulate him, to tell him of my commissions, and to thank him for introducing me to Baron von Werthern. Fortunately, I did *not* see Cosima, who was probably at Tribschen with Wagner. It means so much to me, 'my best friend' to know that neither of us could ever leave the other. Please come soon, so much I miss you."

Elisabet had also learned that to further add to the people's dislike and mistrust of Wagner, in spite of his great music, they not only blamed him for seducing Cosima von Bülow, the wife of the Royal *Kappellmeister,* but also accused him of luring King Ludwig into a homosexual relationship.[12]

With suppressed enjoyment, Elisabet heard the story of how the King agreed to give Wagner, in addition to expensive gifts and subsidies, a cash grant of forty thousand *Gulden,* which infuriated the bankers. When Cosima, acting as Wagner's secretary, went to the bank to collect this money, the bankers paid the amount in coins secured in sacks so heavy that she was forced to hire two carriages to transport the money and to suffer the humiliation of having personally to deliver the weighty moneybags to Wagner.[13]

Early in 1868, Edmund arrived in Munich with his books, microscope, and research equipment and moved into a nearby hotel where he could continue his work because Elisabet's studio could accommodate only her paraphernalia, herself, and Cenci, but at least they could be together again. When Elisabet submitted her sketches and preliminary models of the statues of Iris and Mercury to *Baurat* (architectural counselor) Gottfried von Neureuther, the Royal Special Commissioner for the construction of the new polytechnical school, she discovered that he had his own ideas about the statues which did not always coincide with hers, but realizing how much she had to lose if she displeased the King's architect, she begrudgingly followed his suggestions.

Modeling the bust of the chemist Friedrich Wöhler was easy because he was a mild-mannered, cooperative person, but without a strong personality for Elisabet to project into his statue; however, Justus von Liebig, an eminent chemist, who had established Germany's first school of experimental applied chemistry, had a forceful character. In collaboration with Dr. Wöhler, who specialized in inorganic chemistry, the two of them had become pioneers in Germany in the field of chemistry.[14]

Dr. von Liebig was the sort of person whom Edmund would enjoy; so to bring the two men together, Elisabet invited Dr. Liebig to one of Cenci's excellent dinners. Edmund and Dr. Liebig found that they had mutual interests, and the strong friendship that developed between them lasted long after Elisabet had completed the bust. Dr. Liebig was one of the few persons in Munich who knew of their marriage and even referred to Elisabet as "Frau Montgomery."

At this juncture in her career, Elisabet felt that she had produced enough sculpture to justify having her own exhibit in the galleries of the Munich Art League. Elisabet presented to the public and art critics her busts of Varnhagen von Ense, Jakob Grimm, Arthur Schopenhauer, King George V of Hannover, Joseph and Amalie Joachim, Tom Taylor, Christian Kapp, George von Werthern, Eilhard Mitscherlich, Edmund Montgomery, statuettes of Lady Alford and Lord Brownlow, *Die Brüder Genii,* and *Prometheus Bound,* along with her latest portraits of Giuseppe Garibaldi, Otto von Bismarck, Friedrick von Wöhler, and Justus von Liebig. The reviewers complimented Elisabet's ability to create a life-like portrait, but reserved their praise for the idealistic works of *Prometheus* and *Die Brüder Genii.*[15]

Although other artists exhibited with the Munich Art League, the show was practically devoted to the sculpture of Elisabet Ney. She was gratified with this success, but she was still annoyed by her inability to have an audience with King Ludwig, especially because her contract specified that a bust of the King was to be placed in the Polytechnic Building. From Baron von Werthern, Elisabet learned that the King disliked court life and the crowds in Munich, and spent much of his time at his mountain retreats. Knowing about the King's current emotional difficulties with Wagner, Elisabet realized that there was slight chance that he would sit for a portrait any time soon.

In the late summer of 1868, Edmund suffered a relapse in his fight against consumption. He had spent so much time concentrating his attention on his microscopic studies, without sufficient physical exercise, that he weakened his eyes and aggravated his lung condition. Knowing how cold the winters were in Munich, Edmund decided to return to the warmer climate of Italy, at least until spring.[16]

"For you to leave, I will be sad," Elisabet said, "but you *must* cure yourself of this consumption. You realize that I must stay in Munich to try to have an audience with the King. I promise you, my 'best friend,' that we'll be together as soon as possible."

In light of the delay in starting Ludwig's portrait, Baron von Werthern shared Elisabet's anxieties about a meeting with the King because he knew that Elisabet could accomplish nothing in the way of influencing His Majesty unless she could talk to him; furthermore, Baurat von Neureuther could not complete the Polytechnical Building until the King's bust could be placed inside.

Neureuther suggested to Elisabet that she model a miniature of the King's head from a photograph; perhaps it would please the King enough to grant a sitting. To supplement these efforts, Elisabet wrote the following letter to King Ludwig:

Munich
6 December, 1868

Most Enlightened, All Mightiest King,
Most Gracious King and Lord:
Your Majesty

Has deigned to grant permission for the execution of the small sketch which I made and sent through Baurat Neureuther, with the request that I be permitted to do a portrait statue of Your Majesty. . . .

My ill health obliges me to seek a milder climate, and always my bigger and better works have been created far from

the noise of the cities, in all quiet. If I might be furnished
with just a few lines, done from life, I should be able to execute the statue anywhere. The Christmas holidays which are
bringing Your Majesty back to town, will be most full and
crowded, and they hardly let me hope for the sittings before I
am forced to leave Munich.

Would Your Majesty most graciously signify what time
I may hope for?

Your Majesty's
Most Humble
Elisabet Ney[17]

With *Weihnachten* and the holiday festivities fast approaching, however Elisabet agreed with Neureuther that she had
scant hope of meeting with the King until after the new year.

Edmund's letters reassured her that the mild climate and
the sunshine in Italy had improved his health. When she read
this welcome news and after spending Christmas alone with no
recognition from the King, Elisabet felt a longing to be with
her "best friend," which prompted her to write another letter
to the King on January 5, 1869, telling him that she would like
to go on a short vacation in Italy, but did not want to leave
Munich without modeling a bust of His Majesty.[18] Still no reply
from King Ludwig.

After this setback, Elisabet connived with Neureuther to
place busts of Liebig and Wöhler in the Palace where the King
would be most likely to see them. Then Elisabet wrote another
letter to the King asking that, if he had no time for a sitting,
would he inspect the two portraits that she had just completed
for the *Polytechnikim*. These statues would speak for themselves as to her ability.[19]

Later, on the strong urging of Baron von Werthern, the
King finally agreed to pose for Elisabet, but he insisted that all
details be handled through his Secretary of Chancery, Baron
August von Eisenhart, an aristocratic Bavarian who was
nevertheless a friend of the Prussian Ambassador Werthern.
When Baron von Eisenhart finally summoned Elisabet to the
Palace, she explained that she needed a room with proper
north light where she could set up the equipment necessary for
the King's modeling sessions. Through Baron von Eisenhart's
efforts, a room in the wing known as Odysseys–Saal, facing
the Palace gardens, became Elisabet's atelier. Because in the

afternoons this room was open to the public, the King could only pose in the mornings; after midday, Elisabet had to cover the unfinished model before sightseers appeared, a circumstance which shortened considerably the length of time that she could spend on her work.[20]

In spite of these obstacles, Elisabet was determined to create a likeness that would please even His temperamental Majesty, King Ludwig II.

Travel in the Near East

*Travel gives a character of experience to our knowl-
edge and brings the figures on the tablet of memory
into strong relief.*

Henry Theodore Tuckerman

When the King arrived for his first appointment, accompanied by several men and women Royal Attendants, who stood
around the King anxiously, as though the inconvenience of
posing might cause His Majesty's displeasure, Baron von Eisenhart presented Elisabet to King Ludwig. As she curtsied
gracefully before the twenty-four-year-old monarch, she observed that he was tall and athletically built, with sloping
shoulders, but that his features had an effeminate look en-
hanced by his carefully coiffured dark brown curly hair.[1]

She asked the King to be seated on a stool which she had
positioned to receive the proper light; however, she did not ask
him to remove his shirt (as she did with most of her other subjects), but stood before him looking at his face with a focused
concentration that the King did not enjoy.

"Begin your work," he snapped authoritatively.

"I'll begin when I'm ready, Your Majesty," she said as she dipped her hands into her bucket of clay.

The King relaxed as though he were a child being told what to do by his mother as Elisabet proceeded to take measurements and confidently began to create his features in clay.[2] Other sittings proceeded without incident. During the afternoons, when the temporary studio was open to visitors, Elisabet noticed that a large number of people came into the Odysseys-Saal to admire the painted frescoes on the walls, which told the story of Homer's *Odyssey*. This audience might provide an excellent opportunity to display some of her works: she persuaded Eisenhart to allow her to bring the plaster model of *Prometheus Bound* and busts of Schopenhauer, Garibaldi, and Bismarck into the room, and when she covered her equipment before the public arrived, she left uncovered her statues and the unfinished bust of the King.

Because the King had been evasive and uncommunicative during his sittings, Elisabet felt that she had not gained the sort of insight that she needed to create a true portrait. With this in mind, she studied the King whenever she had an opportunity. One day she saw the King walking along a corridor wearing an elegant gold-embroidered robe and a sword, the attire of the Order of the Knights of St. Hubert.[3] Obviously enjoying this magnificent costume, the King was actually more at ease wearing theatrical trappings and the dress of make-believe than he was wearing customary gentleman's apparel.

When Elisabet observed the King dressed in this fashion with a look of wild detachment in his eyes, she knew that she had "seen" King Ludwig. Hurriedly she sketched the King as she had perceived him and excitedly sent the drawing to Herr Baurat Neureuther with a letter asking him to show the sketch to the King.[4]

After Neureuther supposedly had done this, Elisabet wrote still another letter to the King:

> I dare with greater happiness and confidence to make this request as I was fortunate in having the opportunity to make a most excellent sketch for it which in a wonderful way charms by its striking likeness.
> The sketch is designed by Elisabet Ney.
> Working only under the impression gained by the artist, when, on the day of the festival of the Knights of St. George, she saw Your Majesty walking through the castle's corri-

dors, the artist not eager to catch single details, attempted
only to reproduce the general impression of the nobel ideal
appearance as completely as possible. . . .
    Completion in marble would take 2 years. Therefore I
feel urged even in these days of seclusion of Your Majesty, to
lay the sketch before Your Most Highest Majesty and to request the most gracious permission to carry it out.[5]

Because the sketch of Elisabet's proposed sculpture
pleased the King, he consented to pose in the vestments of the
Order of a Knight of St. Hubert; yet he grew impatient with
the sittings, especially when he had to remain in a standing
posture. The King's restlessness caused Elisabet to rush her
modeling, which she never liked to do; furthermore, she
wanted this statue to be a masterpiece, but she had no choice
but to speed her work for fear that the King would decide to
leave Munich for one of his many retreats in the countryside,
which, nevertheless, he did.

Elisabet was frustrated, then broke into tears, then decided, as true to her spirit, to do something. Taking the unfinished bust and the preliminary work on the King's statue to
her studio, she copied the bust into marble and sent it to Neureuther to be placed in the Polytechnic Building, and, according to her contract, to be paid 5,500 Marks (approximately
$1,256).[6]

When the Polytechnic Building was opened to the public, a
critic remarked that Fräulein Ney's bust of King Ludwig
lacked character and looked more like his younger brother Otto,
which infuriated Elisabet, who suggested that the critic wait
until he saw her life–sized statue of the King before stating
that her work did not have character. The statues Iris and Mercury on the outside of the edifice received no mention and the
busts of Liebig and Wöhler were passed over with scant praise.
A suggestion that the King's bust be removed and replaced by
a more fitting statue of His Majesty created by Elisabet's rival, Julius Zumbusch, incensed her even more.[7]

In the past year, Elisabet had become acclimated to success and had grown to feel that any criticism of her art was un-
justified. Angrily, she confronted Neureuther, even though he
was the King's Royal Architect, that he had deliberately dis-
criminated against her, placed her statues in the darkest most
inaccessible spots; he also failed to point out to the critics her
two statues on the outside of the building. She told him that

she intended to see that her work was properly displayed. Neureuther was sorry that she was upset, but, *nein,* her statues would remain where he had placed them.

Angry and disappointed, Elisabet returned to her studio and informed Cenci that she would see no visitors except Herr Dr. von Liebig. After her temper cooled, she realized that she had been foolish to antagonize the King's architect, who could prejudice the King against her. As she realized this, Cenci informed her that Herr Baron von Werthern and Herr Baron von Eisenhart were there to see her about the King's statue.

From Cenci's message, Elisabet thought that the two Barons might have talked with Neureuther, who possibly told them of their argument. To refuse to see them might worsen the situation; so she told Cenci to show them in. Apparently Werthern and Eisenhart chose to ignore Elisabet's fracas with Neureuther and told her, rather, that the King realized that he had not allowed her as many sittings as she needed for the bust and that the King agreed to give her more time for the St. Hubert statue. Because His Majesty was rarely in Munich during the spring and summer, and because Elisabet had requested time to visit Italy, they suggested that she make the trip and return in the fall to complete the King's statue. Baron von Werthern reminded Elisabet that he and Count von Bismarck still expected her to develop a friendship with King Ludwig; he further promised to assist her in achieving this rapport after she returned and the King resumed sittings.

"I will join you soon in Italy," Elisabet delightedly wrote to Edmund. His reply brought her even more elation: he had recently received a bequest of three thousand pounds plus an annual legacy of two hundred pounds from one of his patients, a Mrs. Mary Jane Forbes, who had followed him from the Riviera to Rome and who had died February 25, 1869.[8] Now they would have some financial security and could travel to Egypt and Greece, as Elisabet had wanted. How soon could she join him so that they could plan their trip?

Leaving Cenci in charge of the studio, Elisabet departed for a happy reunion with Edmund in Rome. On April 21, 1869, they left for Naples, where they spent a week visiting museums, Pompeii, and Mount Vesuvius. But Elisabet could not ignore the filthy, crowded streets, nor the poverty of the city. "The loud songs and howling of these Neopolitan street sing-

ers kept me awake until late in the night," she complained to
Edmund. After leaving Naples, they boarded a steamer, the
Cairo, bound for Egypt. During their two day voyage, whereon
they occupied separate cabins, they read Lord Byron's "Childe
Harold's Pilgrimage" and decided that each would keep a
diary of the trip in English (German–English, as it resulted).[9]

After crossing the Mediterranean, they arrived in Alexandria where an official inspected their passports and asked Edmund if Elisabet were his wife, to which Edmund replied that
it was none of his business. In the streets the native women,
completely covered in thick black clothing with only their eyes
showing from what looked like a shroud, were appalling to
Elisabet, and when she saw some women from a harem being
pushed into a carriage, the blinds quickly drawn, and oranges
being hastily tossed inside, she indignantly remarked, "How
can such inhumanity as this exist in the nineteenth century?"

"It's not just the treatment of women that is frightening,"
Edmund agreed, "but a Frenchman told me that, in spite of
the prohibition, slave trade still occurs."

Being slightly reassured because Egypt was a protector-
ate of Great Britain, they welcomed the sight of the many red-
coated British soldiers about the streets. After a short ride
from Alexandria, they arrived in Cairo. To make arrangements
for transportation to the ancient site of Heliopolis, they hired a
dragoman, smartly dressed in white, who escorted them
through the streets on their donkeys as the awakening male
populace sat with "croped legs," as Elisabet noted in her journal, in their small shops drinking cups of thick syrupy coffee
and smoking pipes. After a day's donkey ride to Heliopolis,
they reached the spot where Joseph, of the Old Testament, al-
legedly married the daughter of a priest of Heliopolis, and
where Moses, Pythagoras, Euclid, and Plato received instructions from these same priests. Now all that remained was one
stately obelisk.

While in Cairo, Elisabet wore clothes that she had especially designed for this trip. Edmund described them in his diary:
"El put on her white costume of novel invention. Wide trousers inserted into boots coming up above the ankles and a kind
of blouse reaching just under the knees. It looked very smart
and becoming, though somewhat unusual. The natives did not
stare much at it — only the Franks [French]."[10]

On this journey back into man's first, dimly understood, unsurpassed civilization of ancient Egypt five thousand years B.C., both Elisabet and Edmund "longed to get acquainted with the religion and philosophy of the old Egyptians." In awe they stood before the Pyramids and the Sphinx, while Edmund reported in his diary that his climb to the top of the pyramid was very strenuous because the Arab attendants insisted on pulling his arms to help him to the summit.[11] Their dragoman later took them on a journey up the Nile in a *dahaliyeh* (private sailboat). Along the way they passed little villages of mud huts and palm trees, with soldiers riding their dromedaries, and herds of water buffaloes, flocks of "sheaps and gots" as well as people—all coming to the river for water. At the river they saw women balancing large amphoras full of water on their heads, graceful, in spite of their awkward clothing and veils over their faces.[12]

After the Nile trip the two peripatetics departed Alexandria on an Egyptian steamer bound for the Aegean Islands and Constantinople (Istanbul). While aboard the steamer, Elisabet noticed that several black women and children of five years and older were being kept in the hold of the ship. "I'm fairly certain they'll be sold as slaves," Elisabet told Edmund.

"As soon as we reach port, I'll telegraph the English Governor in Alexandria," Edmund promised. "This practice of slavery must be stopped."

During the voyage in the Aegean Sea, Edmund made the following notation: "Edmund was before a little naughty, Elisabet a little, too, but very much hurt. They will not be anymore angry at each other, certainly not! Then it is nothing almost what occurs."[13]

By the next day when their ship stopped at the island of Rhodes, both of them had forgotten their misunderstanding in the fun of sightseeing at the many stops among those historic islands, one at the island of Kos, the birthplace of Hypocrates, another at Smyrna (Ismir), where Elisabet purchased a Turkish shawl and rug. Briefly they visited at the ancient site of Troy (Ilium), then sailed through the Hellespont (the Dardanelles) before entering the Sea of Marmara to reach Constantinople.

In this great, ancient city of the Bosporus, where Oriental and Western civilizations rub noses, neither Elisabet nor Edmund could believe the filth and dirt in the narrow streets, populated with even more beggars and more poverty-stricken urchins than they saw in Egypt; however, the people looked cleaner than their environs because of the Moslem custom of washing before their five-times-a-day prayer.

While in Turkey, the two took a side trip on a steamer into the Bosporus through the Golden Horn and stopped at a bazaar filled with men in fezes and turbans selling great varieties of Oriental finery: jewelry, vases, and tapestries, which Elisabet could not resist purchasing. They visited the famous mosque — Hagia Sophia (Holy Wisdom), which was dedicated in A.D. 537. This church had been constructed in A.D. 330 as a Christian cathedral by the Roman Emperor Justinian, long before the birth of Mohammed when Constantinople had been the capital of the Roman Empire, but after the Moslems defeated the Roman Christians, the church was transformed into a mosque.[14]

To complete their journey, they traveled from Constantinople, again through the Aegean, to make their last stop in Athens, where they explored the remains of the Acropolis and the Parthenon and the other ancient ruins. In Athens some of the originals of the great Greek sculptures of gods and goddesses, which Elisabet had admired and copied as a student, were still standing; however, Elisabet deplored the fact that the most beautiful of these statues resided, not in Greece, but in the British Museum in London.

Not until the latter part of June did the weary Elisabet and Edmund return to Naples, and, after a rest in Rome, finally arrived in July to greet Cenci in Munich. After such a wonderful trip Elisabet told Edmund that she was almost afraid to think about King Ludwig. "What if the King should decide not to pose for me again?"

"He will pose, believe me. I've a feeling that forces around him will be certain that he does," observed Edmund.

King Ludwig II

Max died too soon.
Queen Marie of Bavaria

Surprisingly soon after her return to Munich from her trip to the Middle East, Elisabet received a summons to the Royal *Residenz* to report to Baron August von Eisenhart, Secretary of the Chancery and his wife, a professional writer known as Luise von Kobell. They would arrange for a sitting by His Majesty and if Elisabet were to influence the King, she must gain his interest and friendship. The King was erratic and unpredictable, according to Luise von Kobell, and although men seemed to have difficulty communicating with him, women apparently better understood His Majesty. Elisabet must find a way to hold his attention as an attractive woman, not just a sculptress. Luise von Kobell suggested that the King was still fascinated by Wagner; so Elisabet might show an interest in Wagner's music.[1]

Although Elisabet appreciated these suggestions, when she told Edmund about her conversation with the Eisenharts, he said that it appeared to him that the Prussian elements in

the court were in a conspiracy against the King.[2] If Elisabet let
herself become involved, she might find herself in trouble. Excited by the prospect of modeling King Ludwig again, Elisabet
gave slight heed to Edmund's prediction.

Meanwhile Edmund received three thousand pounds when
attorneys probated Mrs. Forbes's will, July 12, 1869, which
was in addition to his two hundred pound annuity.[3] With this
bequest, Edmund suggested to Elisabet that they purchase a
villa that could serve as a home, her studio, and his laboratory
and study.

On Maria-Josepha-Strasse 8 in the fashionable suburb of
Schwabing, they bought a house built in the style of an Etru-
scan villa in a country setting; yet near enough to drive to the
Palace. The architect, Degan, had built the house in 1862 for
Karl Mossbauer, who sold it to Edmund and Elisabet, registered under the name of Elisabet Ney. To meet their requirements, Elisabet added a large northeast atelier and a sunny
study for Edmund to the two-and-a-half storied house.[4] As
soon as the renovations were completed in early 1870, Elisabet
and Edmund moved into their new home. Because the estate
was equipped with a coach house and stable, Elisabet purchased a pair of spirited matched ponies for her carriage and
enjoyed driving them herself, to the consternation of the proper ladies of the neighborhood.

Cenci happily presided as *Hausälterin* over the estate,
which they named *Steinheil Schlosschen* (little stone castle).[5]
There Edmund contentedly resumed his experiments and writing of a book about Immanuel Kant, in which he attacked
Kant's failure to realize the experimentally proven facts of biology.[6] As usual there was gossip about the Prussian Fraülein
Ney, favored by King Ludwig, and the British Dr. Montgomery, who were openly living together in an unmarried state.

While Elisabet was waiting for some word from the King,
she often went to the Palace and walked through a long corridor which was hung with portraits of the royal personages of
the Whittlebach dynasty that had ruled Bavaria for seven hundred years. Among them King Maximilian II, Ludwig II's father, who had been King when Elisabet first came to Munich,
and the former King Ludwig I, Ludwig's grandfather, who was
still living in Munich, were faces whom Elisabet recognized.

The Duchy of Bavaria was created in 1180, and Munich became the ruling city with the construction of the *Residenz,* begun in the fourteenth century. Each of the various Dukes, over the centuries, expanded and added his own personal style to its architectural grandeur. During the Thirty Years' War, Duke Maximilian made Munich the bastion of German Catholicism, opposing the Protestants of the north.

Elisabet heard Ludwig II compared to his grandfather, Ludwig I, who had become so infatuated with a beautiful, unscrupulous Spanish dancer, Lola Montez, and had spent such sums of the public money on her, that the people forced him to send her into exile and to abdicate in favor of his son.[7] Now young Ludwig's extravagances with Wagner were repeating his grandfather's mistakes. Would this Ludwig II repeat his forebear's debacle?

One day while in the *Residenz,* Elisabet encountered Baron von Eisenhart, who told her that His Majesty had agreed to sit for her. The Baron and his wife then explained their plan for Elisabet to attract His Majesty's attention: the King became bored with posing and had asked them to have a Court Gentleman-in-Waiting read to him during the sitting; because the King was fond of poetry, especially the dramatic, they suggested that the reader select Goethe's "Iphigeneia in Tauris," then stop reading while Elisabet recited the remainder of the passage.

The scheme appealed to Elisabet, who agreed to the performance and spent her time before meeting with the King memorizing and polishing Iphigeneia's selected speech. She would wear her white Grecian toga to dramatize the reading. When the King arrived in the Odysseus-Saal, he paid slight attention to Elisabet, nor did he notice much the Court Attendant, who was reading from "Iphigeneia in Tauris." But when the man stopped, and Elisabet began reciting Goethe's verse in her eloquent, melodius voice, the King looked at her in surprise. At once he no longer saw her as an intent female stone worker, but as a beautiful, auburn-haired woman, looking young for her thirty-six years, dressed as the white-robed goddess Iphigeneia, dramatically reciting one of his favorite poems: she *was* Iphigeneia, goddess of chastity and truth. The King was delighted. "*Ja wohl,* Fräulein Ney, your reading has pleased me. I'll send you jewels."

Although pleased and flattered by the King's show of appreciation, Elisabet answered, *"Danke schön,* Your Highness, but I've no place for jewels; when my friends wish to honor me, they send me flowers." For months afterwards, Elisabet received flowers sent daily by His Majesty.[8]

While she was modeling the King, she now conversed with him and he no longer demanded a reader. He told her of his unhappy childhood and how he had become infatuated with Wagner's operas when he first heard *Lohengrin* at age fifteen and had ordered the entire opera performed again just for himself.[9] When the King spoke of Wagner, Elisabet noticed that his eyes shone and his face became agitated.

Elisabet knew that the King had a fondness for architecture and building as well as for music; so she asked him if he planned to build a castle. He told her that he laid the cornerstone for castle Neuschwanstein on September 5 of last year (1869) and had begun Linderhof Castle a few months ago.[10] This friendship with the King was the rapport that Eisenhart and Werthern had expected Elisabet to initiate; however, now that she had established this amity, she realized that she could not conscientiously be a part of any intrigue to undermine the King.

That night at *Steinheil-Schlosschen,* Elisabet told Edmund of her doubts about the Prussians' military organization. Edmund expressed his opinion that Bismarck apparently intended to unify all the states of Germany under the rule of the Hohenzollerns;[11] furthermore, Edmund said that he had heard that Garibaldi also had become disillusioned with Bismarck.[12] As for Bavaria, after having been on the losing side of the Seven Weeks' War, the country was now bound by treaty to support Prussia if Prussia were attacked. Such a happening would prove to be a dilemma for befuddled King Ludwig.

"Edmund, you're right," Elisabet agreed. "The King told me how he hates the Prussians, even more it seems because the Hohenzollerns are his relatives. If he thought that he might become a puppet–King, under the domination of his uncle, King Wilhelm, and could no longer pamper his favorite, Wagner, nor build his fantastic castles, I believe that he'd go insane, as did so many other Wittlebachs.

The current gossip in the Court is that Prince Otto acts peculiarly, at times almost like a madman. If I can befriend the King, I will, he's distraught and many persons are against him."[13]

Not long after Elisabet's conversation with Edmund, Eisenhart congratulated her on reports that she and the King were very friendly and that he sent her flowers every day. Eisenhart wanted to know if the King had asked her about politics, or about whom to appoint as advisors, or had expressed his opinions on France or Prussia.

These questions irritated Elisabet who had begun to dislike Baron von Eisenhart. Although he was a Bavarian, the Baron obviously thought that his country's best interest lay with Prussia and attempted to tutor Elisabet on how to influence the King on Prussia's behalf.

Elisabet could have finished the King's statue with a few more sittings and was pleased with the character of Ludwig that she had created, even to portraying the King's inner fears and compulsions in the look in his eyes,[14] but she prolonged the sittings. The King was agreeable and during their continued conversations she counseled him about his duty to his people and agreed with his desire for peace.[15] Often after she returned to *Steinheil–Schlosschen* from a sitting at the Palace, she wrote a long letter confirming their conversations, to be delivered to the King the next day through the channel of his Secretary Baron von Eisenhart. That Eisenhart not only read everything she wrote to the King, she began to suspect, but also that he did not send her letters to His Majesty, for she never received a reply from the King.

In a letter to the King dated "Thursday Night," discussing religious beliefs, Elisabet expressed her own view of life as follows:

> In this consciousness I am able to regard my individual life as worthwhile, but I consider it a sacred duty to dedicate the full earnestness of my life to freeing my individual self from the meanness and baseness hemming me in.
>
> Certainly what I thus achieve for myself as an individual, and as a part of humanity can never be lost. Herein lies the source of my proud, inspiring self-awareness. How significant I as an individual become! To live this becomes so worthwhile, so full of meaning. Oh, how insignificant in comparison with all this is what the priest calls the goal — heaven or hell. And if Schopenhauer had so believed, he would never have been able to say: "Salvation, the highest goal, is the negation of the will to live." Lives filled with good deeds are threefold more in value than lives filled with individual vir-

tue. This to me is not belief nor supposition. The entire past gives me thousandfold evidence of its reality.[16]

The King did not mention her letters, but he confided in Elisabet that he felt that he could trust no one in the Palace, that everyone was plotting against him. Elisabet suggested that her friend Dr. Herr von Liebig was someone who could be trusted. When the city of Breslau wanted to honor Dr. Liebig with a villa or a large sum of money, he asked instead that they present a medal as a yearly award to a person who had earned special merits in agriculture.[17] The King, however, was not interested in Liebig.

The conversations with the King and the work on his statue continued while Elisabet became aware, from talk in Court circles, that war between Prussia and France appeared imminent. "I've heard rumors," Edmund told her, "that Bismarck wants to provoke Louis Napoleon into attacking Prussia.[18] If this happens, what do you think Ludwig will do?"

Edmund received the answer, when on July 19, 1870, France declared war on Prussia, and, under terms of their treaties, all the smaller German states, including Bavaria, had no choice but ally themselves with the Prussian forces. Realizing the inevitable, King Ludwig left for his mountain castles, leaving Elisabet's statue still incomplete. Eventually, upon the insistence of his ministers and advisors, the King was forced to mobilize the Bavarian army under the command of his disliked cousin, Prussian Crown Prince Friedrich. Bismarck's plans were well-drawn and on the first of September the Prussians severely defeated the French at Sedan, where Napoleon's army capitulated. But in the city of Paris, the people revolted against Louis Napoleon's Second Empire, declared a new French Republic, rejected the humiliating Prussian peace terms, and continued to fight, even though the Prussian army surrounded their city.[19]

Elisabet and Edmund admired and supported the people of Paris, fighting against almost certain defeat to be free from absolute rulers, and they had also learned that Garibaldi felt as they did and had switched his allegiance to the beleagured French.[20]

At the same time that the war was taking place, on July 18 in Berlin, Hans von Bülow divorced Cosima on the grounds of her desertion for Richard Wagner. A month before the divorce,

Cosima had given birth to a son, Siegfried Wagner. On King Ludwig's birthday, August 25, 1870, Cosima married Richard Wagner and the King had sent a congratulatory telegram.[21]

This event incensed Elisabet, who fumed to Edmund, "To be divorced by Hans, then to immediately marry that ingrate Wagner *after* the birth of their child is scandalous. I know how much this marriage will agitate the already harrassed King Ludwig; he's always resented Cosima's share of Wagner's attentions. Perhaps now he'll return to Munich so that I can finish his statue."

Edmund told Elisabet that he was afraid that this turn of events would leave her at cross purposes with Eisenhart and Werthern and that because of her sympathies for the King, she might find herself in a difficult situation.

"*Ach,* Edmund, my 'best friend,' I'm afraid it's already too late. I've heard at the Palace that Bismarck tried to coerce King Ludwig to write to his Prussian uncle, King Wilhelm, and invite him to assume the throne of all the German states, including Bavaria, and was furious because Ludwig refused.[22] I also heard that Bismarck was angry with Eisenhart and Werthern and accused them of failing in their mission to induce Ludwig to accept a 'Kingship' under Emperor Wilhelm. I'm sure now that Eisenhart and Werthern will think that I did not exert influence on the King for that purpose, and I suspect that traitor Eisenhart probably read all my letters to the King. What shall I do now, Edmund?"

"Be patient, *Liebchen,* we can only wait and see what develops."

With war and political turmoil boiling, the siege of Paris continued through September, October, and November, and the besieged population was literally starving. Bombs fell continuously, damaging the entire city. The Prussians, and also the Bavarians, gloated over the devastation of Paris, much to the distress of Elisabet and Edmund.

On November 20, 1870, Elisabet learned that Bismarck had forced King Ludwig to send a letter (the *Kaiserbrief,* as it became known), which was practically dictated by Bismarck, wherein Ludwig asked King Wilhelm to assume the title of Emperor of Germany.[23] When Elisabet thought of King Ludwig being pressured and threatened into signing away his Kingship to his hated Prussian relative, she felt ashamed that she had done so little to help him. Now he could only rule as a puppet-king under the "Emperor."

In conjunction with the distressing happenings around her, Elisabet began to realize that a new development was taking place within herself. She first refused to accept what her body was telling her, but she finally realized the full meaning.

She was pregnant.

After her initial disbelief, she began to face the truth. Edmund would be pleased, she knew, but she had never intended to have a child. Her career was to be a sculptor, not to be a *Hausfrau* with children; yet here inside herself was a new life that she and Edmund had created. She was awed and frightened. Her years of Catholic training were not easily forgotten; she respected the unborn soul she carried. And, as tears rolled down her cheeks, she experienced an excited happiness in the thought of becoming a mother. *Ja, ja*, she thought, now is the time to tell Edmund.

When she did, he exclaimed, "I'm so happy, *meine* Elisabet, *meine kleine Mutter* [my little mother]. Son or daughter, no matter, just to have our own child."

"I want a daughter," Elisabet decided. "I'll teach and train her. She'll be a famous person, an artist, perhaps. But, Edmund, she must not be born into this war-torn country to live under these dictatorial rulers. She must grow up in freedom to live and do as she pleases with her life."

Edmund agreed that he wanted the same sort of life for their child. "But where? Where can we go?"

As if to answer Edmund's plea, a letter arrived postmarked Thomasville, Georgia, United States of America, from Baron Vicco von Stralendorff of Mecklenburg, whom Edmund had met in Italy in 1868, where they both sought a warmer climate to alleviate the symptoms of consumption. Edmund had prescribed the same treatment that he was himself following, and the two became friends.

Elisabet read the letter with him in which Stralendorff narrated that while vacationing in Europe in 1869, he fell in love with Margaret Russell, a nineteen-year-old American girl and had followed her to Boston, where they were married a little over a year ago.

After searching the East Coast of America for a suitable climate for his health, they had selected a small town, Thomasville, in southwest Georgia, located in a forest of pine and live oak trees. Here, surrounded by warmth and sunshine in the presence of his beautiful young wife, he felt that he was living in paradise, but he did miss his European friends and believed that Dr. Montgomery and his good friend, Fräulein Ney, would find the sort of life that they would enjoy in this new country. Why not leave Europe and join him in America for a healthier, happier life? Perhaps, together, they might start a colony of displaced Europeans.[24]

"That is our country!" Elisabet exclaimed. "Reply to his letter, Edmund, and tell him that we'll come as soon as we can make arrangements to leave."

When Elisabet told Cenci of their plans to emigrate to America, Cenci never thought of not going with Miss Ney and Herr Doctor, for they had by now become her family. When Elisabet divulged that she was pregnant, Cenci was overjoyed with the prospect of having a baby to care for.

With Christmas approaching, King Ludwig returned to Munich. Immediately Elisabet wrote asking to be granted one more sitting to complete the King's statue before leaving for America. After dedicating three years of patient waiting on the capricious behavior of King Ludwig, she did not want to leave the King's statue unfinished, and further, she wanted to assure the king that she was not one of those who had plotted against him. When she received no reply, she sent other letters, probably intercepted by Eisenhart, telling His Majesty that she wanted to go to America, but not before completing his statue. Finally Elisabet received a curt, almost insolent, letter, presumably from the King, but again probably dictated by Eisenhart without the King's knowledge, which commanded her presence at the Prussian embassy by Baron von Eisenhart and Baron von Werthern.

At once Elisabet indignantly dispatched the following note to the King, knowing that Eisenhart would intercept it: "Schwabing Villa, 1870: Have stayed. Quite enchanted by your thoughtful benevolence, by so many gifts from you. Am not coming to the Palace. Too tired. Besides, I am neither egotist nor slave. Elisabet Ney."[25]

When she told Edmund what had transpired, he agreed that Eisenhart and Werthern were not above reprisals and that they and Cenci should leave Munich quickly. After sending the

King's statue to the sculptor Friedrich Ochs in Berlin to be finished and executed into marble,[26] Elisabet, Edmund and Cenci
packed bags and trunks, covered the statues and furniture, dis-
charged the servants, sold the ponies, and shuttered and
locked the villa. Then Elisabet realized, with regret, that she
was not only leaving her incompleted statue of the King, but
also the statue *Prometheus Bound,* in the Odysseys–Saal in
the Palace. Because Edmund believed that it would not be safe
for them to remain in Munich until they could book passage to
New York, Elisabet telegraphed her parents to expect them in
Münster.

As far as Adam and Anna Ney were concerned, Elisabet
was returning home in disgrace rather than triumph. Even the
assurance of a legal marriage would have made little difference; their marriage was not performed in the Catholic Church;
so the Neys would not have recognized it as a legitimate marriage. Elisabet and Cenci stayed in the Neys' home, but because Herr and Frau Ney did not accept Edmund as Elisabet's
husband, he lodged at the Köng von England Hotel and spent
his time busily securing steamship accommodations, which
were difficult to obtain because of the war; negotiating necessary changes in his financial affairs; and reading proof for his
soon–to–be published book on Immanuel Kant.

While in Münster, Elisabet was saddened to learn that
Bishop Müller had died a short time before; she knew that her
parents were glad that he did not know of her manner of living.
Cenci enthusiastically discussed the coming baby with Frau
Ney, never realizing that the Neys considered it an illegitimate
child and were glad that it would be born in far away America.
On *Die Weihnactenabend* (Christmas eve), the Neys attended a
midnight mass without Elisabet, but with her brother Fritz,
now a forty–year–old schoolmaster, and his wife, Leonore Ney-
Stoetmann.[27]

After the Neys returned from the Cathedral and Elisabet
saw the grieved look on their faces, she regretted that they felt
that she had dishonored them, especially when she saw tears in
her father's eyes. But her life had changed drastically since she
was last in Münster; she could no longer successfully communicate with her parents. She tried to explain that she and Dr.
Montgomery wanted a new environment where they could live

in freedom, away from the war, turmoil, and repression in Europe, to start a new life and family.

When they left Münster, after a two weeks' stay, for their steamship departure from Bremen, Elisabet sadly kissed her parents, her father, age seventy and her mother, age sixty-eight, and bade them *"Auf Wiedersehen,"* as she wondered if she would ever see them again.

Self–portrait, 1864
— **Courtesy Texas State Library Archives**

Edmund Montgomery, 1856
— **Courtesy Texas State Library Archives**

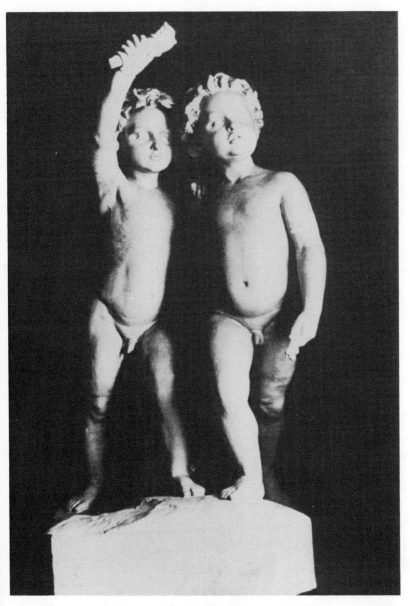

Sursum (Die Brüder Genii), *1864*
— *Courtesy Texas State Library Archives*

Elisabet Ney standing beside **Prometheus Bound** *in Odyessey-Saal, Royal Palace, Munich, 1869*

Courtesy Texas State Library Archives

King Ludwig II of Bavaria as a Knight of St. Hubert, 1870
— **Courtesy Texas State Library Archives**

Liendo Plantation Mansion, 1853
— *Courtesy Texas State Library Archives*

Statue of Sam Houston, 1893

— *Courtesy State Department of Highways and Public Transportation*

Statue of Stephen F. Austin, 1893
— *Courtesy State Department of Highways and Public Transportation*

Lorne Montgomery, 1898
— *Courtesy Texas State Library Archives*

Formosa 1892–1902
— **Courtesy Texas State Library Archives**

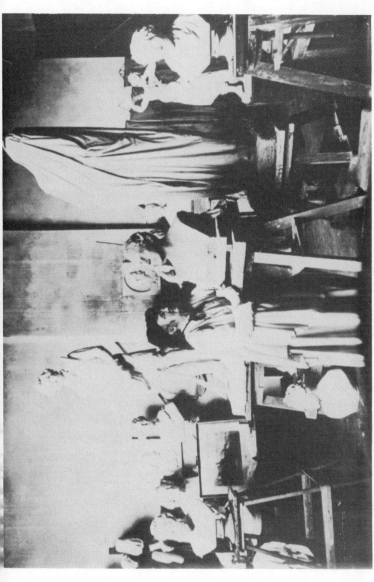

Elisabet Ney in her studio with the bust of William Jennings Bryan, Lady Macbeth covered, 1900

— Courtesy Texas State Library Archives

Afternoon Tea at Formosa, 1905
— *Courtesy Texas State Library Archives*

Lady Macbeth, *1905*
— *Courtesy DeGolyer Library — Southern Methodist University*

II

The New
World
1871–1907

14

Flight to Thomasville

Our life is closed, our life begins.
The long, long anchorage we leave,
The ship is clear at last, she leaps!
Walt Whitman

"We're fortunate to book this passage," Edmund told Elisabet and Cenci. "Until recently, the French had blockaded Bremen harbor, but now their navy is in such disarray that our Captain, Herr von Oterendorp, feels that we can leave without problems."

The three ascended the gangplank, registered their passports with the purser, and boarded the *SS Main* of the North German Lloyd Line on January 14, 1871, with New York as their destination. On the purser's list, they signed themselves as Dr. Edmund Montgomery, Miss Elisabet Ney, and Fräulein Crescentia Simath, and were assigned to three consecutive first class staterooms. This ship of three thousand tons, fully loaded with merchandise and 250 passengers, was one of the first ships to sail from Bremen after the French could no longer enforce their blockade.[1] Most of the thirty or more first class passengers were German businessmen; a few women were also aboard.

These voyagers were anxious for news from the war. "What's the latest word?" they wanted to know as they grabbed the newspapers along with the ship's bulletins. "Has Paris surrendered?" According to latest information, "Not yet."

Along with the other passengers, Elisabet worried about this siege of Paris, but unlike her German fellow-travelers, her concern was for the French; however, she realized that because the ship carried no wireless, they would probably reach New York before they learned the outcome. After the *Main* entered the English Channel, the passengers put aside their uncertainties about the siege of Paris for anxieties about the possibility of being stopped by a French gunboat, or being sunk by a mine planted off the French coast. After reaching the Atlantic Ocean safely, the men relaxed to the extent of placing bets as to whether Paris would fall before the last of the month when they were due in New York. The odds were that it would.

As they steamed toward the mid-Atlantic, a winter storm descended with huge, dark frothy waves, howling winds, and hard-driving rain that rolled and tossed the ship, sending most of the passengers to their cabins, seasick. All this turbulence scarcely registered with Elisabet because of her troubled doubts and misgivings about this venture into an unknown future. Would this New World really be so much better than the Old?

Because of the storm, Elisabet and Edmund spent their time reading the books and essays that Edmund had brought along to keep their minds from anxieties while they were confined to the innards of the ship by the weather. Edmund suggested that Elisabet read the essay called "Self-Reliance" by the American writer and philosopher, Ralph Waldo Emerson, who wrote: "Trust thyself: every heart vibrates to that iron string."[2] After reading several of Emerson's *Essays,* Elisabet read *Leaves of Grass* by another American, Walt Whitman. Then they read and discussed Thomas Paine's two books concerned with the rebellion of the American colonies during their war for independence: *The Rights of Man* and *The Age of Reason,* as well as accounts of the British reformers Robert Owens and Frances Wright.[3] After reading this literature on freedom,

Elisabet suggested that perhaps they could organize a colony in Thomasville like Garibaldi's at Caprera. America needed a freedom village where liberated Negroes and freedom-loving people could learn what it meant to live the words, "equality and freedom."

After so much absorption in literature and enforced inactivity, Elisabet was delighted when the storm abated. She and Ceni wrapped themselves in the heavy, embroidered shawls, which Elisabet had purchased in the Near East, and briskly walked around the ship's promenade deck to exercise and to breathe the fresh sea air. Sometimes Edmund joined them. Elisabet noticed the curious sidelong glances that they received from the other passengers, especially from the women, who sat in the deck chairs bundled in blankets against the cold. Even the men interrupted a game of shuffleboard to eye the three strollers. Elisabet laughed as she said to Edmund, "I'm sure a nosey *Hausfrau*-passenger has managed a look at the passenger list and spread the tidbit of gossip that, since we aren't registered as man and wife, we must be lovers, with Cenci as our chaperon."

When Elisabet made this remark, simultaneously she and Edmund repeated: "The meager, stale, forbidding ways of custom, law, and statue."

This same passenger curiosity followed them into the ship's dining salon where Elisabet had difficulty making the waiters understand that her bread must be "wind-dried" to a certain crispness and that, under no circumstances, should the steward serve her any meat. The fellow-diners observed Elisabet's special diet with amusement and, as Elisabet anticipated, also commented upon and disapproved of her self-styled clothes. "Let's speak English in the dining room," Elisabet suggested. "Then perhaps most of these Germans won't understand us."

As usual Elisabet and Edmund ignored the gossip but inadvertently caused more of it when, on January 26 they celebrated Elisabet's "thirty-sixth natal day" (actually her thirty-eighth) with a special dinner. To insure as much privacy as possible, the three waited until many of the diners had left before entering the dining room. Elisabet dressed in her white Grecian-styled tunic with a gold girdle, which now had to be loosened around the waist; Edmund dressed more elegantly than usual in a Prince

Albert coat with an embroidered pearl–grey waistcoat, black broadcloth trousers, and patent leather boots, complimented by a wide white satin cravat; Cenci wore a colorful Turkish shawl over her best brown silk dress.[4]

After they were seated at their usual table, Edmund raised his glass of *Sekt* (a sparkling German wine), "A toast to my beloved Elisabet: May her natal day and every day be filled with happiness and love and may our child be worthy of her." Then he turned to Cenci for another toast: "To our valued housekeeper and friend, may she realize how much we value her loyalty and affection."

After Edmund's salutations, Elisabet lifted her glass toward him: "To my 'best friend,' whom I love dearly, may you find in America all the success and happiness that you deserve." Then they drank a toast to the Stralendorffs and another to their future in Thomasville. This festive meal lasted until almost daybreak. Quickly, tales about the *Geburstag Feier* (birthday party) circulated among the passengers, but the gossip was quickly forgotten in the excitement of the ship's approach to New York Harbor on January 28, after fourteen days at sea.[5]

The cry, "land in sight," sent Elisabet to the porthole in her stateroom to see the passengers excitedly assembled on deck, where she, Edmund, and Cenci quickly joined them as they steamed into the harbor. Although snow was falling heavily, Elisabet could discern the tall buildings of New York City rising before her. A tugboat chugged out to meet the *Main* and to tow her to her berth at a pier on the Hudson River in Hoboken, New Jersey for quarantine and customs. As soon as the ship docked, the German passengers rushed to buy newspapers from the vendors who came on shipboard.

The newspapers told the story that Paris had indeed surrendered on January 18, and that King Wilhelm of Prussia was crowned Kaiser, Emperor of a new German Empire consisting of all the German states except Austria. How unpalatable this coronation must have been to the defeated Parisians! Bismarck had triumphed. With a lump in her throat, Elisabet read that King Ludwig had sent a representative to Versailles to read the letter, dictated by Bismarck, in which he requested that his uncle, King Wilhelm of Prussia, be proclaimed Emperor. Under the peace terms, Germany extracted an indemnity of a great sum of money plus the territories of Alsace and Lorraine from France.[6] On receiving this news, passengers who won their bets collected their winnings and everyone disembarked for New York City.

Edmund hired a carriage to take them to a hotel where they could rest, acquire "land legs," and become acquainted with America; however, a bitter New York snowstorm kept them hotel-bound for the following several days. While they remained in the hotel, Elisabet dreaded to read the *New York Times,* which was filled with reports of the German victory over France.

While Edmund also read the papers, he noticed a small dispatch from London, which announced the approaching marriage of Princess Louise, the fourth daughter of Queen Victoria, to John Southerland Campbell, The Marquis of Lorne and heir to the eighth Duke of Argyll. Edmund showed this notice to Elisabet and remarked, "He's a cousin, a distant cousin, from the same part of Scotland as my forebears." Although Edmund had not discussed the fact, Elisabet knew that he was related to important persons, but now she was impressed to learn that Edmund could claim as a cousin the son-in-law of Queen Victoria.[7]

Although Elisabet and Edmund had planned to sightsee in New York, the continuing storm prevented it. They were also eager to begin their journey to Georgia and left New York on the first clear day and were not able to observe much of the city except to note that it seemed as busy and bustling as London, only not so large. They traveled to Jersey City by ferry and from there they boarded a railroad sleeping car to begin their long journey south along the coastline where the war between the North and the South was fought. Edmund explained that the hostilities had lasted for four years; so they would be passing through a war-ruined countryside.

After Philadelphia, they had a brief stop in Baltimore, where Edmund remembered that some of his friends who had fled the 1848 revolution from Frankfurt had settled. At the end of the day they arrived in Washington, D.C., only to learn of a twenty-four hour stopover between trains. Until now Cenci had stoically accepted the inconveniences of travel, but when she experienced the multitude of black faces around her, she panicked. "Herr Doctor," she wailed, "I've never seen so many

Negro people together before. Are they the 'Darkies' who were slaves? Why are there so many in the capital city? Are they dangerous?"

To calm Cenci's anxieties, Edmund explained that in the period immediately following the end of the conflict between the Northern and Southern States, freed slaves, as well as Negroes from the North, responded to President Lincoln's promise of a better life and crowded into the already overcrowded national capital. People from other parts of the country descended on the triumphant Federal Government in the expectation of jobs, which further increased the population that was already swollen with Union troops stationed in the city to prevent an invasion. Because of these new arrivals, Edmund discovered that accommodations were scarce and inadequate. Fortunately, Edmund found a respectable place for the night with the help of the station-master, who was impressed with Edmund's dignified, if foreign, appearance. When they registered at their small hotel, the clerk told them that in the past six years, Washington had grown from a population of 20,000 to its present 120,000, creating a difficult situation.[8]

Before leaving Washington, they saw the Capitol, the Executive Mansion, the adjoining government buildings, the tidal basin, and the Potomac River. Edmund pointed out Ford's Theater where President Lincoln had been assassinated and told Elisabet that Lincoln had been watching a play by their friend Tom Taylor, *Our American Cousin,* at the time that he was shot.[9]

"Who is the President now?" Elisabet asked.

"Ulysses S. Grant," Edmund told her, "the victorious Union General."

From Washington the travelers chugged through Virginia toward Richmond, the former capital of the Confederacy, through a damp, dreary countryside of unkept farms and muddy, deeply rutted roads, which provided slow transportation for wagons and buggies. From the train window Elisabet saw people dressed in worn, homemade clothes; however, the tattered Negroes, with some of the children barefooted in the cold, looked even more pathetic than the white people. Elisabet heard the ragged black children called "pickaninnies," and the women, many wearing a red bandana kerchief tied around their heads, called "black mammies," and all referred to as "the niggers" who apparently lived in the rundown shanties beside the railroad track.

Besides the pitiable humans, the ravages of the war were only too obvious in the burned-out capital of Richmond. The city had begun to rebuild, but at a slow pace. Even from the railroad car window, Elisabet could sense the dull, weary feeling of defeat in this once beautiful and prosperous city. "Where are the fine old Southern mansions I've heard about?" Elisabet asked as the monotonous journey continued amidst soot from the coal-burning locomotive, whistles and clanging signals at the cross-roads, and bleak, poverty-stricken landscapes all the way to Wilmington, North Carolina, where the train was again delayed several hours before continuing along the seacoast to still another delay at Charleston.[10]

At Charleston, even though the weather was damp and cold, the three walked around outside the train for exercise before going inside the depot to warm themselves at the pot-bellied, woodburning, iron stove in the center of the waiting room. Elisabet noticed that the persons crowded around the stove were all white, with the few Negroes in the depot seated on a far bench under a sign, "Colored." The strangeness of the depot, the unintelligible accents, and the black faces confused and bewildered Cenci and only her unbounded faith in Herr Doctor kept her from giving way to her fears.

Cenci was obviously relieved to board the train again with Miss Ney and Herr Doctor as it resumed its crawl to reach what was left of the city of Savannah after General William Tecumseh Sherman's destructive, scorched-earth march. Sherman's soldiers had not been content to pull up the railroad spikes, but also heated the rails and wrapped them around trees so that they could not be used again.[11] At Savannah, another change of trains was necessary to the Brunswick and Florida railroad, built in 1860, for the last leg of the trek some two hundred miles across swamp country to Thomasville.[12] Before leaving Savannah, Edmund sent a telegram to the Stralendorffs that he, Miss Ney, and their housekeeper expected to arrive that evening. Because the roadbed and rails were still being overhauled and the terrain was soft and boggy, the train could only proceed at cautious speeds of fifteen to twenty miles per hour.

Elisabet complained wearily, "In all my life and in all my

travels, I've never had such a miserable journey. This country is so poor, so *ugly*. In spite of Stralendorff's colorful description, I dread to see Thomasville."

Although she was tired and concerned about the new life ahead for her, Cenci never considered that she would not be a part of it. Edmund was also fretful, worried about whether or not his telegram had been delivered, for he had noticed along the way the disrepair of the telegraph lines. At long last, after dark, the train inched to a stop in Thomasville, Georgia. In the dim light of a so-called railroad depot, Elisabet discerned an elegantly dressed couple.

"The Stralendorffs!" Elisabet exclaimed happily as she gratefully embraced Margaret von Stralendorff without waiting for an introduction. The young bride, scarcely twenty, was poised and beautiful — a tall, slender, blue-eyed blond dressed in fashionable blue velvet. The Baron standing beside her was a handsome, north-German blue-eyed blond, ten years older than his wife. He had a somewhat distant look in his eyes, not unlike Edmund's, but his beard and good looks could not conceal the flushed appearance of a consumptive.[13] After greetings of welcome, the Stralendorffs and their Negro servant loaded the three bone-weary travelers into a carriage, which the servant drove, while the Stralendorffs rode in their two-seated buggy through the darkness to their home.

Inside the house, hospitable candles and kerosene lamps greeted the wayfarers in a large parlor tastefully furnished in Victorian-styled elegance with appointments apparently assembled from many travels: a German crystal chandelier, gilded, rococo-style framed mirrors, Belgium lace curtains, and even a grand piano.[14]

A Negro maid appeared with sandwiches and wine and showed Elisabet and Edmund to their rooms where pitchers of warm water were waiting for baths in a tin, sit-down bathtub. The hosts gave Cenci a room in another part of the house, and for her assuagement, the Negroes had quarters outside.

The next morning Elisabet awoke, as she usually did after a sound sleep, alert and energetic. Before the others were awake, she left the house to explore the town. As she walked along the clay-dirt street she saw that the Stralendorff's home was a two-story white house with green shutters, hidden away from the street in four acres of pine trees, which provided pri-

vacy as well as shade from the sun in summer. Along this main
street, she passed many small shops, some with trees in front
to serve as hitching posts. Because it was so early, the town
was not yet awake; the fresh morning air smelled of pine and
oak trees from the surrounding forest. As a climax of her impressions, in the center of the town she came upon a magnificent live oak tree up-raising its strong branches as though to
bless all beneath. As Elisabet stood silently before this enormous tree, she felt that any land that could nourish such a tree
would be an agreeable place to live.[15]

When Elisabet walked quickly back to the Stralendorff's,
she found everyone eating breakfast. Stralendorff asked her
what she thought of their village. She replied that it was
charming and what she admired most was a huge oak tree in
the center of the town. That tree was called the "Great Oak,"
Stralendorff told her and was two hundred years old. He and
Margaret loved the tree and had found this little community
an ideal place to live.

Margaret interrupted, "Miss Ney, don't let the special
breakfast Cenci prepared get cold." But when she saw Elisa-
abet's three eggs, sugar and cognac, along with dry bread, the
well-bred young Baroness could not restrain from a look of
puzzlement.

"Is everything the way you want it, Miss Ney?" Cenci
anxiously inquired, only too happy to resume her role as housekeeper, especially when Elisabet replied, "*Ja, ja, es ist ausgez-
eichnet* (excellent)."

After breakfast they toured the large, rambling house with
servant's quarters outside in the rear; the kitchen was built
apart from the house, but attached by a covered walkway, with
an ample wood fireplace for cooking. Stralendorff then proudly
showed them the study that he had added to the upstairs,
above the trees to receive sunlight, with windows on four sides
surrounded by an outside gallery.[16] This light, comfortable
study appealed to Edmund, who told Elisabet they would find
a house like this, or they would build one.

Stralendorff explained that in antebellum days, Thomasville, located in the extreme south-central part of Georgia, was
a prosperous Southern city with more than fifteen hundred inhabitants, over nine hundred of whom were white, in a slave
culture of wealthy plantations, each of which included hun-

dreds of acres maintained by slave labor. Now in 1871, of the
town's sixteen hundred inhabitants, only six hundred were
white; however, they included the mayor and city council.[17] Although General Sherman missed Thomasville in his march
through Georgia, the area was nonetheless devastated. Thomasville, like most villages and towns in the South, had seen the
end of an era.

Now that Elisabet and Edmund had decided to live in
Thomasville, Stralendorff was eager to show them his "Mecklenburg Farm," named after the duchy in Germany where he
was born, consisting of 350 acres on Coffee Road.[18] During the
drive there, they passed a stately, once-white colonial plantation homestead with a wide gallery and white columns across
the front. When Elisabet saw a "For Sale" sign, she insisted on
inspecting the place. She and Edmund liked the design and
beauty of the old mansion, even in its run-down condition;
however, Stralendorff pointed out that if Edmund bought the
house and could find labor to maintain the land, he would need
a tremendous fortune, with slight chance, in this post-recon-
struction economy, of the plantation's ever becoming profitable.

In all parts of the South, mansions such as that one remained unsold. The once luxurious mansions of the great plantations of Millpond, Boxhall, and Greenwood, in the vicinity of
Thomasville,[19] were vacant and deteriorating like raped and
abandoned ladies: they displayed peeling paint, broken windows, rotting woodwork, overgrown lawns and gardens and
disintegrating slave quarters.

When they reached the Mecklenburg Farm, Stralendorff
showed them a one-room "hunting lodge," (as the Germans
called it) and a barn and stable for the saddle horses, where he
and Margaret could come from town to ride horseback and to
enjoy the wooded countryside. Within a few days after seeing
this country format, Edmund purchased one site of fifty and
another one hundred acres adjoining the Mecklenburg Farm
for $1,250.00. The tract contained a horse-powered cotton gin
with the capacity of ginning one to two bales per day, but no
dwelling. A short time later Edmund bought additional land,
until his holdings were almost four hundred acres.[20]

While Elisabet and Edmund were still guests in the Stralendorffs' home, Margaret told Elisabet that her parents had

bought and furnished the house before she and Vicco moved in. She also said that they planned a formal party to introduce Miss Ney and Dr. Montgomery to their neighbors. Indeed, in these dreary days in Thomasville, few could afford to give parties, certainly not stylish receptions such as provided by the German Baron and his bride. Many of the guests were people who had once owned grand plantation homes, but now lived at a level near poverty. They came dressed in whatever old finery was still available for this rare opportunity to dine in fashionable elegance; they were happy for a chance to live the luxurious life again, if only for a few hours. Added to this was an occasion to meet these "peculiar" rich Europeans who had bought land in their town.[21]

For this event Elisabet wore her gold, loosely hung, Grecian-styled tunic, which disguised her pregnancy, but certainly was not the fashion of the day, gold sandals, rather than high-top shoes, and the diamond bracelet given to her by Queen Marie of Hannover. Edmund made his usual handsome appearance in elegant gentlemen's attire. At the reception Elisabet was vivacious and charming; she talked of Europe, the Franco-Prussian War, King Ludwig, and listened to the guests tell of their European travels "before the War." To these Southerners, Elisabet was an enigma. They asked each other: "Why was she called 'Miss Ney' and introduced Dr. Montgomery as her 'friend'? Were they married or were they free lovers who planned to start a colony in Thomasville? Why did she wear such unusual clothes? Was 'Miss Ney' pregnant?"

Margaret chose to ignore the gossip among her guests until one asked her if "Miss Ney" was "in a family way." Then Margaret replied, properly, "I'm sure I don't know. I also consider that it is only the concern of the Doctor and Miss Ney."

When Margaret informed Elisabet that the neighbors had asked her questions about "Miss Ney's" condition, Elisabet said: "The world must be taught to trust and not suspect. A union of man and woman, designed to pass on to another the gift of life, is the most noble and most beautiful of human relationships, transcending all convention, too binding in itself for any law or statue, too sacred for any so-called holy rite or ceremony. 'Let me not to the marriage of true minds admit impediments.' Are things personal and precious shouted by a crier at every street corner?"[22]

After Elisabet's enunciation, Margaret told Vicco that she

could no longer be happy with Miss Ney and the Doctor living in the same house. To appease her, Stralendorff suggested that by adding four rooms to their one-room hunting lodge, Miss Ney, the Doctor, and Cenci could stay there until they completed a house on their own land. Both Elisabet and Edmund sensed the tension that their presence was causing; so when Stralendorff suggested that he add rooms to the hunting lodge for temporary quarters, everyone welcomed the idea.

After examining their property, Elisabet and Edmund decided to construct their home in a small grove of pines and oaks three and a half miles northeast of Thomasville on Old Coffee Road, near the Mecklenburg Farm.[23] They undertook this new project with more enthusiasm than they had felt since leaving Europe. Edmund's first purchase was the best buggy available and a fine two-hundred-dollar spotted horse that they named "Ulysses" to transport them back and forth to town; then he purchased the finest supplies that he could locate for the construction of the house.

Although Elisabet had experienced the luxuries of King Ludwig's palace, now that she was living in this rough homespun country, she decided to build accordingly. She drew up plans that called for the house to be constructed of hewn logs with spaces between filled with mortar and to include a wide veranda across the front, where she and Edmund could sit and admire the sunsets, the surrounding forest, fields, zig-zag fences, and the travelers along Old Coffee Road. The ground floor would consist of a large parlor, hall, dining room, kitchen, and two small rooms in the rear, with the bedrooms for herself, Edmund, and Cenci, including a nursery, located on the second floor.[24]

The rustic German-styled house was soon completed in April, for there were plenty of workmen available and Edmund had the money to pay them. Elisabet invited the Stralendorffs to dinner to inspect the new home, to the delight of Cenci who would have the opportunity to show the Stralendorffs that her "family" also understood gracious living. Happily, Cenci prepared an Austrian dinner of *Bauernschmaus,* but no meat, only vegetables for Miss Ney, along with Tyrolean *Kuchen und Kekse* (cake and cookies). To accompany the meal, Edmund discovered a few remaining bottles of good vintage *Rhein Wein* that he had packed from Germany. To decorate the rough-finished interior, Elisabet displayed her Oriental rugs and draperies, festooned the staircase with Spanish moss, and scattered pine cones and branches for garnish and gaiety.

When the Stralendorffs arrived and admired Elisabet's handiwork, Stralendorff asked if they had named the house.

With a grin Edmund suggested, "From its magnificent elegance, it looks like a *Holzlotzschloss* [log castle] to me." Everyone agreed that the name was a good one and drank toasts to the new home. As the evening flowed gaily, Edmund and Stralendorff sang German student songs acappella; Margaret recited original verses, and Elisabet repeated portions of Goethe's "Imphigeneia in Taurus" in the melodious voice that had charmed King Ludwig. Although her child was expected soon, Elisabet looked lovely in her loose Grecian tunic. Edmund proposed a toast to the future health and happiness of the Stralendorffs, who in turn toasted the future of the soon-expected heir.

"*Prost!*" [cheers] Let's drink to our lives in Thomasville," Stralendorff proposed, "and may *Holzlotzschloss* always be filled with happiness and love."

Travel in America

. . . Let us strive on to finish the work we are in,
to bind up the nation's wounds. . . .

Abraham Lincoln

Shortly after the housewarming party for *Holzlotzschloss*, the Stralendroffs left for Boston to spend the summer with Margaret's parents, but Elisabet and Edmund were too busy to be lonely: Edmund was occupied with last-minute revisions of his soon-to-be-published book in German, *Die Kant'sche Erkenntnisslehre*, which was critical of the philosophy of Immanuel Kant; Elisabet was engaged with the planting of flowers and shrubs around the house and with the damming up of one end of a drainage basin to form a pond, which she called a lake. Although she had no knowledge of farming, she insisted upon supervising the planting and cultivating, and the buying of supplies, seed, and corn rations.[1]

Because Elisabet would soon be giving birth, she needed to hire someone to assist her with the farm. She found an intelligent ex-slave, Uncle Archie Cone, who not only was a good farmer, but also knew how to supervise the Negro workers,

many of whom had yet to adjust to their freedom and to working for wages.[2] Some of the Negroes available as farm hands
did not like Uncle Archie; they called him "nigger-driver," but
he was fair and they desperately needed to earn a living. Even
with Uncle Archie's assistance, Elisabet insisted that she was
to make the decisions as to what crops to plant and when, but
Uncle Archie was experienced in dealing with the "white
folks" and, by subtle suggestions, let "Mistress Ney" think
that his ideas were her own.[3]

When imports were curtailed or impossible during the war,
the Southerners had been forced to plant crops which were
self-sustaining rather than raising the one crop of cotton for
export, as had been the custom in the past. As a slave Uncle
Archie had worked as a plantation field hand and knew the soil
and what it best produced. If this neglected land were to be
profitable, Elisabet needed the expertise of someone like Uncle
Archie and she grew to depend on his farming ability.

While driving Ulysses and the new buggy back to *Holzlotzschloss*, after buying supplies in town, Elisabet felt contractions in her abdomen which she identified as the beginning
of labor. She applied the buggy-whip to encourage Ulysses to
canter. As soon as she arrived, she rushed into the house and
called, "Edmund! Cenci!" When they both appeared, she exclaimed, "I believe my labor's begun!"

"What do we do, Herr Doctor? What do we do?" Cenci im-
plored.

Although he had practiced medicine, Edmund had never
delivered a baby, but he told Cenci to have warm water and
sterile cloths available and to make Miss Ney as comfortable
as possible while he went to bring the doctor from Thomasville.

"*Sich breeilen*," Herr Doctor, "*bitte, sich breeilen* [hurry,
please, hurry]," Cenci pleaded.

After he determined that Elisabet's pains were not acute
or occurring too frequently, Edmund calmed both women by
telling them that there was time for a doctor to arrive from
town before the baby. Poor Ulysses was not eager for a fast return, but Edmund saw to it that they covered the three miles
to Thomasville at a fast pace. Through the Stralendorffs, Edmund had met Dr. James R. Reid, an old-fashioned family
physician who had delivered dozens of babies; so he drove to

Dr. Reid's office and explained that Miss Ney was in the beginning stages of labor.[4]

Sympathetically, Dr. Reid informed Edmund to locate Aunt Dolly, who was the best midwife around, and to take her to his place as quickly as he could. The Doctor said that he would come as soon as he could dismiss his patients and drive out. Edmund gave directions to his home, but the Doctor knew, for he and everyone else in Thomasville was aware of where the eccentric Europeans lived.

Edmund was unfamiliar with midwives, especially black ones, but in rural towns in the South, the help of a midwife in the birth of a baby was standard procedure. Following Dr. Reid's directions, Edmund found Aunt Dolly, a rotund, pleasant–faced older black woman dressed in "mammy" fashion with a red bandana tied around her head and a clean white apron over her ample front. She quickly packed her bag of supplies and climbed into the back seat of the buggy, while Edmund urged a tired Ulysses to pull them as fast as the horse could be persuaded to go over the bumpy road.

By the time that the two reached the "Log Castle," Elisabet's pains were occurring at closer intervals. Without formalities Aunt Dolly took over kindly and efficiently. As she patted Elisabet's cheek and held her hand, even Cenci was glad to take orders from her. Although the pains had become body-wrenching, Elisabet did not cry out. Edmund did what he could to ease her suffering, and by the time Dr. Reid arrived, the baby was practically born. Then, after a mighty, wrenching effort, through her pain, Elisabet heard a newborn wail. "Is it my girl?" she asked weakly.

Dr. Reid announced: "Congratulations, you have a fine baby boy," as he handed the newborn to Aunt Dolly.

"I'm so proud and happy, *meine Lieb*," Edmund said as he bent over and kissed Elisabet. "We have a perfect little son. So very much I love you both."

Elisabet was so relieved that the ordeal was over and that the baby was healthy that she did not dwell on her disappointment of not having a daughter. Cenci was ecstatic, even to the extent of hugging Aunt Dolly. "Miss Ney, Herr Doctor, I've never seen such a beautiful baby!" exclaimed Cenci.

Aunt Dolly was happy too. After years as a midwife, she always enjoyed the happy experience of bringing a new life into the world, but she was disconcerted when she heard this rich white lady referred to as "Miss Ney"; however, Edmund gave her such a generous amount of money that she decided that they be "quality folks," sort of queer from the "furrin" way dey talk an' act, but still "quality folks." Elisabet said "thank you" with warmth and gratitude.

"What will you name him, Miss Ney?" Cenci was anxious to know.

Certain that she would have a daughter, "Elisabet" was the only name decided upon. Then Elisabet remembered how well Schopenhauer had liked his name, "Arthur," and how he had proudly explained that the name was the same in German, French, and English. She remembered also that it was Schopenhauer who first started her professional career. "My best friend," she said to Edmund. "What do you think of the name, Arthur Montgomery?"

"That's a fine name," Edmund agreed.

And little "Arti-dee," or *Männchen*, or *Liebchen*, as his mother and Cenci called him, prospered. Soon Elisabet had hung a hammock between two shady pine trees, where she happily nursed the baby during the hot, muggy Georgia summer.[5]

The birth did not go unnoticed in a town as small as Thomasville where every white person knew his neighbors and every Negro knew his and also delighted in knowing about the whites, especially since most of the Negroes had formerly been their slaves. Soon the villagers' main topic of conversation was about the "European free-lovers" who had brought a bastard child into the world. Because most of the townspeople were conservative Baptists or Methodists, they had no tolerance for such un-Christian behavior, or for what they considered to be living in sin. Although the tradespeople sold Elisabet and Edmund merchandise, they had no more personal contact than necessary, and they warned their children to come inside whenever these "strange people" came into town.

With the problems of the farm and raising a new child, neither Elisabet nor Edmund had time to socialize, even had they wanted to do so. To facilitate the supervision of the farm, Elisabet had learned to ride Ulysses astride wearing loose-fitting trousers stuffed into knee-high boots, a practice that further alienated the townspeople. When Elisabet wore dresses they hung in loose, Grecian style, the complete opposite of the fashionable women's tight waists, bustles, and high-laced pointed-toed shoes. Because Baron and Baroness Stralendorff were not in town to sponsor their friends and soften disapproval, the ostracism of Elisabet and Edmund was unrelenting.

These people castigated Elisabet for her unwomanly behavior more severly than they did the aristocratic Doctor, but he, too, received criticism when copies of his recently published book in German arrived in the local express office. The talk was that he was writing atheistic books and intended to set up a Godless, free-love colony of Europeans in Thomasville.[6]

As in the past, Elisabet and Edmund ignored the gossip and continued their assumed roles, with Elisabet supervising and Uncle Archie managing the farm, the sharecroppers, the field hands, and the operation of the small cotton gin (when any of the townspeople patronized it through necessity). Edmund buried himself in his study with his microscope, books, and writings; Cenci, with the help of Uncle Archie's wife, Aunt Nelly, cared for baby Arti and the household chores. The semitropical heat of the summer was difficult for everyone except Arti, who seemed to thrive regardless. When the crops were finally harvested in the fall, Elisabet balanced the books and discovered that the farm had operated at a deficit.

In the middle of October when the torrid heat ended, the Stralendorffs returned to Thomasville. When Elisabet and Edmund welcomed them home, the change they observed in Stralendorff was alarming: he was twenty pounds thinner, his face was haggard, his voice was hollow, and his walk was labored.[7] Edmund, the physician, recognized the symptoms of the last stages of consumption. Remembering the unfortunate Lord Brownlow, they realized that it would take an heroic effort to save Stralendorff. Although Edmund knew well the contagious nature of the disease and of his own susceptibility, he felt that with his knowledge of the treatment of consumption, he must do everything within his capability to help his friend.

Margaret presented another problem because she wanted to remain constantly with Vicco and refused to accept the contagious nature of the disease. Elisabet and Edmund forgot their own problems in their efforts to befriend these young people who were so desperately in need of help. Using every skill and medicine he knew in the treatment of consumption, Edmund worked with Stralendorff, while Elisabet tried to divert

Margaret from the sickbed with visits to little Arti, who was a delight for Margaret, and with horseback rides through the fall foliage of the countryside.

On these rides on a side-saddle the Baroness dressed in a blue velvet riding habit with an ostrich plume in her hat, while Elisabet, also riding side-saddle, wore a gold-trimmed ensemble which matched the spots on her horse, Ulysses.[8] Elizabet became fond of the lovely young bride, who was very much in love with her doomed husband. Under Edmund's solicitious care, Stralendorff rallied to the extent that he went for drives in his buggy and for visits to *Holzlotzschloss* and baby Arti.

By February of 1872, Stralendorff's health improved to the extent that he became obsessed with the idea of returning to Germany, to Mecklenburg, his family estate. After a visit there, his plans were to spend the summer in Germany, then go to the dry desert of Algeria and to return to Thomasville the following winter. When he heard of Stralendorff's intentions, Edmund said, "Poor Vicco wants to go home so badly that I must concur that he should go. Although the journey will be difficult, he should be at home when he dies."

When the Stralendorffs began serious preparations to return to Mecklenburg, Edmund suggested, "Why not go with them? They're the only friends we have in this unfriendly New World. Why not go back to the Old World that we know and make a life for ourselves there?"

"And admit failure," retorted Elisabet. "How could I return to Munich or Berlin after all that's happened?"

"But we could go to Italy, or to the south of France, or Spain — even to Madeira," Edmund insisted.

"*Nein, nein, nein,*" replied Elisabet. "Our home is now in America."

With a sense of loss, Elisabet and Edmund accompanied the Stralendorffs to the railroad depot and bade them "*Auf Wiedersehn und Gluckliche Reise*" (goodbye and pleasant journey). On the drive back to *Holzlotzschloss,* Elisabet confided to Edmund that she had received a letter from her father with the news that her mother had died a month previously in January.[9] Because she did not want to bring any more sadness to the Stralendorffs' departure, she had not mentioned it before now. With their friends gone, Elisabet knew that she had burned her bridges behind, and that she could never resume her life in Europe again. In a country as big as America there must be some desirable place for them to live other than the prejudiced backwoods of Georgia.

Elisabet had a plan: as soon as the crops were harvested, they could travel the country until they found a place where they could live and raise their children.

"Children?" Edmund asked.

"Edmund, 'my best friend,' you said that you wanted children, and I want a daughter so very much that . . . *ja,* I'm expecting another child in the fall. I hope she'll be as beautiful as Arti. At my age [thirty-nine] I can no longer put off having children."

Dropping his buggy reins in surprise, *"Liebchen,* I'm delighted," Edmund said. "We'll have a son and daughter, who will grow up in this free country. I know that we can find a suitable place for a home for our family."

A few months later, as Elisabet and Edmund had feared, Margaret wrote that Vicco had died on June 10, 1872, in Gamehl, near Wismar, in Mecklenburg.[10] Her plans were to return to Boston to be with her family; her father would attend to the sale of their property in Thomasville. This news of Stralendorff's death, plus the torpid summer heat, strengthened Elisabet and Edmund's resolve to leave Thomasville. In July, Elisabet arranged for Uncle Archie to manage the farm and cotton gin, and for Cenci and Aunt Nelly to care for young Arti and to take charge of the house, while she and Edmund set out on a journey through America in search of a new home.

Although their trip from New York down the East Coast to Thomasville had been wearisome and difficult, Elisabet and Edmund decided to retrace their course because Margaret had invited them to visit her family at their summer home in York Harbor, Maine. They also wanted to visit Baltimore, New York, Boston, and nearby Concord, where Edmund had been in correspondence with professors of the Concord School of Philosophy and the Free Religious Association of America. Although they wanted to evaluate the cities, they actually hoped to find a place in the country where they could live in privacy without interference and criticism.

After their brief visit in New York, they had a sad reunion with Margaret in the Russells' spacious and hospitable home on Beacon Street in Boston.[11] On their arrival the Russells were most gracious. They said that Margaret had told them how kind Miss Ney and Dr. Montgomery had been to her and to Vicco, while he was so ill. It had meant much to him to know and talk with his friends from Germany, and he had improved under the Doctor's care. Although his death saddened them, at least they knew that he died in his own home, in his own country where he had wanted to be.

Before Elisabet and Edmund's arrival, Margaret had explained Elisabet's eccentricities; so Mrs. Russell graciously overlooked Elisabet's dress style. She and Mr. Russell cordially entertained her and Edmund, talked of the cultural activities of Boston, and showed them the fine, old New England–styled homes, the Commons, and the environs of Harvard University, which to Elisabet and Edmund resembled a European university.

Before leaving Boston, the two visited Concord, where Edmund left a copy of his book, *Die Kant'sche Erkenntnisslehre widerlegt vom Standpunkt der Empirie*[12] at the Concord School of Philosophy, and as sightseers, they stood on the bridge where the colonists fired the first shots of the American Revolutionary War. "This is the town where the philosopher Ralph Waldo Emerson lives," Edmund told Elisabet, "and also Bronson Alcott and his daughter, the writer Louisa May Alcott. I only wish we had a letter of introduction to them, for I know we would find them congenial."

After a day in Concord, Elisabet and Edmund returned to Boston to drive to the Russells' summer home on the Atlantic Ocean, approximately fifty miles north of Boston, in York Harbor, Maine. While there, Elisabet received a letter from Cenci, which assured her that she and the baby were doing well and that affairs on the farm were about the same.

After a week's stay at the Russells' cool seaside home, Elisabet and Edmund were refreshed and invigorated and ready to travel by rail across Massachusetts and New York State to Buffalo on Lake Erie. From Buffalo they continued to Cleveland, Ohio, and through Indiana to Chicago. Neither Elisabet nor Edmund liked the bigness and crudeness of Chicago, and although that part of the country looked more prosperous than the South, they realized that the winters were extremely cold.

Because they were traveling almost constantly, they did

not stay in one place long enough to receive mail from Cenci; so Elisabet made an effort to put aside worries about Arti, Cenci, and the farm. She knew that Cenci loved and would care for Arti the same as if he were her own child. Elisabet had expected to return to Thomasville before her child was born, but she and Edmund had yet to find a suitable location. Because they preferred a German environment, they decided to continue their search to Wisconsin, where they had heard of a German colony. Before Edmund left Germany, he had obtained names of Germans who had emigrated to America in the 1850s. One was a liberal freedom fighter, Karl Bayrhoffer from Frankfurt, who had settled on a farm in Wisconsin in 1852, where a German settlement was already established.

With this in mind, Elisabet and Edmund traveled north to Milwaukee on Lake Michigan and to Wisconsin, where they learned of a German community at Rhinelander in the northern part of the state. Because stagecoach was the only means of travel available in that part of the country, to get there required an uncomfortable, arduous journey for Elisabet in her advanced state of pregnancy. After much seeking and questioning, they finally located Karl Bayrhoffer living on a farm in the vicinity of Rhinelander. He graciously invited the two wanderers to rest and to visit in his home, an invitation which Elisabet especially needed and appreciated. Although he had prospered over the years, Bayrhoffer told them that he had encountered the same sort of prejudice and bigotry alluded to the South, and that the extremely cold weather kept everyone indoors for four or five months out of the year."[13]

After this hospitable visit with Bayrhoffer, they realized that they must look for their Utopia in a warmer section of the country. Bayrhoffer suggested the new states of the Southwest, which had a warm climate and, reportedly, cheap land. Another of his suggestions was that they could go West across Wisconsin to St. Paul, Minnesota, located across the Mississippi River from Minneapolis, there board a Mississippi steamboat follow the river through the midwest farm country, and, if they wanted to go so far, to New Orleans and the Gulf of Mexico.

If they took such a trip, they could stop off and explore interesting looking places, then continue the river route on another steamboat. These recommendations sounded logical to Elisabet, who would soon be giving birth. On the first of October, they began their trek toward the Mississippi River, once again, by means of the nerve-wracking stagecoach.

Upon arriving in St. Paul, they secured passage on a Mississippi steamboat, a steam-powered paddlewheel vessel which traveled approximately fifteen miles per hour. "What a welcome relief from the railroads and the wretched stagecoaches," Elisabet commented as she observed the red, plush-covered furniture, curtains with ball fringes, and crystal chandeliers decorating the ship's rich accommodations.[14] The boat reminded her of the trips on the Rhine except that the Mississippi was much wider and bigger with sparce habitation along its banks unlike the villages and castles along the Rhine. On the boat she could relax, be comfortable, and enjoy the trip. After leaving St. Paul, the steamboat docked for the first stop at Red Wing, a hamlet on the Minnesota side of the river. By this time, Elisabet was experiencing labor pains. "Edmund," she cried, "my pains have begun! We must do something!"

When Edmund determined that no doctor was aboard the vessel, they decided to go ashore in search of a doctor or a midwife. Although they could not find a hotel, they did locate a respectable boarding house, but they encountered no black midwife in that pioneer village, not even a local doctor. As Elisabet's pains intensified, Edmund knew that he must take charge. He was shaken, but he had been with Elisabet when Arti was born and had observed Aunt Dolly and Doctor Reid. In his concern he asked help from the proprietor of the boarding house, a stout woman and mother of six, who quickly provided the necessary boiled water and cloth, while Edmund sterilized his instruments on the kitchen stove.

With his love and medical knowledge, Edmund assisted Elisabet through her labor until they heard the welcome cry of their newborn. With the ordeal over, Elisabet heard Edmund say, *"Meine kleine Mutter* — another fine little son. *Liebchen,* I'm happy and thankful. A new life is wonderful."

"And you are wonderful, my 'best friend,' " she murmured as she drifted into exhausted sleep from the sedative Edmund had given her, while the helpful landlady looked after the baby.

While recovering the next day, Elisabet asked Edmund about a name, because again she had not thought of a boy's name. "Let's call him 'Lorne,' for my cousin the Marquis of Lorne, oldest son of the Eighth Duke of Argyll," Edmund suggested.[15]

Elisabet liked the name. "Let's name him Lorne Ney Montgomery — born on October 9, 1872, in this faraway hamlet of Red Wing, Minnesota." [16]

After a week's recuperation, Elisabet felt well enough to travel with her infant son. Now that she had two sons, she wondered if by some prescience she had chosen two little boys to model for *Die Brüder Genii*. As she nursed and fondled her healthy infant, she longed to return to Arti. Now that he had a brother, she must raise them together. Edmund was as weary of travelling as Elisabet and agreed they must return to Thomasville regardless of whether or not they had found a place to live. Because Elisabet was nursing the baby, they decided that the most practical plan would be to continue on another steamboat.[17] Even though the going was slow, Elisabet could care for the baby and regain her strength. Possibly they could discover the place for their home on this trip back to Thomasville. If they wanted, they could leave the boat in St. Louis and travel by railroad through parts of Illinois, Kentucky, and Tennessee.

As they again boarded the paddlewheel steamer and chugged down the Mississippi, they saw the prosperous middlewest farm country of Minnesota, Wisconsin, Iowa, and Illinois. They both enjoyed the slow pace and the pleasant fall weather. On the steamboat Elisabet rapidly recovered her strength and baby Lorne thrived. By the time their boat finally docked in St. Louis, they were anxious to return to Georgia and decided to continue by rail.

After visiting the Blue Ridge mountains of Kentucky and the Carolinas and not finding a satisfactory site, early in December they reached Georgia — the devastated city of Atlanta. From there Elisabet wrote to Cenci about the birth of another son, of their failure to find an acceptable place for a home, and of their plans to arrive in Thomasville before Christmas. As they reached the final lap of their travels, both Elisabet and Edmund's spirits soared at the prospect of seeing Arti, Cenci, and their home again. In the middle of December, on the day before they were due to arrive in Thomasville, Edmund sent a telegram telling Cenci when they were scheduled to be there.

When their slow train stopped at Thomasville, Elisabet, holding the baby, and Edmund stepped eagerly from the railroad car, Uncle Archie and Aunt Nelly, with Arti, greeted them, but Cenci was not with them. "Where's Cenci?" they both asked.

Worridly twisting his hat, Uncle Archie explained, "Oh, Mistress Ney an' Marse Doctor, Miss Cenci, she's bin terrible sick wid de swamp fever. She ain't able ta come ta de depot."

"Then we must get to her as fast as we can," Edmund said as he and Elisabet embraced Arti and Aunt Nelly happily took over baby Lorne from Elisabet. Uncle Archie loaded everyone into the buggy and drove Ulysses back to *Holzlotzschloss.*

When Elisabet and Edmund saw Cenci, they were shocked at her emaciated body and hollow eyes brimming with tears to see her "family" again. She said that she had been very sick with what the doctor had called "malaria fever," even Arti had been ill with it. She had suffered so much that she had almost believed that she would never see Miss Ney and Herr Doctor again. Now that Herr Doctor was home to care for her, Cenci was sure she would improve. "I must get well now that I have two babies to look after," she told them.

Under Edmund's concerned attention, Cenci's health did improve; however, she was still very weak and subject to recurring flare-ups of the fever, which made Edmund even more aware of the unhealthy climate of this muggy Georgia swampland. Elisabet discovered still another deficit when she balanced the accounts of the farm operation.

After their return, the attitude of the townspeople toward Elisabet and Edmund grew even more hostile, especially when they learned that "another little bastard" had been added to the family. One of the men who was sitting on a bench in front of the general store, remarked, "That Miss Ney an' the Doctor jes' went off an' left their baby with a nurse an' two niggers; then, danged, if they didn't come back with another brat. An' I wish they'd git tharselves out of this town before iny more of thar kind shows up."

The man's wish was exactly what Elisabet and Edmund intended to do as soon as possible. To accomplish this, they made inquiries and received literature about the Southwest and read about the mild climate, open prairies, and good cheap land available in the new state of Texas.

In the local newspaper, the *Southern Enterprise,* Edmund read letters from ex-residents of Thomasville, who had moved to Texas after the Civil War and who described their prosperity, especially in growing cotton. They also wrote that ample land and water existed for ranches and livestock.[18] Elisabet and Edmund had received reports that the town of Brenham, Texas was a German farming community located on a railroad line to Austin, the state capital. This might be a place where they could find educated Germans to whom they could relate. Elisabet wrote to the German consul in Galveston for information as to what property was available in the vicinity of Brenham.

During this time of indecision, Cenci suffered another severe attack of fever, which made certain to Edmund that she would require all his medical skill if she were to recover. Because Edmund could not leave Cenci, and also a journey would be strenuous for the little ones, he suggested that Elisabet go to Texas alone. With Aunt Nelly's help, he would care for Cenci and the children. He would attempt to sell their property and to make necessary arrangements to join her whenever she could find an appropriate and affordable place in Texas.

Although Elisabet was apprehensive over the prospect of leaving her young sons and dreaded another long and tedious journey, she was determined to discover a place of refuge and freedom where they could establish their longed-for home. With these feelings in her heart, she set out for Texas.

16

Plantation in Texas

Away, away from men and towns
To the wild woods and to the downs....
            Percy Bysshe Shelley

With doubt and hope, Elisabet began her journey to the Lone Star State. She knew that Texas had been a "slave state"; however, she had been assured that actually in pre–Civil War days only a few large, slave–run plantations had existed in Texas. Until 1836 Texas had been a part of Mexico, but won independence and remained a self–governing Republic until December of 1845, at which time it became the twenty–eighth state of the United States. Texas seceded and joined the Confederacy at the onset of the Civil War in 1861 and was readmitted into the Union in 1870, just three years prior to Elisabet's arrival.

After the Civil War, thousands swarmed into the state, bringing with them whatever they had managed to salvage from the war — horses, livestock, and what household goods and farm implements that could be transported, along with the family, in a covered wagon.[1] Emigrants from Germany and

other parts of Europe also arrived in large numbers,[2] all feeling, as did their fellow emigrant, Elisabet Ney, that their path
toward a better future led to Texas.

After leaving New Orleans on the New Orleans, Opelousas
and Great Western Railroad to Brashear City (Morgan City)
on Berwick's Bay, she boarded a steamer to cross the Gulf of
Mexico to Galveston.[3] On shipboard she noticed the strange
assortment of passengers: Southerners dressed in shabby gen-
tility, homespun–clad adventurers, city–dressed Yankee op-
portunists, as well as rough–clothed European peasants, many
of whom were sturdy blond Germans with families ranging
from nursing babies to old grandparents.

When the steamer docked at the island port of Galveston,
Elisabet was pleasantly surprised to find a bustling city, with
a prosperous business district and blocks of fine Victorian
mansions surrounded by tropical palm trees, magnolias, and
oleanders. Fortified with a letter of introduction to Henry
Runge, the German Consul, Elisabet called upon his office. Although Consul Runge was not in, his nephew Julius Runge
was, and Elisabet conferred with him about the purpose of her
trip to Texas. "Are there any distressed plantation homes in
the vicinity of Brenham like the ones I saw for sale in Georgia?"
Elisabet asked.

Mr. Runge explained that although his business was not
real estate, he would give her a letter of introduction to his
friend in Brenham, Robert Leisewitz, a land agent and also a
cotton broker for a firm in Bremen, Germany, who could show
her whatever property in the area was available.[4] After this
cordial conversation in German and Runge's assurance that
Brenham was a "garden spot" and a solid German community,
Elisabet left for Brenham that afternoon by way of Houston
on the Houston and Central Texas Railway, which necessi-
tated a change of trains in Houston and again in Hempstead.
Inefficient and poorly equipped, the train required almost ten
hours to complete the 125 mile trip.

At two o'clock in the morning, Elisabet wearily arrived at
the deserted station in Brenham.[5] The stationmaster appreciated her fatigue and directed her to a small German hotel
which compared with those in the Rhine Valley: furnished with
heavy, hand–carved furniture, with pictures of castles and
villages along the Rhine in the German countryside, and was

staffed by German-speaking employees. After a sleepy porter showed her to her room, she thankfully fell into a big, heavy bed, covered herself with the eiderdown *Steppdecke* (comforter) such as she had known as a girl in Münster and was quickly asleep like a Grimm Brothers' Snow White who had found a home.

When Elisabet awoke the next morning to look at her environs, she discovered a prosperous, small-town farming community heavily populated with immigrants from Germany, who had been pouring into Texas since the 1830s. In the hotel dining room, Elisabet directed a surprised waitress to bring her dry bread, raw eggs, and brandy for breakfast. When she complained about the difficulty that she experienced in traveling the relatively short distance from Galveston to Brenham, the hotel manager explained that the change of trains in Hempstead was necessary because the farmers in Brenham realized that they must have some means to transport their products to market. To accomplish this, they financed and built the Washington County Railroad connecting Brenham with the Houston and Texas Central Railroad at Hempstead, but to reach Brenham, a change of trains was necessary at Hempstead.[6]

After receiving directions to Mr. Leisewitz' office, Elisabet walked along streets with German names, noticed the German-styled houses and shops, and heard the townspeople speaking the language. When she met Mr. Leisewitz, an intelligent young man with European manners, he greeted her courteously in German. After explaining her mission, Elisabet specified what she wanted: "First, my friend Dr. Montgomery's health requires a warm, dry climate; second, we need enough acreage to insure our privacy; third, we want to be near a cultured German-speaking community such as Brenham; and fourth, we would like a plantation homestead, such as those in the South, for a reasonable price. Do you know of any such place?"

"*Ja,* Miss Ney, I do indeed," Mr. Leisewitz told her. "The plantation known as 'Liendo' near Hempstead, if you are interested."

"Most certainly I am. Can you show it to me now?"

To reach Liendo, located approximately five miles southeast of Hempstead, Elisabet and Mr. Leisewitz boarded the

twenty-one mile spur railroad to retrace Elisabet's journey
from Hempstead to Brenham. Upon reaching Hempstead, they
rented a "gig," a two-wheeled buggy, to complete the five
miles to Liendo plantation. Mr. Leisewitz drove the gig over
the muddy, deeply rutted road where the Brazos frequently
and had recently overflowed. Although Elisabet was excited
by the prospect of viewing Liendo, she was depressed by the
desolate scenery along the way, especially when Mr. Leisewitz
called the shallow, muddy stream which they forded, "Clear
Creek." The next stream across their path, however, *was* clear
and fast-running.

"This is Pond Creek, which is on Liendo Plantation property and an asset in supplying clean water," Mr. Leisewitz explained. Because the recent flood had washed away the bridge,
they were forced to leave the gig, hitch the horse to a tree,
cross the stream by means of a flat log, and walk the remaining
quarter of a mile to the house. The growth of the thicket and
the Spanish moss-covered trees prevented Elisabet from dis-
cerning anything until she found herself standing before the
house.

Immediately, she was impressed with the stately white
frame, two-story, Colonial Greek-Renaissance style mansion,
trimmed with green shutters and four tall columns across the
front veranda, supporting an upstairs balcony. Elisabet's gaze
fell upon an eye-catching bronze star, the emblem of Texas, on
the gable of the roof immediately above the front entrance. It
bore the date, 1853, the same year that she had met Edmund in
Heidelberg.

On entering the house from the veranda, she stepped into a
large entrance hall, then into another hall which separated the
spacious, high-ceilinged rooms. Two parlors were on her left,
both with large brick fireplaces; a large dining room was across
the hall. When they inspected the dining room, Mr. Leisewitz
told her that in antebellum days the owners, Colonel Groce and
his southern-born wife, entertained with lavish dinners for
sometimes as many as two dozen guests seated at the table.

As she went through the house, Elisabet was glad that it
was empty so that she could visualize the ways that she could
use the eleven spacious rooms. "But where's the kitchen?" she
asked. Mr. Leisewitz showed her the large outside kitchen connected to the house by a runway, an arrangement similar to

the Stralendorffs'. As he pointed out the huge oven, he remarked that it was large enough to roast a whole ox, which
should have been sufficient meat for even the Groces' many
guests. Adjoining the kitchen was the "spring house," which
enclosed a cistern and was the place where butter, eggs, milk,
and meat were kept cool. Directly behind the house stood a
guest house called "Bachelor Hall," which had been used to
house young male guests when the main house was full. Mr.
Leisewitz explained that the smaller houses clustered around
the rear were former slave quarters.

He could remember when Liendo had the reputation of being the center of entertainment and hospitality for all of south
Texas, especially because Liendo was a convenient stopover
for stagecoach or horseback riders coming and going between
Houston and Galveston to Austin. In those days, guests would
stay from overnight to months to avail themselves of the generous hospitality of the Groce family. During this time, Colonel
Groce owned at least three hundred slaves, including field
hands and the "house Negroes," who served his family and
guests.[7]

"I don't believe in slavery," Elisabet asserted. "I'm glad
it's abolished. If we buy this plantation, we'll operate it with
paid workers. Are servants and tenant farmers available?"

Mr. Leisewitz assured her that servants and tenants were
no problem because the population of Waller County was approximately nine thousand and over half of them were ex-
slaves who needed employment.[8] Our economy is poor now,
whereas, when this was Groce's Country, Liendo Plantation
was practically self-sustaining; the Colonel even maintained
his own schoolhouse for his ten children. The Texas hero, Sam
Houston, was one of the Colonel's personal friends and was
often a guest at Liendo before the Civil War. After the war,
however, Houston no longer visited Liendo because he opposed
Texas joining the Confederacy, and Colonel Groce was a
strong supporter of the South.

Liendo was also a prisoner-of-war camp, housing forty-
six soldiers and eighty-six Union sailors captured by the Confederate forces in their Battle of Galveston victory.[9] Colonel
Groce's son William established Camp Groce at Liendo, where
he recruited and trained troops for the Confederate Army. After the defeat of the South, Liendo's Camp Groce became the

headquarters of the Union Army of Occupation for the area under the command of General George Custer.

"I can understand what you meant when you told me that Liendo Plantation has been a part of Texas history," Elisabet said. "Tell me what happened to Colonel Groce after the war?"

"The Colonel 'went broke' like all the other plantation owners," Mr. Leisewitz explained. "With the slaves freed, credit unavailable, and the country dominated by Yankee scalawags and carpetbaggers, in 1866 the Colonel was forced to sell the plantation, but later had to repossess it. Now it is again for sale."[10]

Elisabet had been too intrigued with Mr. Leisewitz's tales to inspect the upstairs; so she climbed the outside stairway in the rear to look at the large, sunny bedrooms. While standing on the upstairs balcony, she admired a grand live oak, standing tall and free, spreading its branches three hundred feet into the space around it. Oblivious to Mr. Leisewitz, Elisabet felt the tree's majesty as she had that of the Great Oak in Thomasville; stretching her arms outward toward the tree and the sunset, she proclaimed: *"Here* will I live, and *here* will I die!"[11]

This unexpected outburst surprised Mr. Leisewitz, who was even more amazed when Elisabet said that she wanted to return immediately to Hempstead to locate Colonel Groce and to make an offer on Liendo plantation. Even though Mr. Leisewitz wanted to sell the property, he felt that he should honestly warn Elisabet about the cost of maintaining such an estate and told her that without slave labor a sizeable fortune would be required to make the plantation successful, but Elisabet did not hear him because her mind was too full of happiness and hope for the future.

At Elisabet's insistence, she and Mr. Leisewitz returned to Hempstead, where they learned that Colonel Groce was ill, but that his son, Leonard Jr., was empowered to sell the plantation. The price of the plantation was ten thousand dollars. Elisabet made an offer, then sent a telegram to her "best friend": *Wunderbar!*

Because it was dark when Elisabet and Mr. Leisewitz completed this business and the day had been long and tiring, Elisabet gladly accepted Mr. Leisewitz's invitation to stay for the night in Brenham with him and his bride of three weeks, also of German ancestry. When Elisabet entered the Leisewitzes' tastefully furnished German–style home, she realized that they were educated, cultured persons and decided not to make the mistake that she had made in Thomasville of refusing to discuss her relationship with Edmund. She explained that she was married to Dr. Montgomery, but preferred to be known by the professional name that she had used in Europe where she earned her reputation as a sculptor, "Miss Elisabet Ney."

The Leisewitzes knew that some time would be required before Elisabet's family could arrive from Georgia and invited her to remain as their guest. Mr. Leisewitz also introduced her to two lawyers in Hempstead, Thomas Reece and Abner Gaines Lipscomb, who could assist in her purchase of Liendo Plantation.[12] The lawyer Mr. Lipscomb had bought Bernardo Plantation, where Colonel Groce had lived before building Liendo, and thus was also in a position to advise Elisabet concerning the problems in the management of a plantation.

While Elisabet was in the Leisewitzes' home, she received a letter from Edmund, who wrote that, with quinine treatments and good care, Cenci had regained her strength, and that the two babies were healthy. He had made arrangements to leave Uncle Archie and Aunt Nelly in charge of the farm, the cotton gin, Ulysses, and the Log Castle. As soon as arrangements were completed and everything packed for shipping, within two or three weeks, they should arrive in Texas.

While Elisabet was waiting for her family to arrive, she divided her time between the Leisewitzes' home in Brenham and the unpretentious Snell Hotel in Hempstead. Because she felt confident that Edmund would feel the same as she did about Liendo, she made arrangements with local carpenters and artisans to build sturdy, functional furniture to be available for them to move into Liendo as soon as possible. To facilitate her traveling between Brenham and Hempstead, she purchased a buggy and a saddle–and–buggy horse named Asta.

In Hempstead, as in Thomasville, Elisabet's unorthodox appearance and apparent wealth, at least to the poor townspeople, caused speculation about this peculiar German woman, dressed in "queer–looking" clothes, who wanted to buy Liendo Plantation. The Hempsteaders' appearances were equally displeasing to Elisabet: men in buckskins, wearing pistols, women in drab cotton dresses, wearing sunbonnets. Mr. Leisewitz told her that since the end of the war, Hempstead had become such a lawless place that it was known as "Six-shooter Junction" and the "Hell Hole of Texas."

"Don't worry," Elisabet told him. "Our family plans to remain on our plantation and to mind our own business with as little contact as possible, except for Mr. Reece and Mr. Lipscomb, with the wild men of Waller County."

"You're wise in that judgment," Mr. Leisewitz agreed and explained that the reason for this lawlessness was that when the State separated Waller County from Washington County and made Hempstead the County Seat, the citizenry took law enforcement into their own hands, and aided by Yankees from the North, they encouraged gun fights, killings, saloons, and houses of ill–repute. When Hempstead had been part of Groce's Country, Colonel Groce and the law–abiding Germans in Brenham saw to it that law and order was maintained, but now it was a different story.

"It's good to be forewarned," Elisabet said. "We'll also be five miles away from the town."

At last Elisabet received a telegram from Edmund stating that they were on their way to Texas. When their ship docked in Galveston, Elisabet was waiting joyously to welcome her family — her "best friend," her sons, and her faithful Cenci. They were forced by necessity to ride the slow, tedious railroad from Galveston to Hempstead and did not arrive at the Snell Hotel until eleven o'clock at night and all went exhaustedly to bed.

Even though Edmund was very tired from the long trip from Georgia, he was as anxious as Elisabet to complete the necessary transactions to acquire Liendo, which Edmund accepted from Elisabet's description as their long–searched–for home. He conferred with the lawyers Reece and Lipscomb to complete details for the purchase of Liendo Plantation. Edmund agreed to pay $10,000 for eleven hundred acres of land, $2,500 in gold on that day, March 4, 1873, and signed notes for $4,000 to be paid December 1, 1873, and $3,500 on December 1, 1874.[13] With this agreement consumated, the deed to Liendo Plantation was recorded with Dr. Edmund Montgomery and Miss Elisabet Ney as the purchasers.

Happily Elisabet and Edmund, now plantation owners, ordered their furniture delivered, and Edmund loaded Cenci and the children into the buggy, harnessed to another recently purchased horse, while Elisabet riding Asta, led the way over the deeply rutted winding road through the budding countryside to their new home. When the little caravan crossed Pond Creek and stopped before the imposing homestead, both Edmund and Cenci were delighted, but Cenci appeared to be the happiest, now that she had a home where she could care for her family.

Enough of the furniture had been delivered to set up housekeeping, and Cenci discovered a cradle, apparently left behind by one of the Groce children, which she used as a bed for Arti. A basket that Elisabet had brought from Madeira served for baby Lorne. Edmund selected the large, sunny, southwest bedroom for his study and laboratory and installed his microscope on a make-shift desk, his books in crude bookshelves, and expected to sleep on a wooden cot which constituted his bed. Elisabet's bedroom was opposite and Cenci's room was located down the hall across from the nursery. All the furniture was simple and uncomfortable, with narrow plank beds, crude tables and benches, and folding chairs.[14] Kerosene lamps and the wood-burning fireplaces provided light and heat. Sanitary facilities were also primitive, including one tin sit-in bathtub. But the house was roomy and spacious, in a lovely rural setting, with tenant farmers and sharecroppers already working the land and gossiping neighbors miles away.

As was their pattern in Thomasville, Elisabet assumed the supervision of the farm and enjoyed wearing breeches and riding astride Asta across the prairieland to inspect their crops. After what she learned about the lawlessness in Hempstead, Elisabet purchased a couple of six-shooter pistols and taught herself to shoot. Whenever she had to ride a long distance or through an unfamiliar countryside, she felt more secure wearing the guns around her waist. When Edmund saw the pistols, he threw up his arms in surrender and joked, "Those guns are fine protection, that is, unless you have to engage in a shoot-out with a Hempsteader."

To commemorate their new home, together Elisabet and Edmund planted a grove of live oak trees near the house, calling the place the "Sacred Grove." Edmund said, "these trees are dedicated to you, Elisabet, 'the goddess of Liendo.' Some day we'll be buried here, side by side."[15]

During Elisabet's supervision of the plantation, she discovered that her nearest neighbor was Mrs. Jared Kirby, who lived at the adjoining Alta Vista Plantation. She was the first resident of Waller County to visit Elisabet. Mrs. Kirby said that her husband had been murdered without justification during the lawlessness following the Civil War, leaving her with five young children to support. She finally obtained sufficient financial backing to operate a boarding school for girls in the plantation homestead, and with the help of her children selling butter and milk from their cows, they managed to survive.[16] Now, however, the children were older, and she felt that they must move to Austin for an environment more suitable for their education. She advised Elisabet to stay away from Hempstead as much as possible, advice with which Elisabet was in agreement.

When it was necessary for Elisabet to go into Hempstead, her demeanor, like that of a visiting Grand Duchess, only amplified gossip about her as this "crazy" artist from Germany, who wore "breeches" and other peculiar clothes and lived with a rich doctor, who must be the father of her children, although he called her, and she referred to herself as, "Miss Ney."

After hearing the much repeated gossip about Miss Ney and Dr. Montgomery, to satisfy their curiosity four of the prominent matrons of Hempstead drove five miles in a carriage to Liendo Plantation with the intention of paying a social call on Miss Ney. Lottie Cameron Effner, whose father came to Texas with Austin's colonists, and who was a writer and also a supporter of women's suffrage, was one of the visitors; also a daughter-in-law of Colonel Groce, who in times past had lived at Liendo.

When the ladies arrived, Cenci courteously ushered them into the parlor, where they sat stiffly on the folding chairs, while she hurried upstairs to inform Elisabet of the callers. The ladies noticed the Oriental rug on the floor and the richly woven tapestries on the wall, art objects which were in sharp contrast to the parlor's rough-hewn furniture.

Elisabet was in the nursery and said, "Cenci, tell the women that my child is ill, and that I have no time to visit with them." Cenci left with the message, but soon returned to tell Elisabet that the ladies said that they had children and would be glad to help. Their solicitousness irritated Elisabet. "This time, Cenci, thank the *Hausfrauen* and tell them that if I need their assistance, I'll send word to them in Hempstead."[17]

When an embarrassed Cenci delivered Elisabet's message,

the visitors left indignantly and spent the returning five miles to Hempstead making unflattering observations concerning this immoral woman and her illegitimate children, living without marriage with a lover. The offended ladies agreed that Miss Ney and her family were a disgrace and an affront to the decent, church-going citizens of Hempstead.

The fact that her rudeness had ruffled the sensitivities of the self-styled Hempstead socialites was of no more concern to Elisabet than the rumors and insinuations circulating about her. A new challenge was before her: she would shape and mold the lives of her two young boys, she would teach them the ideals of fredom, educate them to achieve their birthright — roles of prominence and leadership. This achievement will be an even greater one than creating beautiful statues in marble, she promised herself as she cradled her two infant sons in her arms.

Death of a Son

"Twas thine own genius gave the final blow, and helped to plant the wound that laid thee low. . . .
Lord Byron

Elisabet, Edmund, the two children, and Cenci settled into life at Liendo with Elisabet managing the plantation, Edmund studying and writing, and Cenci attending to the housework and the babies. The idyllic springtime of their arrival soon materialized into a long, hot Texas summer, as hot as summers in Georgia, though not so humid. Elisabet in her parasol hat, breeches, and pistols strapped to her sides as a protection against rattlesnakes and dangerous Waller County folk, mounted Asta and rode through the plantation under the relentless sun to oversee the tenant farmers and the field hands. What she saw in the plantation's sun-scorched fields was a dishearteningly inept operation begrudgingly performed by lazy and ignorant laborers.

Elisabet told herself to be tolerant: only a few years before these Negroes had been slaves, and even after freedom, they had had little opportunity or incentive to improve themselves.

She and Edmund had promised each other that they would do all that they could to rehabilitate these unfortunate people. The wages that Elisabet paid were more generous than customary, and she tried to be fair and kind with the workers in directing the work necessary to operate the plantation. But without Uncle Archie to understand and interpret the Negroes' feelings and to manage them accordingly, the day laborers considered "Missey Ney" and "Marse Doctor" as "queer furriers."

Because half of Waller County's population consisted of ex-slaves, illiterate and unskilled field hands and house servants, and with few jobs available, the lives of the freed Negroes continued in much the same pattern as they had during slavery, but with less security. The white population was only slightly better off, because they too, had been dependent on the patronage of the plantation economy, and they also had been victimized by unscrupulous Yankees during Reconstruction.

The forlorn field hands were as relieved as everyone else when the scorching heat, chiggers, ticks, stinging-nettle, and snakes finally abated with the onset of fall. For Elisabet, however, the new season brought new trouble. One day she noticed that some of the dairy cattle had become infected with a frothing at the mouth, and several days later a few of them died. Soon after Arti became ill with a swollen red throat and high fever, symptoms that Edmund recognized as diptheria. Because of the contagious nature of the disease, he immediately quarantined Cenci and baby Lorne, less than a year old, to the back wing of the house away from Arti.

Edmund knew of no physician in Hempstead or Brenham who might assist him in this critical situation. Then he thought of his friend, Arthur Lefevre, superintendent of schools in Victoria, with whom he frequently corresponded on philosophical ideas, who might know a doctor to send from Houston. As quickly as he could get to Hempstead, Edmund sent a telegram to Lefevre, who wired in return that as soon as he could make arrangements, a Dr. Conway Nutt from Houston would come to Liendo.[1]

Now that another doctor was coming, Elisabet and Edmund faced a perplexing decision: should they summon their friends Reece and Lipscomb in Hempstead, the Leisewitzes in Brenham, or Mrs. Kirby at Alta Vista at the subsequent risk of contagion or of starting a diptheria epidemic? They decided to treat their baby without risking exposure to others. Edmund tried every remedy he knew to minister to his dangerously sick son; yet the child's condition grew worse. Not having a rocking chair, Elisabet sat in a straight-backed wooden chair and held Arti in her arms to soothe and comfort him while Edmund treated him to reduce his fever.

Arti had been ill for two days before Dr. Nutt arrived from Houston. He and Edmund used all their skill and medical knowledge trying to save the desperately ill infant, who, in spite of their efforts, died in Elisabet's arms. When Dr. Nutt realized that the baby was dead, he advised that to avoid the danger of contagion the body should be cremated.[2]

When Elisabet heard these words, she grasped Arti's lifeless body to her breast, ran upstairs to her room, and locked the door. There she remained all night, while Edmund paced the hall outside. The next morning she opened the door and showed Edmund a clay model that she had spent the night sculpting, a replica of the still figure of their small son.

"*Ach* Edmund," Elisabet sobbed as he held her in his arms, "Can we do this? Can we cremate our little Arti?"

"We have no choice, *meine* Elisabet," he said, "as difficult as it will be."

Heartbroken, Elisabet agreed. "Then we must do it ourselves — in our 'Sacred Grove.' " Together with Cenci, they assembled a stack of logs in the center of the Grove among the live oak trees, gently wrapped the infant body with cloth, saturated it with oil, and placed it on the firewood. With her strong hands trembling, Elisabet ignited the flame and ran to the upstairs balcony. For an hour she stood motionless in grief-stricken silence, staring at the fields and the grand live oak tree before her, feeling as if she were a spectator watching what took place, as if what happened were not real, but rather a stageplay.

While she was still standing on the balcony, Edmund and Cenci came to her. "The fire has burned out," Edmund said gently as he held her close. "We must collect the ashes."

Sadly the three returned to the Grove and the extinguished pyre as Elisabet shoveled the ashes into a leather pouch. Only after they had left the Grove could Elisabet finally release her grief and tears. After her crying had subsided, she took the sculpted death mask of her son to a small trunk that she kept at her bedside, placed it inside, and turned the lock.[3]

What events had occurred at the big house could only be conjectured by the Negroes on the plantation. They knew that the baby had been ill and that he had died. Why was there no funeral? The ritual and sociability of a funeral were an important part of the lives of the people in Waller County, especially the Negro population. For them a death without a funeral was an event that could not be easily understood. No one had been allowed in the house while the child was ill, and then when the baby had died without a funeral, or even a burial that anyone knew about, speculations abounded. Tales of little Arti's ghost haunting the mansion spread quickly among the Negroes and townspeople.[4]

Because the local population was already alienated by the unconventional style of life of Miss Ney and Dr. Montgomery, they were eager to disparage the two, calling them free-lovers, atheists, queer foreigners, and, when they heard rumors of cremation, even murderers. Gossip was that the "blasphemous pair" would be run out of town by the Ku Klux Klan, which was active in the county. Only the earnest intervention of Judge Tom Reece and Gaines Lipscomb, respected lawyers in the community, spared Elisabet and Edmund the humiliation of a visit from the Klan, of whose existence Elisabet and Edmund were only vaguely aware.[5]

After Arti's death, Elisabet and Edmund kept to themselves even more than before, rarely going into Hempstead. To absorb his interest and to lessen his grief, Edmund kept busy reading scientific and philosophical books and articles, and studying through his microscope the complex forms of amoebae that he procured from the marshy banks of Pond Creek. To keep herself occupied, Elisabet worked harder than ever to make the plantation prosper. Whenever a trip to Hempstead became necessary, Elisabet wore a heavy veil and engaged in as little conversation as possible with the tradesmen. They, in turn, were just as eager to avoid contact with her.

After months of such reclusive living, Elisabet felt older, discouraged, defeated. Looking in the mirror, she noticed a few wrinkles around her eyes and streaks of grey in her short auburn curls. Her successful life in Europe seemed very long ago. Since coming to America, she had received several letters from Herr Baurat Neureuther regarding the completion of King Ludwig's statue; her father had written also that Friedrich

Ochs needed her permission to finish and sell Ludwig's statue. In her depressed state, however, she no longer cared about her sculpture in Europe.[6]

One night when she could not sleep, she walked out on the upstairs balcony into the cool, star–flecked moonlight of the South Texas nighttime. In the massive live oak, in the middle of the night, a mockingbird was singing in pure exhuberance. As Elisabet listened to the bird's joyous song, gazed up into the face of the full moon, and felt the night breeze on her face, she experienced a tranquility that she had not known since the death of her child. Surely a tiny soul as young and fresh as Arti's would be at one and at peace in the universe. Standing in the moonlight, enveloped in a healing embrace as if from God, Elisabet absorbed this serenity and returned to her bed to a restful sleep.

Refreshed the next morning, she played with baby Lorne, as attractive a child as Arti. "I still have this other *Bruder Genii*," she told herself. "This son, Lorne Ney Montgomery, will be proud of his name and heritage. He'll be an *Edelmannisch* (little gentleman), be educated in the best university in Europe, have estates in Texas and in Europe, become wealthy and important. We will be proud of him." Hugging the boy, she left him in Cenci's care as she resumed her horseback supervision of the plantation.

After several months, living returned almost to normal at Liendo. Not quite a year after Arti's death, in the spring of 1874, Edmund received word that Duncan McNeill, Lord Colonsay, had died on January 31 of that year at eighty years of age. According to his will, he bequeathed to Dr. Edmund Montgomery, the son of Mrs. Isabella Davidson or Montgomery, the sum of one thousand pounds (approximately five thousand dollars at that time). Edmund's mother was left a stated amount and an annuity.[7] Because legal procedures were involved, Edmund consulted with Judge Reece in Hempstead, which occasioned rumors to circulate that Dr. Montgomery was a Scottish nobleman who had inherited a great estate. (Five thousand dollars was a fortune in impoverished Hempstead.)

Further gossip circulated that Miss Ney was a granddaughter and heir of Marshal Ney, Napoleon Bonaparte's famous commander. Although the townspeople still mistrusted

the domestic arrangement of Miss Ney and the Doctor, they
now regarded them as prominent, wealthy, and highly eccentric Europeans, who had selected Hempstead, Texas as a place
to settle where they could live as they pleased.

After receiving this legacy, Edmund spent some of the
money to purchase more acreage adjoining Liendo. Elisabet
had urged him to amass an "estate" for Lorne; however, this
additional land only added to the losses of the plantation and
increased Elisabet's worries and responsibilities. Because
most of the owners of plantations had as many difficulties as
she did, Elisabet, with no background in farming, received no
cooperation from the other plantation owners, except from her
friend Gaines Lipscomb. Although she made inquiries, she
could find no intelligent plantation supervisor whom she could
trust as she had trusted Uncle Archie Cone, and because she
did not understand the Negroes, and because they, in turn, did
not understand her, the crops were not planted and harvested
at the most propitious time, cattle not properly looked after,
and farm equipment not properly maintained. Such inefficiency and wastefulness forced Edmund to borrow money continually to keep the plantation in operation.

Becoming more and more involved with the problems of
the plantation, Elisabet had almost forgotten her friends away
from the plantation vicinity until a letter arrived in the spring
of 1875 from Margaret von Stralendorff inquiring about Miss
Ney, the Doctor, their two children, and their new home in
Texas. In this letter Margaret wrote that she was soon to
marry again,[8] and that she and her fiancé had attended a concert of the Boston Symphony Orchestra where Hans von Bülow, as soloist, introduced Peter Ilych Tschaikovsky's "Con-
certo in B flat minor, Opus Twenty-three" to an enthusiastic
audience.[9] Knowing that he was a friend of Elisabet's, Margaret wrote that they went backstage to congratulate Bülow,
who seemed pleased to hear from his friend, Elisabet Ney, and
had asked to be remembered to her.

This letter brought back memories of the concerts and the
culture she had enjoyed in Europe. "*Ach*, Edmund," she said,
"how I miss Europe — the great music of Beethoven, Liszt,
even Wagner, in spite of the way he treated Hans von Bülow,
the art galleries and museums, the theaters, and all the culture
in that beautiful city of Munich. In contrast, Texas is crude

and uncultured, the people of Hempstead act like uncivilized peasants, and the Negroes are ignorant and downtrodden. I know, however, with repression still in Europe that we can never return. Here the ideal of freedom is still possible, although further from realization than I'd hoped; yet we can try to better our lives."

To better their lives in their precarious financial situation, Elisabet and Edmund realized that they must obtain more capital. Because the plantation was already heavily mortgaged, the only possible source of money would be the sale of their property in Georgia. After they decided that because of the detrimental effect of the Georgia climate on Edmund's health, Elisabet should return to Georgia in an effort to sell the property. Because the deed was in Edmund's name, to enable Elisabet to sell the land Judge Reece drew up a deed to Miss Elisabet Ney in return for the payment to Dr. Montgomery of $5,200, the amount that Edmund had originally paid and the price that Elisabet hoped to receive.[10]

After a tedious journey, Elisabet arrived in Thomasville in December of 1875, where she was received by the residents with indifference and, in some instances, hostility. The economic condition of the town had not improved in the two years since she had left: the large plantations were still for sale and all the property values were depressed. When Elisabet returned to *Holzlotzschloss,* the dilapidated Log Castle brought tears to her eyes. Although she knew that the house had been poorly constructed, she was unprepared for its state of disrepair after two years of vacancy and neglect.

The only people in Thomasville who seemed genuinely glad to see her were Uncle Archie and Aunt Nelly, who were grieved to learn of Arti's death. With Cenci, they had cared for him for almost a year and had grown to love him. The kindness and intelligence of these two trustworthy individuals impressed Elisabet to the extent that she told them about her troubles in Texas and promised good wages if they, their family, and any of their friends would return to Texas with her to work on her plantation. The Cone family and a few of their friends agreed to come with her because there appeared to be no future for them in Georgia.[11]

After two weeks in Thomasville, Elisabet found a buyer

for the property, Mr. Benjamin F. Hankins, who owned adjoining acreage and was one of the few inhabitants who had been
friendly. All he could offer to pay for all the land, the cotton
gin, and what remained of the Log Castle was $2,200. Because
she was anxious to sell and leave Thomasville, Elisabet accepted the loss from the original cost of the property and completed the deal on December 16.[12]

Elisabet was delighted to return home, especially to see
the fast-growing Lorne, now in his fourth year. Everyone welcomed Uncle Archie and Aunt Nelly, who were installed in former slave quarters near the main house; the other workers who
came with them from Georgia were housed in the nearby shanties. Elisabet's return with some money temporarily eased the
plantation's financial crisis. Although the influx of capital and
labor encouraged Elisabet and Edmund, the monetary requirements of the plantation had greatly increased by the cost of
the additional acreage, the multiplying expenses and interest
on indebtedness, and the inefficiency of labor and lack of
knowledgeable supervision, they both realized exacerbated the
situation.

Once again, however, Liendo's worsening fiscal condition
was reprieved when Elisabet received a small legacy from her
father, who died in Münster on December 21, 1879, although
she first had to settle a lawsuit filed by her brother Fritz'[13];
however, the money did not ease Elisabet's problem in supervising the plantation. She could not depend on Uncle Archie's
management as she had in Thomasville because the Negro laborers in Texas had no respect for his authority and refused to
change their irresponsible work habits. With regrets, Uncle
Archie and Aunt Nelly decided to return to Georgia, but their
two grown children and grandchildren remained at Liendo.

In her efforts to oversee the field hands after Uncle
Archie's departure, Elisabet equipped each of twelve yoke of
oxen with a different toned bell; so that whenever she heard a
certain bell sound, she knew how much work was being done
by the worker driving that particular yoke.[14] This ingenious
improvisation highly amused the Negroes and the neighboring
farmers, and only increased their conviction that Miss Ney
was "peculiar."

This opinion was further confirmed when Lorne was five
years old, at which time Elisabet began designing his clothes.

Because she considered her son born to a heritage different from the rough people around him, she thought that he should dress in the manner befitting a young nobleman. As she did with her own clothes, she designed patterns, imported expensive fabrics, and instructed a Hempstead seamstress to make a wardrobe for the boy. The sort of apparel that Elisabet requested amazed the seamstress as Elisabet showed her a copy of the suit in Thomas Gainesborough's *Blue Boy* portrait, a copy of a suit worn by "Little Lord Fauntleroy,"[15] a design for a white woolen Grecian toga, and another for a Scottish kilt. Because Elisabet paid well, the dressmaker sewed the clothes, but nothing prevented her from telling her neighbors in Hempstead about what a spectacle Miss Ney was making of her son. To Elisabet, Lorne's clothes were elegant and princely; Lorne was too young and isolated to know that he wore costumes from Europe.

The only playmates available for Lorne were the children whose parents worked on the plantation. His favorites were Uncle Archie's two grandsons, Jimbo and Little Willie, who called him "Lore," which soon became his nickname. Although Cenci, now in her late forties, was his adoring "nanny," she could hardly be his playmate. Only when the Robert Leisewitzes came from Brenham with their daughter Henrietta, younger than Lore, and left her for a visit, did he have a friend of his mother's approval. But Henrietta was a girl; Lore preferred rougher play with the black boys.

Once when the three boys were playing, Jimbo, age eight, asked Lore, "Why you allus wearin' clothes thet look like a gurl?"

Lore replied, "Because that's the way Miss Ney says I'm supposed to dress."

"But effin' she's yore mammy, why ya call her 'Miss Ney'? Is ya shore she's yore mammy?" Little Willie, age nine, wanted to know. "An effin' da Doctor be yore pappy, why ya call him 'da Doctor'?"

Not able to answer these questions, which made him very uncomfortable, Lore asked Elisabet if she and the Doctor were really his mother and father.

Elisabet exploded, "Of course, I'm your *Mutter!* And the Doctor is your *Vater.* Have you been playing with those Negro boys again? You know I've forbidden you to have anything to

do with them. You have your status to maintain. Pay them no
mind. You must learn to fight against the bonds of convention,
to live in freedom. I'll find a tutor to teach you what you need
to know. And, Lore, if you ever play with those boys again, I'll
send you to the tower room for the rest of the day. Do you understand?"

"I understand," he said, but he could not understand why
he was forbidden to play with his friends. Was there something
different about him from the other children? He did not know
because the only time he left the plantation was for an infrequent visit to Hempstead with "Miss Ney" to make purchases.

On one such occasion, dressed in his white toga and sandals, he rode into town in the buggy with Elisabet, who was
also dressed in her white Grecian toga. The Hempsteaders
stared at the two in disbelief. "Maybe thar in a circus," an old-
timer conjectured.

Elisabet told Lore to wait in the buggy as she tied the
horse to the hitching post and went inside the general store.
When she returned in a short time, she discovered several local
youths, ages ten to fourteen, dressed in rough homespun
clothes, coarse stockings, and heavy boots standing around
her buggy shouting to Lore.

"Hey, lookit tha kid in his nightshirt. Hey, shirttail, come
on out an' let's see yer dress. Hey, shirttail, is ya supposed ta
be dressed like Jesus?" they taunted as they laughed and
pointed to Lore, who had hidden under the buggy seat.

As soon as Elisabet confronted the boys with her haughty
stare and commanded, *"Gehen Sie! Gehen Sie!* Leave immediately, every one of you ragamuffins!" They quickly ran in all
directions. When she pulled Lore from underneath the buggy
seat, he burst into tears as Elisabet tried to comfort him.

Elisabet was indigant. "Give no heed to those uncouth urchins — they're nothing but scum. Imagine those big boys
taunting a boy only six years old. They're jealous of you because you're better-bred and better-dressed, a young nobleman, while they're nothing but uneducated peasants. You're
my fine, brave son. You don't have to associate with such riff-
raff." [16]

Lore was comforted, and Elisabet was more than ever determined to keep him away from the crude youths of Hempstead; yet he must be educated; she must hire a suitable tutor.

No public education existed in Hempstead in 1878, but Elisabet would never have considered a public school. At age six, Lore was handsome, well-built, large for his age, and quick to learn. He spoke English and German interchangeably and could understand his father's French and Italian. Thanks to Elisabet, he was also an expert horseman.

As well as teaching him languages, Edmund customarily took a walk on Sunday mornings with Lore, which was the most time they normally spent together, to impart to him a knowledge of nature. Edmund taught him to recognize different kinds of flowers, trees, rock formations, birds, and small animals. On this particular Sunday, Elisabet told Lore to dress in his Scottish kilts because his forebears were Scotsmen. To Elisabet's amazement, Lore screamed to her, "I won't wear that ugly skirt. What's more, I won't wear any of the clothes you make me wear. I'm going to wear regular clothes!" He then pulled all his clothes from the chest in his room and stomped on them. "You can't make me look funny any more. I won't do it!"

Elisabet had never seen him in such a rage. "Be calm, Lore, be calm. I thought you liked your beautiful clothes."

"No!" he stormed, "I hate them, and I hate you."

Stunned and hurt, Elisabet felt that she must quiet him. "I'm sorry you feel the way you do, although I don't think you meant what you said. But, all right, if you'll apologize, I'll let you wear 'regular' clothes, as you call them."[17]

With tears streaming down his cheeks, Lore ran to Elisabet. "I'm sorry . . . I really didn't mean that I hate you. I'm sorry, but you did promise that I could wear regular clothes."

"*Ja,* that's what I said," Elisabet agreed, acknowledging defeat.

After this episode, Elisabet had clothes made for him similar to those worn by the other local boys, but from good quality fabric. As Elisabet looked at Lore in his Hempstead-styled clothes, in a moment of recall, she thought about her own mother, and how as a child she had rebelled against the clothes that her mother had required her to wear. Had her rebellion hurt her mother as much as Lore had hurt her? *Nein, nein,* her mother had never understood her.

To offset the negative influence of his environment, Elisabet realized that she must find a qualified teacher for Lore, pref-

erably with a German background, to begin his formal education. With the help of the Leisewitzes in Brenham, Elisabet
hired a tutor, who soon proved unsatisfactory because Lore
learned that if he were uncooperative, played tricks, and set up
obstacles, the instructor would leave. With this behavior, Lore
dispatched several male teachers.

Lore's contrariness caused Elisabet to be continually in
search of a tutor. Once when Elisabet was returning from a
trip to Galveston to visit her friend Julius Runge, now German
Consul, on the train she met a well educated, well brought up,
eighteen-year-old Englishwoman, Miss Dora Gray. Elisabet
decided that the young lady would make a suitable schoolmarm
for Lore. Miss Gray was agreeable, but her parents would consent only if her eleven-year-old sister (the same age as Lore),
could accompany her older sister so that Dora could teach both
children.[18] Because she felt that their feminine presence would
be a refining influence for Lore, Elisabet gladly accepted the
younger sister.

Unfortunately this harmonious arrangement lasted for
only a year. After that time Lore became even more unruly
than before. Elisabet confided to the Leisewitzes that she was
worried about her son. He refused to take his studies seriously
and continued to be defiant toward his tutors and toward her.
Somehow he had become acquainted with the Hempstead
roughnecks. The other day she had found him with some of the
uncouth juveniles teasing Jimbo and Little Willie, calling them
"kinky-headed niggers." He seemed to have forgotten how he
felt when the ruffians in Hempstead had teased *him*. She had
sent Lore to the tower room and had forbidden him to see those
Hempstead boys again. He had resented her and her discipline.
Sometimes she wished that he had been a girl like the Leisewitzes' charming Henrietta. She had wanted a daughter so
much.

The Leisewitzes were sympathetic toward Elisabet's problems with her son and also agreed as to the crudeness and lawlessness of Hempstead. Edmund also was aware of the undesir-
ability of the town; yet he realized that whether or not they
liked the situation, they would probably spend the rest of their
lives in Texas.

This realization prompted him to apply for American citizenship in Waller County on October 31, 1884, as a forty-nine-

year-old citizen of Great Britain. Before he filed this application, Edmund procured a copy of his marriage certificate from
the British Consulate in Funchal, Madeira,[19] a document which
allowed his wife Elisabet also to become a citizen of the United
States. Two years after the application, they were granted citizenship on September 16, 1886.[20] Curious householders, who
inspected the records of Waller County, discovered that Miss
Ney and Dr. Montgomery were legally married, regardless of
whether or not they acknowledged the fact.

Elisabet was glad to become an American citizen, especially because her son was born an American. Although Lore was
becoming more antagonistic and harder to control, Elisabet
did not unburden all of her problems to Edmund because she
knew that at that time he was particularly preoccupied with
his writing. Several of Edmund's articles attacking the theory
of "Transcendental Philosophy" were published in a Boston
periodical, *Index*, a semi-popular journal propagating liberal
religious views. Because many members of the Concord School
of Philosophy were known as "Trancendentalists," when the
school organized a symposium to discuss this topic in July
1885, Edmund was invited to be a participant, an invitation
which could have meant recognition for him, for members of
the panel were distinguished scientists and philosophers. But
because of his delicate health, lack of funds, and natural reticence, Edmund did not make the long trip to Massachusetts.
His proxy, Thoreau's friend and biographer Frank B. Sanborn,
read Edmund's paper.[21]

Both Elisabet and Edmund had become totally engrossed
in trying to live their "ideal life" in Texas, which had become
something less than "ideal," and it seemed they had almost
forgotten Europe. A letter brought the past forcibly back into
Elisabet's consciousness. King Ludwig had died on June 13,
1886, the letter related, drowned in Lake Starnberg under mys-
terious circumstances. His doctor, Bernard von Gudden, also
drowned with him.[22] The facts were confused as to how these
drownings occurred, although there was much speculation
from the *Müncheners*. King Ludwig had been officially declared insane on June 6 and had been incarcerated in *Schloss*
Berg the week before his death.[22] This news shocked and
grieved Elisabet, for she was fond of the hapless King Ludwig
and realized how he must have suffered from such humiliation.

He was not insane; he was eccentric and emotionally imma-
ture, but not insane.

The letter also contained a disconcerting article written by
Auguste Schiebe, July 17, 1886, for the Munich newspaper the
Dresdener Tagblatt. This story appeared, along with many
others after the death of King Ludwig, "because the sculptress
Elisabet Ney had modeled a life–size statue of King Ludwig."
Auguste Schiebe stated that the possibility, previously mentioned in the press, that Miss Ney had met a terrible fate was
unlikely, but not inconceivable. The conclusion of the article
read:

> Shortly before she left for America where she disap-
> peared, Miss Ney made the remark: "After so many great
> men of the civilized world sat for me, I would like to model
> the greatest of wild men!"
>
> And really, some time after she left Europe, a notice
> of adventurous coloring went unnoticed through the news-
> papers: A tribe of wild Indians in North America carried
> away a German sculptress who had dared to enter its ter-
> ritory.
>
> Since that time, ten years have passed without any
> news of Elisabet Ney.
>
> Did the papers bring that notice to render more dense
> the veil which the artist had possibly drawn about her life,
> or was there really some truth in the notice? [23]

Elisabet laughed and cried. Was she buried alive in this
backward country? Was there no way out of this quicksand of
a plantation that was slowly swallowing her? The hope that
saved her from despair was that perhaps someone in Texas
would recognize her talents and commission her to create, once
again, a work of sculpture.

18

A Son in Rebellion

Gods! How the son denegrates the sire!
Alexander Pope

In her depression Elisabet no longer pushed herself to oversee the plantation. The situation seemed hopeless: the harder she tried, the more she slipped backward. When Edmund was in Hempstead on business, one day in 1878, he met Judge Oran M. Roberts, a landowner in Waller County, who was campaigning for the Governorship. Each man was impressed with the breeding and intelligence of the other. To become better acquainted, Edmund invited Judge Roberts to visit Liendo and to meet Miss Ney, who also recognized Judge Roberts as an educated, cultured gentleman. During their conversation, Judge Roberts told them that he was born in South Carolina and studied law at the University of Alabama before coming to Texas. One of the principles in his platform in his bid for Governor was to transform Texas from a frontier state to one with an appreciation of art, education, and culture.

He was surprised and delighted to find a well-known European sculptress and a distinguished scientist living in the vicinity of the wild town of Hempstead. If he should be elected, he told them that he would need the help of both of them in his efforts to bring refinement to the state. To Elisabet, his words had brought a ray of hope that she had longed for ever since coming to Texas.

The following year, 1879, Judge Roberts was elected Governor, then reelected two years later. During his second administration, on November 9, 1881, the State Capitol in Austin was destroyed by fire. After this catastrophe, the members of the State Legislature decided to rebuild the Capitol at the origination of Congress Avenue and to construct the biggest and the best State Capitol in the United States. No money was available for such a grandiose project because the State Treasury was almost bankrupt, but the enterprising Texans made a deal with two Chicago brothers, John V. and C. B. Farwell who, with British backing, agreed to build a three million dollar Capitol in exchange for three million acres of land in the Texas Panhandle.[1]

After this deal to build the Capitol was accepted, Governor Roberts appointed a building committee to consider plans for the new Capitol. He invited Elisabet to consult with this committee and also to be his guest in the Governor's Mansion. Upon receiving this invitation, Elisabet hurried excitedly to Edmund. "My 'best friend,' read this. Perhaps now I will receive commissions. This is the opportunity that I've been hoping for."

When Elisabet appeared at the Governor's Mansion dressed in a grey silk cloak which completely covered her and a black velvet close–fitting headpiece draped with a veil of rare lace,[2] quite different from the prevailing style of women's fitted coats and large, ornately adorned hats, Governor Roberts welcomed her politely and graciously. The Governor's Mansion, built in 1855 in the style of the old Southern Colonial homesteads with stately white columns and wide verandas, was the pride of Austin and also impressed Elisabet. She felt honored to be given a room once used by Governor Sam Houston.

Being a guest of the Governor, Elisabet was treated with respect by the members of the Legislative Building Committee, with no allusions made to her unorthodox attire. Elisabet considered herself to be regally dressed in her white Grecian-styled toga accented with white kid gloves, which she habitually wore to protect her hands. Although the committee members may have been surprised by her unexpected appearance, her artistic background, poise, and intelligence impressed these officials that she was capable of creating statues of Texas heroes for the new Capitol's vestibule and bust portraits for the rotunda. When a member of the legislature asked for an estimate of the cost of the proposed fourteen statues and busts, she answered, "fifty thousand dollars," a sum which apparently staggered the committeeman, who knew little about the art of sculpture.[3] He remarked to a colleague, "She must think that she's Queen Victoria dealing with Her Majesty's humble subjects."

No commitments for the sculptures came from the Building Committee, not only because of the high price, but also because of a change from the first plan of constructing the building of Texas limestone to red granite from Marble Falls in Burnet County, which was plentiful and cheaper. This choice meant that Elisabet would receive no commission because red granite was not suitable for sculpture.

This turn of events was a disappointment for Elisabet, but Governor Roberts assured her that there would be other opportunities now that her reputation as a European sculptress was becoming known; however, recognizing the provincialism of Texas, Elisabet foresaw the obstacles. Austin of 1881 was a village–like town located in the bend of the Colorado River, with ten thousand inhabitants more interested in earning a decent living than in attaining education or culture.

The year following Governor Roberts again visited Liendo plantation, and during his stay, Elisabet persuaded him to sit for a bust portrait. In 1883, upon the opening of the University of Texas, which was established mainly through the efforts and insistence of Governor Roberts, the plaster bust that Elisabet had sculpted was prominently displayed on the speaker's platform.[4] Although the statue brought her no money, and as badly as she needed funds, she felt rewarded to be recognized as a sculptor after ten years away from her art.

Even though this reexperiencing of her art of sculpture uplifted her state of mind, nothing had changed at Liendo. With the additional purchases of land, the size of the plantation had doubled to include twenty–two tenant families, but its productivity had declined. Elisabet found no market for the plantation's cotton and heavy competition for its farm products, while worker's wages and money for supplies and equipment maintenance continued to be paid; nevertheless, an even greater worry to Elisabet than the plantation was Lore, who had reached puberty at the age of fourteen. Although he had grown into a tall, handsome boy, he was openly defiant and rebellious.

Against her orders, Elisabet knew that he often rode horseback into Hempstead and associated with the local youths, refused to study with his teachers, who continually resigned in frustration, and often purposefully used the coarse language of Hempstead, knowing how much she disliked it.

Edmund remained unaware of the seriousness of Lore's situation until one evening when Elisabet told him what had occurred that afternoon. Lore had come riding to the house at a gallop. After he dismounted and started toward his room, Elisabet had stopped him. His eye was black and his lip was cut, obviously from a fight. When she had tried to question him, he became angry.

"Yes, I had a fight," he had stormed. "And I had to fight because you're such a miserable mother." He had told Elisabet that the boys in town called her and the Doctor free-lovers and called him a bastard. He had fought the boy who said it. "You can be sure, *Miss* Ney, that boy won't be saying such things to me again. I hate you for what you do to humiliate me before my friends," he had screamed at her and slammed the door to his room.

This recital of Lore's actions hurt and upset Edmund who said, "I will not tolerate such behavior. I can understand why Lore had a fight over being maligned—I've had that experience — but he's no bastard. I promise you, Elisabet, I'll see to it that he never again speaks to you the way he did. I see that it is now time that I come down from my isolated tower and take charge of my son. First, I intend to see that he's disciplined; next, we'll find a boarding school for him. Obviously he can no longer remain in this unhealthy environment."

"*Nein*, Edmund," Elisabet protested, "don't send him away to school. I know he's unruly and rebellious, but we can teach him to act like a gentleman. He's our only child. He's the reason I work so hard on this plantation—to provide him with an inheritance. If he leaves, I'll have nothing to work for, to fight for. *Nein,* he must be educated here. We'll find a tutor who will really teach him."

Elisabet's objections to Lore's being sent away to school was their most serious disagreement. She used all of her ability of persuasion, including how much she loved her son, to convince Edmund that Lore should remain at Liendo; however, in this instance Edmund remained adamant. He wrote to his friends in the East regarding a good preparatory school where his son could receive quality education, discipline, and instruction on how to behave like a gentleman.

After heated arguments, when Elisabet realized that there was no way she could sway Edmund from his determination to send Lore away to school, she told Lore of his father's intention, explaining that they wanted him to have a better education and quality of life than was possible in Texas. Lore agreed to try a school away from Texas because he thought that he might enjoy living on his own.

Before Lore left Liendo, Elisabet modeled a sensitive, somewhat sentimentalized, bust of him. When she asked Lore what he thought of it, he said, "That stupid statue doesn't look like me. How can you call yourself a sculptor and model something that ridiculous?"

Because Elisabet knew the portrait was an excellent work of art, Lore's remark hurt her deeply. *A Young Violinist* is the title that she gave to the bust and always referred to it by that name, not admitting that it was a likeness of her son. Lore's behavior had equally disturbed Edmund to the extent that his agitation brought on a malarial attack; however, regardless of his physical infirmities, he was determined to find a suitable school in the East for Lore.

After numerous letters and inquiries, Edmund decided that Swarthmore, a small college operated by the Society of Friends (the Quakers) in Philadelphia, would provide the proper environment, but the school could not accept Lore in their college preparatory department until the following fall. Regarding the school, Elisabet wrote to her friend Julius Runge that this college seemed the most appropriate for a boy touched by the "Texas nature."[5] Edmund was very anxious to get his son away from Waller County, and early in 1887, he decided to take Lore to the East and to arrange for a suitable living place and a tutor until he could enroll in Swarthmore.

With Elisabet still protesting, he and Lore left Texas for Baltimore, where Edmund found lodging for himself, and a teacher and boarding house for Lore. To be certain that Lore was being properly taught and looked after, Edmund wanted to remain nearby; also, because of his fever, Edmund did not feel well enough for a return trip to Texas.

While he was convalescing in Baltimore, Edmund continued writing and sending papers to the Concord School of Philosophy, which were read and discussed at the school. Although Edmund had been expected to appear at a meeting of the school in 1887 to deliver a lecture on "Aristotle's Theory of Causation in Its Relation to Modern Thought," instead he sent the paper for his proxy, Frank B. Sanborn, to read for him. After Edmund's repeated failure to appear in person at any of the Concord School's symposiums, a Boston newspaper reporter expressed doubt in an article as to whether a Dr. Edmund Montgomery, PhD from Hempstead, Texas existed; however, Edmund was too filled with fever and worry over his son to make an appearance, even though he was in nearby Baltimore.[6]

After her "best friend" and son left for the East, Elisabet felt excluded from this trip. Although she had been strongly opposed to Lore's being educated away from home, she hoped for his success. She felt that her son was exceptionally intelligent. He had a feeling for languages and a flair for self–expression, as when he memorized famous speeches and recited them with eloquence. If she could obtain a position as a teacher of art at the institution Lore was attending, she could oversee his instruction and keep an eye on his behavior. In an attempt to find such an arrangement, she wrote to Professor Felix Adler, President of the Society of Ethical Culture in New York, to ask if his college could use her abilities as an instructor in *Plastik* (sculpture). Upon receiving a reply that the institution had no funds available for such a course of instruction, she wrote a similar letter to the President of Swarthmore College, offering to teach without recompence except for a studio and living quarters, but again she received no reply.[7]

With Edmund and Lore away, Elisabet had little incentive or desire to manage the work on the plantation. After modeling the bust of Governor Roberts and *The Young Violinist,* an activity that eased her worry and loneliness with creativity, she felt such a need for another project that in January 1887, she wrote to her friend, Julius Runge, German Consul in Galveston, with an offer to model a bust of him and his wife Johanna without remuneration. The Runges were delighted to accept Elisabet's generous proposal and rented accommodations for her at the Beach Hotel in Galveston, from where she made daily trips to the Runges' home for sittings.[8] Both Julius and Johanna Runge had been educated in Germany even though they were native Texans, and Elisabet enjoyed their German conversations and the congenial atmosphere of their home during the several weeks that she worked on the two busts.

When Elisabet went to Galveston, she left the maintenance of the plantation to Cenci, who was not capable of handling the responsibility. In her desperation, Cenci wrote to *Herr Doctor* in Baltimore, telling him that if he wanted to keep Liendo from disaster, he must return as quickly as possible. When Edmund received Cenci's letter, he realized that he should return; yet he did not feel that his mission had been accomplished until Lore was enrolled in Swarthmore. Edmund was distressfully aware of the necessity of keeping the plantation in operation, because before leaving he had been forced to borrow five thousand dollars for payments on notes due on acquired acreage, for Lore's tutors and tuition, and for the trip to Baltimore. He had secured this loan from Dr. Philip Frank, a London physician whom he knew at St. Thomas's Hospital. As security for the loan, Edmund was forced to mortgage a large portion of the plantation.[9]

Even though he realized the seriousness of Cenci's predicament, Edmund felt that his first duty was to his son; furthermore, his own health at that time would not permit a trip to Texas. Not until September 30, 1887, almost six months later, after Lore was settled in Swarthmore's preparatory school, did Edmund answer Cenci:

> Our wild and obstinate boy is now in an entirely new and diversified environment in which he has to adjust himself, in which he has to find his way before he has time to write to us. I have had no letter, but am sure that as soon as he has gotten used to his new surroundings, he will again show more attachment and kindly feelings to us. . . . He is taken care of extremely well and not cowed at all. He tries to dominate there, too, but will not succeed as he did in Liendo.[10]

Edmund also mentioned in this letter that his health was improving and that he would soon return to Texas. In the meantime, much to Cenci's relief, Elisabet had completed the two plaster busts of the Runges and had returned to Liendo. She was there to welcome Edmund home again after their longest separation since coming to America fifteen years before.

During Edmund's absence, Elisabet had received a letter from her attorney in Munich, Dr. Karl Dürck, whom she had asked to attend to her affairs when they had left precipitously for America, leaving her sculpture, villa, and unfinished business. She also recalled that she had received letters from Neureuther in 1872 in Thomasville stating that because he was responsible for giving her the commission for King Ludwig's bust for the *Polytechnikum*, he would require her instructions before Friedrich Ochs could procure the marble and execute the statue.[11] At the time that this letter was sent, she had been traveling and searching for a home, and had failed to provide Neureuther with a satisfactory reply.

Now Dr. Dürck explained that the Bavarian government had secured a 2,500 *Gulden* mortgage on the Schwabing villa until the delivery of the King's statue; however, the Bavarian government had not supplied the Carrara marble as Elisabet had specified and had wanted the statue to be executed in Munich, which Ochs had refused to do without Elisabet's permission. Finally because of the expense of the marble, storage costs for twelve years, and his need to be paid for his workmanship, Ochs had settled with the Bavarian government to liquidate the mortgage and had placed King Ludwig's statue in the custody of the Bavarian *Landbauamt* (land office).[12] When Elisabet related this news to Edmund, she suggested that perhaps now after King Ludwig's death, the new Regent-Prince Luitpold might buy the statue for a memorial to the poor deceased King.

"That would be good news," Edmund agreed. "What does Dr. Dürck write about the villa? With the lien liquidated, perhaps we can sell it."

"That's what I'll inform him to do," Elisabet replied.

Forced from her dreams of selling the villa by realities, Elisabet wrote to Julius Runge for ideas as to how she might make the plantation profitable; he suggested that she might start a dairy farm and import German immigrants to run it.

"I like that idea," Elisabet answered in her letter, "that is, if we could locate some sturdy, thrifty, hard-working peasants, who wouldn't look at me with sullen, woe-begone faces

while they loafed and lied to me. It is worth trying. I'll write to
my lawyer in Munich. Perhaps he can secure the type of persons I'm looking for. I can allow them the use of a horse, a
plow, and a cow to milk. If they live frugally, by hard work and
diligence, they should be able to make a living. If they prove re-
liable, I could work out a shares system.''[13]

With the assistance of Dr. Dürck and Consul Runge, Elisabet hired several families of Bavarian immigrants. These Germans proved more compatible workers for Elisabet than the
Negroes, and they found companionship in the German community of Brenham. Along with the dairy operation, Elisabet
planted acres in cotton as well as staple farm crops and experi-
mented unsuccessfully with goat ranching. In spite of her renewed efforts, the plantation's deficit continued; furthermore,
Lore's schooling proved very expensive, requiring Edmund to
borrow even more money.

After trying so hard with such disappointing results, Elisabet turned to Edmund for encouragement. ''You know, my
'best friend' that I've done everything I know to do to make
this plantation produce as it should; yet I show nothing but
failure. To add to this defeat, I grieve and worry about Lore,
especially with Cenci constantly reminding me of his absence.
Frankly, Edmund, I'm very tired of trying to manage this
property. I must ask for your help.''

Edmund reassured her that he realized that it was now
necessary for him to put aside his research and writing until
the plantation might be operating profitably. Perhaps by par-
ticipating in local activities he could acquire help and cooperation, and at the same time possibly add a little culture and education to the lives of the citizenery of Hempstead.

As Edmund had promised, he took more interest in plantation affairs. In a discussion between Edmund and the other
planters and farmers in Waller County, they told him that few
of them had made a living since the Civil War. They spoke of
their need for markets and for a fair price for their farm com-
modities; however, these farmers had considered that Dr.
Montgomery and Miss Ney were wealthy Europeans, too rich
to be troubled by the discouraging problems of agriculture in
Waller County.

As Edmund became increasingly busy with the management of Liendo and the affairs of the community, conversely

Elisabet was less active and increasingly moody and introspective. Without her art or her son, she told Edmund that only their love kept her from complete despair.

Elisabet's depression increased when Lore, after a year at Swarthmore, failed in his studies. After consulting with his friends, Edmund transferred him to Chappaqua Mountain Institute in Claverack, New York.[14] Apparently languages and public speaking were the only fields of study in which Lore achieved any success. In 1890, after supporting Lore for three years of ineffective schooling, Edmund sent him to a well-recommended boarding school for boys, Chateau de Laucy, near Geneva, Switzerland. This school, which was very expensive, seemed their last hope. Keeping Lore there strained their finances almost past their limit. When they received a notice that Lore's tuition was delinquent, Elisabet wrote that the money would be forthcoming as soon as the cotton crop was picked, ginned, and sold.[15]

In the meantime, Lore not only spent all the money sent to him, but also accumulated large debts. After Elisabet and Edmund refused to send him any more funds, he ran away from school, leaving a message that he was "going to Italy." When Elisabet and Edmund were notified of Lorne's disappearance, Elisabet was frantic. Then she remembered that their friend, Mrs. Robert Leisewitz, was in Stuttgart, Germany with her daughter Henrietta, who was attending a finishing school. Elisabet wrote to her for assistance and with the help of mutual friends, Mrs. Leisewitz discovered Lore in Italy — broke, lonesome, and glad to see his friends from Texas. Overjoyed to learn that Mrs. Leisewitz had found Lore, Elisabet and Edmund were even more pleased when Mrs. Leisewitz promised to keep him with her until she and Henrietta returned to Brenham.[16]

As Edmund became more involved with affairs of the plantation during the four years that Lore was away, his business transactions brought him into closer contact with his fellow-citizens, who began to realize that the Doctor, whom most had regarded as a wealthy recluse, was actually a friendly fellow with a sly sense of humor. He actively supported the fledgling public schools in Hempstead as well as volunteering as an academic consultant for neighboring Prairie View College, the first institution of higher education in Texas for Negroes, established in 1878–79 on the site of Alta Vista Plantation, the former Jared Kirby plantation.[17]

Elisabet was glad that her "best friend" apparently enjoyed his work in the community, but in her depression and worry over Lore, she preferred to remain isolated from life in Waller County. Edmund, on the other hand, had become so well-known that a group of women from Hempstead asked him to assist in raising funds for the maintenance of a Confederate Veterans' Home in Austin. Edmund held a series of three well-attended lectures, donating his time and the money raised from ticket sales was given to the Home.

While these lectures raised Edmund's esteem in the county, his financial obligations grew increasingly serious. He was troubled by the growing costs of the plantation's maintenance, his son's extravagances, and the infertility of the soil after fifty years of cultivation.

"If I could only receive an outstanding commission for a sculpture," Elisabet sighed to Edmund, "then we could have some funds to use. But who in Texas will give me a commission? Those rustic oafs in the legislature, when I told them what my art was worth, decided that the Capitol didn't need any statuary. I only wish that you could be paid for the worth of all those articles published in the *Open Court* journal, or find a publisher for your book. I remember reading a poem by Paul Carus, the editor of *Monist,* entitled 'Sursum.' In the Latin dictionary, I discovered that the word means 'upwards.' That word seemed like the title I've wanted for my Brü*der Genii* statue,[18] like a word that we might even adopt as our motto."

"Then we'll make our motto 'Sursum,'" Edmund agreed. "'Sursum' reminds me of the Goethean gospel of salvation through ceaseless striving. Apparently our 'ideal life' has now reached such a low point that 'Upwards' is the only direction possible. 'Sursum,' Elisabet."

19

Commissions in Austin

*The art of the sculptor is made of
strength, exactitude and will.*

Auguste Rodin

"My 'best friend,' read this," exclaimed Elisabet as she brought to Edmund a letter that she had received from Governor Roberts. "There is hope. 'Sursum' is a magic word."

The letter, dated October 1890, contained an invitation for Elisabet to be the guest of former Governor Roberts and his wife in Austin to consult with a committee of ladies to plan a Texas exhibit for the World's Columbian Exposition to be held in Chicago in 1893.[1] Former Governor Roberts, now a professor of law at the nine-year-old University of Texas, wrote to Elisabet that he had recommended her to Mrs. William B. Tobin, chairman of the committee, because of Elisabet's reputation as an artist in Europe, and especially because of her experience in exhibiting her sculpture at the 1867 Art Exhibition in Paris. This Columbian Exposition was planned to commemorate the four hundredth anniversary of the discovery of America. The former governor wanted Texas to be represented

by noteworthy statuary created by a Texan to demonstrate to
the other states that Texas was no longer a frontier, but rather
a state where art and culture were appreciated and nourished.

"Here's my chance for a commission," Elisabet said.
"Now perhaps I'll have the chance to show the people in this
uncultured country what an authentic and capable artist can
produce."

Such a possibility brought a sparkle to Elisabet's eyes; yet
when she looked at herself in the mirror, she saw that she was
no longer the beautiful young *Fraülein* who had captivated important men and kings with her charm and artistry. She had
become a fifty-seven-year-old woman with a matronly figure,
with her short auburn curls mixed with grey and with distinct
facial lines from days spent in the sun and evenings spent in
worry. When she reminisced upon her hardships in Texas, she
recalled that she once told a friend that she would rather scrub
floors for her bread in the Old World than to live like a queen in
the New.[2] "That's no longer true," she told herself. "Today I
feel young, renewed, and equal to a challenge. I'll be the first
famous sculptor in the state of Texas."

To make herself as presentable as possible for the committee in Austin, she chose a dark silk tunic, a round, tight-fitting
black velvet hat "that will not blow off my head," with a veil of
fine lace, black boots, and elbow-length black mesh gloves.
Elisabet considered herself to be properly dressed, especially
when she noted the so-called stylish woman's appearance: an
hour-glass waist corseted so tightly that the rest of her body
exploded top and bottom like a sausage tied in the middle, leg-
o'mutton sleeves shaped like a sheep's shank, narrow, pointed-
toed shoes constructed like hobbles for a horse, with the absurd
costume crowned with a bonnet trimmed with flowers and
feathers, looking like a poor bird trapped in its nest.[3]

Elisabet felt so strongly on the subject of dress that she
wrote to Mrs. Frances E. Russell, Chairman of the Committee
on Dress Reform for the World's Fair in 1893:

> By the nature of my work I found myself compelled to
> quit the trailing dress which I admired for its grace. Through
> various stages I came at last to a form which appeared to me
> convenient, protective, and handsome. I adopted and used it
> publicly first in my travels in Egypt, varied the material ac-

cording to the climate, season, work: dark flannel, white flannel, military linen, black velvet. . . .

I have never wished for notoriety for it . . . though I wore daly [sic] for over twenty years now.[4]

Since the first time Elisabet visited Austin almost ten years before as Governor Robert's guest, she had liked the town. Austin in 1890 had grown to a population of approximately 14,400 and could boast of a few distinguished Colonial-styled homes, such as the Governor's mansion, now the home of Governor Sul Ross, and Woodlawn, the elegant homeplace of former Governor Elisha M. Pease.[5] With its new Capitol and the new University located a few miles north of downtown, Austin reminded Elisabet of Munich in her student days. Unlike Munich, however, Austin lacked a center for the fine arts, something that Elisabet dreamed of bringing into existence. Perhaps she and Edmund could establish a school of art and a school of philosophy in this fledgling University of Texas.

Such were her thoughts when she arrived as the guest of the Roberts to meet with the committee of ladies planning art works for the Texas Pavilion in the Chicago Columbian Exhibition. Former Governor Roberts had already suggested that the statues of the two greatest heroes of Texas, Sam Houston and Stephen F. Austin, would make an appropriate representation for the state. When Elisabet met with the members of the committee, she noticed that they were startled at first by her manner of dress, but after she discoursed on art and the important Europeans whom she had modeled, she convinced them by her intelligence and witty stories that she was well-qualified to be given a commission to create the two statues.

One drawback existed, however, which Mrs. Tobin explained: the committee was short of funds and must ask Miss Ney to model the statues as a patriotic duty for the State of Texas. But they could give her a thousand dollar advance for her expenses if she were willing to accept such terms.[6]

Elisabet gladly accepted the proposition because this commission meant that she would be working professionally again, something that she had missed dearly for over twenty years; however, she insisted upon a written contract stipulating that she would be furnished with funds to execute the two statues into marble within ten years after the close of the Exposition.[7]

When Elisabet returned to Liendo after the Austin trip to

bring Edmund the good news of her commission, she discussed
with him her needs for funds to construct a studio and for living expenses; they also discussed their financial situation,
which as usual was precarious and debt-ridden. But Edmund,
delighted to see Elisabet happy in the anticipation of working
with sculpture again, wrote to one of the wealthy scientist-
philosophers with whom he corresponded and obtained a sizeable loan to supplement the thousand dollar advance paid to
Elisabet.[8]

With this reassurance from Edmund, Elisabet enthusiastically returned to Austin and again accepted the Roberts' hospitality for living quarters and set up a temporary studio in a
basement room in the Capitol to begin her work on the statues
of Houston and Austin.[9] In her search for a site for her studio
and future art school, Elisabet discovered an undeveloped section known as Hyde Park, three miles north of the business
district and a short distance north of the University, a place
studded with cedar, mesquite, and live oak trees, with a spring
that was the source of Waller Creek.

The location and terrain appealed to Elisabet, who purchased seven acres, which included a pond that she named
"Bull Frog Lake." As she had done in Thomasville, she drew
plans for a small scale building in Greek-Revival style to be
built of native limestone, containing a basement, a studio with
two small fireplaces and for north light exposure, two ten-by-
twelve-foot windows which could be dismantled to admit a
block of marble too large for one window, a carriage porch on
the south front, and a small reception room on the west. A balcony bedroom, which she planned to furnish with a hammock
and sit-in bathtub, could be curtained off from the studio. This
room was reached by a narrow staircase with a railing constructed with wooden pegs. A ladder and trap door led to the
sun deck on the roof where, in good weather, Elisabet intended
to sleep in a hammock.[10]

After drawing the plans and beginning construction, she
needed a name for her studio. Remembering Formosa in Madeira, where she and Edmund had lived happily, she decided
also to call her Austin studio "Formosa," with the word "Sursum," which seemed to bring good fortune, engraved on the
cornerstone. She had a tent erected on the building site from
where she could supervise the workmen, hung her Oriental

tapestries inside and lived there during the building process.

While still living in her tent, Elisabet received exciting news from Germany in a letter from Friedrich Ochs dated December 26, 1890, asking if she would be interested in exhibiting the finished statue of King Ludwig at the International Art Exhibition at the Berlin Royal Art Academy in the coming summer. He also asked instructions for the disposition of the King's statue after the Exhibition and requested payment for his work in executing the statue.[11]

Elisabet replied to Herr Ochs that she would be glad for her sculpture to be shown in Berlin, and that in regard to his request for payment, he should consult with her attorney, Dr. Karl Dürck in Munich. She also wrote that she was eager for a plaster copy of King Ludwig's statue to be sent to the Columbian Exhibition in Chicago, and asked the assistance of her friend Anton von Werner, Director of the Royal Academy of Arts in Berlin,[12] as well as Dr. Dürck, to send King Ludwig's statue, the bust of Bismarck, and *Die Bruder Genii* to be exhibited in Chicago.

After this recognition in Germany and the possibility of selling her Ludwig statue, Elisabet had renewed enthusiasm for her Texas project, although she experienced a setback when in September, 1892, a fire destroyed her tent, burned her two handsome Spanish blankets, her Turkish shawls, and left her gold watch and table silver as molten pieces; only her silver necklace survived intact. In her notebook, she wrote: "Where shall I get a tent again? I would be sorry to leave my tent life. A real house lacks a good deal of the posie of a tent."[13] Later Elisabet replaced the burned tent with one with a wooden floor and canvas fly and furnished with two cots and a rocking chair, to be used as a guest room whenever Edmund or her friends came to visit.[14]

As soon as she had moved her modeling equipment into the new studio, she invited Mrs. Tobin to see how her work was progressing on Houston's statue. She told Mrs. Tobin that she had selected Houston to model first because she felt an empathy for him, especially because he had many times visited Liendo Plantation when it was owned by Colonel Groce, and also because Houston had stood courageously against slavery.

Mrs. Tobin seemed pleased with the statue and asked to see the rest of the atelier. The cooler basement, reached

through a trap door, "which will enable me to hide from anyone whom I don't want to see," Elisabet joked, was where she
kept her modeling clay and perishable foods, such as her clabber, cream, cheese, and vegetables. At the upper end of the
tour, when Mrs. Tobin climbed through the trap door to the
roof, she was surprised to see a hammock.

When Mrs. Tobin asked about it, Elisabet explained,
"when we lived in Madeira, I followed the natives' example
and often slept in a hammock, which I found less trouble than
a bed. When I traveled in the Middle East, I saw people in
those hot countries sleeping on their roofs in the coolness of
the night, which also seemed a good idea.[15] I enjoy the peace-
fulness of the night sounds of the crickets, bull frogs, and
sometimes a night-singing mockingbird. I'm pleased with my
studio. If only Dr. Montgomery could sell the plantation and
move to Austin, I could add a study where he could experiment
and write."

After inspecting Formosa and the emerging statue of Sam
Houston, Mrs. Tobin was impressed with Elisabet's professional approach, including her research into the lives of Houston and Austin, and her letters to Houston's daughter, Mrs.
Margaret Houston Williams, and to other relatives of both
Houston and Austin asking for clothes, photographs, or me-
mentoes that might help her create the character of the men.[16]

Elisabet conceived Houston as forty years old, dressed in
buckskin as he surveyed the territory struggling to be free
from Mexico. She intended to portray Austin as a pioneer, appearing as he did when he led the first Anglo-American set-
tlers in 1821 into Texas, wearing a buckskin hunting jacket
and holding a map in one hand, with a long musket leaning
against his opposite shoulder.

With sensuous pleasure and lightness of heart, Elisabet
dipped her hands into the wet clay to form these Texas heroes
and felt the figures within her hands slowly coming into being.
She was happy. She was creating.

While Elisabet was living and working in Austin, Edmund
continued to struggle with the woes of the plantation. Whenever Elisabet visited Liendo, she appeared to be filled with enthusiasm about her work and her dream to create a school of
fine arts in Texas. Her optimism encouraged Edmund, who
was inspired to start a philosophic discussion group in Hemp-

stead. A German watchmaker in town who read philosophy, and several others had asked him to lead such a group.[17]

In the troubled reconstruction environment, however, it was difficult to consider discussing only the subject of philosophy; the men of Waller County could not refrain from bringing up, with humiliation and anger, the abuses of the office-holding "scalawags and carpetbaggers."

As a result of Edmund's leadership in this circle and in response to the exploitation by the Yankees running the county at the time, in July of 1892, the Waller County Democrats invited Edmund to become chairman of the County Executive Committee.[18] Edmund accepted because he realized that his fellow townspeople respected his judgment and needed his advice. He further felt that he should at least make an effort to improve the environment of the county for the sake of his son, who might someday live there.

Lorne did return to Waller County in January of 1892 with Mrs. Leisewitz and Henrietta when they returned to Brenham from Europe. The change in Lorne after four years amazed Elisabet: he was almost twenty, tall, strong, and handsome, and easily affected cultured manners whenever it suited his pleasure. Elisabet and Edmund were pleased with his fluency in languages, although they knew that he had done little serious studying of languages or anything else.

When Elisabet brought Lorne to Formosa, he was charming and gracious to her friends and to former Governor Roberts, but when Elisabet asked the now Law Professor Roberts what he thought of Lorne, he replied that the boy was too charming. Everyone spoiled him, most of all his parents and Cenci. Lorne had never done a day's work in his life and acted as if his parents should be expected to support him. Professor Roberts advised Elisabet to insist that the boy either complete his education or find work to do.[19]

With Professor Robert's assistance, Lorne enrolled in the University of Texas Law School under the name of "Lawrence Ney Montgomery," age nineteen, and registered in one law course and in advanced studies in French and German.[20] Although the languages presented no difficulty, he had trouble with his law course because he refused to apply the time necessary to learn the material. Even though her son's behavior distressed Elisabet, she complied with Lorne's request that she write to his law professor, Judge R. S. Gould, and ask that he be assigned "some oratory task," such as delivering an address to the House of Representatives incorporating Judge Gould's ideas and suggestions. "In his various schools here and abroad," Elisabet wrote to Judge Gould, "he was considered the best deliverer of addresses and carried off invariably the medals and prizes for declamations and oratory." She also added how Lorne's behavior worried and grieved her; how his late hours and failure to study "take away my night's rest and deprive me of the necessary concentration for my work. . . ."[21]

Because of her helplessness in dealing with her son, Elisabet had not yet completed the Sam Houston statue nor even started Stephen F. Austin's, and the Chicago Exposition was only six months away. This was the first time that she had been so tardy. What would Rauch think of such unprofessionalism, she wondered? When Lorne lost interest and dropped out of the University, Elisabet rationalized: if he's not interested in a career as a lawyer, he can become a diplomat or ambassador, influencing affairs of governments in America and Europe. With her dreams and ambitions for her son, she could not see him as a pampered and spoiled young man who preferred to dress and act as a Hempsteader rather than as a potential statesman.

But Elisabet was forced to accept the reality of Lorne when, several days after the event, she received a copy of the *Hempstead News,* which stated that on July 13, 1893, Lorne Montgomery had eloped and married Daisy Thompkins, the sixteen-year-old daughter of Judge H. C. Thompkins of Hempstead.[22] Elisabet was incensed. In her outrage she wrote letter after letter, in English or in German or in combination of the two, to Lorne, who had returned to Liendo with his bride.

Regarding the young bride, Elisabet wrote:

> *Mein Sohn:* She is a thoroughly useless, unwelcome guest in our house who has degraded herself in the opinion of any high-minded person, who think marriage ought to be a union of a kindred spirit; who take a wider aim in life than to manufacture children. . . .
>
> People cannot commit rash degrading acts. They can only redeem themselves, not by making the best of such acts, but by retracing their wrong steps. . . .
>
> This union is nothing but animal instinct turned loose without conscience. A marriage thus contracted has not my interest. For me it does not exist.[23]

Elisabet's attitude and her letters, some of which she copied in her journal,[24] only deepened Lorne's animosity toward her. Edmund's attitude toward the marriage, although he was not especially pleased, was to accept the inevitable. Edmund wrote to Elisabet that Daisy apparently was very much in love with Lorne and perhaps the marriage might have a stabilizing effect on him. Edmund also admitted that he needed the help of both young people to manage the plantation. After Lorne and Daisy settled into the plantation under Cenci's watchful attention, Edmund returned to his study and his intellectual pursuits.

Three weeks after the marriage, Edmund left the newly-weds to go to Chicago at the invitation of Mr. and Mrs. Benjamin Underwood, with whom he corresponded, to read his paper, "The Psychological Significance of Dreams," to the annual meeting of the Psychical Science Congress, a part of the Columbian Exposition, which had opened three months earlier in May.[25] Upon visiting the Texas Pavilion to observe Elisabet's sculptures, of which only the statue of Sam Houston had arrived in time for the opening, Edmund wrote to Elisabet that her works received a poor reception and that her name as an artist was not even mentioned. Because she had not completed the Austin statue, Elisabet had no desire to go to Chicago to supervise the placement of her art.

In a letter written August 11, 1893, from the Chicago Exposition, Bernedette Tobin wrote that the statue of King Ludwig II, the *Group of Genii,* and the bust of Bismarck arrived from Germany, but the *Genii* statue was broken en route and could not be exhibited. King Ludwig's statue and Bismarck's bust were placed in the Woman's Building rather than in the Fine Arts Building; however, the statue of Houston was placed on a pedestal in the center of the Texas Exhibit, where it was well-received,[26] but it lacked the companionship of Austin, a circumstance of which the members of the women's committee made Elisabet distressingly aware.

Soon after Edmund returned from Chicago, Elisabet, anxious to hear his report personally, visited Liendo. While she and Edmund were seated in the parlor talking, Lorne and Daisy walked in. Standing up rigidly and focusing her "haughty stare" at the frightened young girl, Elisabet confronted her daughter-in-law with the words, "So you're the hussy who stole my son."

Lorne stepped between them. "Daisy's my wife and I'll not tolerate any more of your insults and abuse. You're no mother. I hate you!" Lorne spat his words at Elisabet.

"And I no longer have a son!" Elisabet exclaimed. "Both of you leave this house!"

Edmund intervened: "This is Lorne's home. He has a right to be here, and I've also asked him to assist me with the plantation."

"Then I'll leave immediately," Elisabet replied as she stormed upstairs, packed her bag, and ordered a servant to drive her into Hempstead, even though it was hours before the train was due to leave for Austin.

Some time later, a visitor in the Formosa studio asked Elisabet if the bust of a young man, displayed in the reception room, was that of her son.

"No," Elisabet replied. "I have no son and my daughter died in infancy. That work is entitled *A Young Violinist*." [27]

As Elisabet had idealized her conception of Lorne, she now attempted, in a closed compartment of her mind, to lock away his cruel behavior, but being a mother, she felt that if she became recognized as a successful sculptor, Lorne would realize that she was a talented artist worthy of his respect and admiration.

To ease her pain through hard work, Elisabet returned to her sculpture and completed the statue of Stephen F. Austin, as she first had conceived his portrayal as a pioneer, even though it was too late for the Chicago Exhibition. Bernedette Tobin and the members of the committee for the Texas exhibit felt justifiably upset by Elisabet's failure to complete the two statues as she had promised and demanded the return of five hundred of the thousand dollar advance. [28] At this time Elisabet had practically no cash, and Edmund's situation at Liendo was no better.

To mollify the ladies of the committee, Elisabet asked that they be patient and invited them to her studio to view the beautiful statue she had created of Stephen F. Austin. As he had done in the past, Professor Roberts came to Elisabet's defense, especially because he understood that her delay resulted from her anguish over her son's behavior. After viewing Austin's statue, the ladies finally agreed to accept the sculpture of Austin as a fitting companion for Houston.

After these two statues had demonstrated Elisabet's ability as an artist, Formosa slowly became recognized in Austin as the gathering place for artists and patrons of the arts. Elisabet became a celebrity of sorts. People came to her studio as they had done in Münster to watch a woman sculptor at work and to view her eccentric working costume of a black velvet tunic that reached a little below the knees and close-buttoned serge leggings, which she wore even in the hottest weather. Her reputation for eccentricity grew when she told her friends about her "private dungeon," a small closet in her studio where she banished her "enemies." At one time when the nose of the bust of George von Werthern was accidentally chipped, Elisabet remarked, "It doesn't matter. He's one of the fellows in the 'dungeon' anyway." [29]

As had been her strategy in the past when she needed a commission, Elisabet selected a person who was well-known and wealthy, then schemed to win his friendship. The person Elisabet targeted for this manipulation was the widow of former Governor Elisha M. Pease, owner of Woodlawn, Austin's finest pre–Civil War mansion, where she lived with her spinster daughter and presided as the "grande dame" of Austin society.

On her first assault on the Pease mansion, the family was out of town, and she was met by a Negro servant, who seemed startled by her unconventional clothes and her ability to handle her horse and gig. The man told her that Mrs. Pease was vacationing in the north. Elisabet informed him, "Tell your mistress that she can expect to make Miss Elisabet Ney's acquaintance when she returns." Elisabet then wrote a note to Mrs. Pease and explained that she was a well-known sculptor temporarily in need of funds and requested a loan of one hundred dollars. [30] She received no reply from Mrs. Pease, who had never heard of Elisabet Ney.

When Mrs. Pease and her daughter returned to Austin, Elisabet, dressed in her white wool tunic, paid a formal call to Woodlawn. She entertained Mrs. Pease and her daughter Julia with talk of her life in Europe in contrast to her life in Texas and of her ambition to establish an Academy of Fine Arts in Austin. Even though she was over sixty, Elisabet's wit and vivacity impressed Mrs. Pease and Julia as well as the two orphaned grand-children, Margaret and Niles Graham, who

were nicknamed the "Brownies," and who also lived in the
Pease mansion.

As a result of this visit, Elisabet not only received the hundred dollar loan, but also an invitation to spend week-ends at
Woodlawn. "I'll be pleased to visit," Elisabet said, "but I
must sleep in a hammock. I don't like too-soft beds. Also I do
not eat meat; the idea of eating the flesh of a dead animal is ab-
horrent to me," she explained to the surprised, yet agreeable,
Mrs. Pease.[31]

Seizing the opportunity to meet Mrs. Pease's circle of
friends, Elisabet soon found herself popular and respected by
Austin socialites, who considered themselves lovers of art and
culture. One friend whom Elisabet acquired was a young writer, Bride Neill Taylor, who became an admirer and unofficial
public relations liaison for Elisabet. Other friends included
Nannie Carver Huddle, widow of a prominent Austin painter
William Henry Huddle, and Mrs. Emma Burleson, sister of Albert Sidney Burleson (who was later to become postmaster-
general in President Woodrow Wilson's cabinet). As always
Elisabet enjoyed the warm hospitality of Professor Roberts,
his wife and stepchildren.[32]

As the result of becoming known and gaining social status, Elisabet received four commissions for marble busts —
John R. Reagan, United States Senator; W. P. Hardeman, a
former Confederate General; Francis T. Lubbock, Governor of
Texas 1861 to 1863; and Caroline Pease Graham, the deceased
mother of the "Brownies." This bust was to be created from
photographs and clothing supplied by Mrs. Pease. Previously
Elisabet had modeled a bust of Bernedette Tobin, which had
not been cut in marble, but now that Mrs. Tobin was threaten-
ing a lawsuit against her for the return of five hundred dollars,
Elisabet was not sure of collecting the commission for that
sculpture. From the other commissions, however, she was able
to secure approximately four thousand dollars in advance payments, which enabled her to have peace of mind to work whole-
heartedly on these ordered pieces of statuary.

Her concentration on her work kept Elisabet from dwelling on her estrangement with Lorne, but she was saddened by
the death of her faithful horse, Asta. "She was only an animal
some people will say," Elisabet wrote to Mrs. Pease, "but with
the sudden death of Asta, a friend seemed to be taken away.

She (Asta) had been the unassuming destroyer of weariness many a time; her swiftness often seemed to carry me from under a weighty cloud which had gathered over my mind; *and!* was she not my conveyer to Woodlawn?"[33]

She purchased another horse, an Arabian stallion, "Pasha," who was big and strong enough to pull her gig the 120 miles from Austin to Liendo. When Elisabet made her trips to Liendo, she would leave Austin early in the morning and drive all day over the prairieland. At sundown she would ask at a farmhouse if she could feed her horse in the field, have water for herself and the horse, and hang her hammock between two trees in the yard.

The surprised hosts would almost always grant her request; many already knew about her from word of mouth. By the light of her kerosene lantern, she would eat her supper of "wind-dried" bread, unparched peanuts, fruit, and well water provided by the farmer. Then, without taking off her clothes, she would sleep in her hammock, and she and Pasha would be on their way again by early daybreak, stopping for the next night at another farmhouse. After four days of this sort of travel, she would arrive at Liendo for a visit with her "best friend."[34]

On one such trip to Liendo in January, 1895, when Elisabet drove up to the big house, Cenci greeted her excitedly to tell her that she must come and see her two-month old *Endelkind* named "Edmund" for Herr Doctor.

"Nein," Elisabet sadly told Cenci. "Until my son changes his ways, I do not wish to see him, his wife, nor his child."

Even though Lorne, Daisy, and the baby were living in a former tenant's house near the homestead, Elisabet did not visit her grandchild. While she was at Liendo, she dreamed that the women of the Exposition Committee had foreclosed on her studio, and that she had lost it forever. The intensity of the dream woke her in the early hours of the morning and compelled her to leave her bed immediately and write a letter to her business agent, Mr. Thomas Taylor, husband of her friend Bride Neill Taylor, telling him to do everything he could to restore her studio to her. When the reply came from Mr. Taylor that she should not be disturbed by a dream, and that Formosa was still hers, she felt relieved, yet slightly foolish. Mr. Taylor wrote that he felt certain that the committee would not foreclose on the studio.[35]

Elisabet did not tarry at Liendo because her work was now in her studio in Austin. Edmund, with Lorne's help, was attempting to manage the plantation, which had now grown to 2,200 acres, making Edmund the largest landowner in the county. Because of this, Edmund felt some responsibility for the welfare of Waller County. He added his voice to plans for better schools, better roads, and improved public facilities. As a result of his words and actions, Edmund was asked to be a candidate for Road Commissioner from his precinct. In May 1894, Edmund delivered the commencement address for Hempstead High School[36] and in it stated his philosophy of government and civic responsibility. Apparently the audience approved and many told him that he had their vote.

In the county elections in November, Edmund was elected, and in 1896 he was reelected for a second term. He also accepted the presidency of the Waller County Melon Growers Association[37] and became a member of the Texas Academy of Sciences, which met semi-annually at the University of Texas.

Whenever Edmund came to visit Elisabet, where he stayed in the guest tent, Elisabet's friends were impressed by his tall, aristocratic appearance, his side whiskers and flowing white hair, his distinguished way of speaking, and his Old World manners. Unfortunately Edmund's success in political and academic affairs did not carry over into his plantation management which, even with Lorne to assist him, was as great a financial failure as ever. "It will take a miracle to save Liendo," Edmund admitted to Elisabet.

20

Return to Europe

Art is long, life short;
Judgment difficult,
Opportunity transient.

Johann Wolfgang von Goethe

"*Wunderbar!* We have our miracle," Elisabet exclaimed as she read a telegram from Dr. Karl Dürck, her attorney in Munich, informing her that he had sold the Schwabing villa on February 1, 1895 and the King Ludwig statue on February 22. Elisabet's portion of the payments would be 39,500 Marks. "Now we can pay our debts and I can take my sculpture to Germany to be executed. *Ach,* Edmund, I'm filled with joy."

Later Elisabet received a lengthy letter from Dr. Dürck, dated April 19, 1895, with details of the sale of the villa and the statue. Adolph Fürtzwangler bought the villa for 75,000 Marks and assumed the remaining mortgage; from this amount Elisabet would receive 30,000 Marks. After King Ludwig's statue was exhibited at the International Art Exhibition at the Berlin Art Academy, at the suggestion of Prince-Regent Luitpold, the Bavarian government purchased the statue as a memorial to King Ludwig for 15,000 Marks, Elisabet's share being 9,500 Marks. In his letter Dr. Dürck wrote:

> The gentlemen from the Administration said that the determining factor in placing the statue [of King Ludwig] at Linderhof, near Oberammergau, was the fact that this castle in particular was the first to be conceived in the King's imagination and the first to become a reality, whereas the concept and realization of the other two castles fall in the time of the King's mental derangement. Also I am told that as a work of art and in the framework of artistic taste, the statue is best suited for this place. . . .
>
> I thought it appropriate to ask for an audience with the Prince-Regent to convey to him your thanks for his approval of the purchase. . . . He inquired about you with a great deal of concern and was well aware of the fact that you had often visited the late King, that he had been fond of you and sat for the statue. . . . He also asked me to tell you how happy he was to own one of your works.[1]

After this good fortune, Elisabet busied herself in her studio with finishing touches on the plaster statuary. She wrote to Dr. Dürck of her plans to come to Germany and requested him to rent a studio for her and to file suit for damages against Wetsch Brothers Shipping Company for improperly packing *Die Brüder Genii*[2] statue and, if possible, to determine the whereabouts of her statue *Prometheus Bound*, which she had left in the Royal Palace. With this turn of events, Elisabet felt that she should go to Germany to attend to her business affairs and to retrieve the sculpture that she had left behind, as well as to execute in marble her commissioned works. In September of 1895, Elisabet sailed from Galveston on a North German Lloyd steamer for Hamburg,[3] after an absence from Europe of almost twenty-five years.

To be once again on German soil rejuvenated Elisabet. She found that Hamburg was a large, bustling industrial port, alive with commercial activities. Being in Germany brought memories of her childhood in Münster and a yearning to see the town again. She knew that her brother Fritz and his wife Eleanor had no children, that Fritz had retired as a schoolmaster at the age of sixty-five, and that he lived in the family home at Bohlweg, No. 101.[4] Impulsively she telegraphed Fritz to expect her for a short visit.[5]

When Elisabet arrived in Münster, she was happy to discover that although the population had grown to 57,000, the town still retained its quaint Old World charm. She scarcely recognized her brother, however, for he was old, fat and grey-haired. He appeared equally surprised by his sixty-two-year-old sister's changed appearance: she was no longer a slender, attractive young woman, but a stout matronly grandmother, although she still dressed in her own idiosyncratic style. The two embraced, both glad to renew their kinship after their many years apart. After Fritz made Elisabet comfortable in the familiar surroundings, he asked about Lorne, who had visited them several years ago when he was in school in Europe. Elisabet said that he was married, had a son, and was presently helping Dr. Montgomery, his father, manage their plantation, but Elisabet expected him to enter law or diplomacy. To change the subject, she asked Fritz to show her their parents' grave.

Fritz and his wife took her to the family plot in the St. Mauritz Cemetery[6] where Johann and Anna Ney were buried beside their monument — a life-sized marble Madonna that looked like one that Elisabet herself might have created. While in the cemetery, Elisabet visited the grave of Bishop Müller. Her eyes filled with tears when she thought of the fine old man, who had been sympathetic and understanding toward her as a troubled child. He had commissioned her first piece of sculpture, *San Sebastian, Martyr,* and had continued to believe in her even after she had left the church. What piece of sculpture would be a fitting memorial? A large head of Christ — that would surely please the Bishop. As a memorial to Bishop Müller, she decided to create such a work of art.

While still in Münster, Elisabet received an invitation to visit the family of her maternal aunt Frau Elisabeth Röper-Wernze, who lived in Werne, a town twenty miles south, with her son Peter, her daughter Maria, Maria's husband, Herr Dr. Joseph Lueder and their two children. As soon as Elisabet met this family, she felt welcome and at home. The Lueders were as charmed by Elisabet as she was by them. To the Lueders she was a famous celebrity, and they were entranced by her anecdotes and tales of famous personages as well as by her stories about life in America. Elisabet called their home the "Magic Hut"[7] after the tale by her friend Jakob Grimm and his brother Wilhelm.

The visit was such a pleasant one that Elisabet departed with regret to attend to her business in Munich. Elisabet had wired Dr. Dürck to expect her, and was glad to see him and his wife and to accept their invitation to be a guest in their home. Elisabet had known Frau Dürck as the daughter of Wilhelm von Kaulbach, Director of the Bavarian Art Academy.[8]

When Elisabet inquired about Friedrich Kaulbach, Frau Dürck told her that he was a successful artist, was happily married, and lived in Hannover. From the tone of her voice, Elisabet sensed that Frau Dürck had probably heard gossip from years past about herself and Friedrich Kaulbach, and also sensed that Frau Dürck did not approve of her style of dressing, but because Elisabet was a client of her husband, Frau Dürck treated her politely and formally.

Concerning Elisabet's lawsuit against the shipping company, Dr. Dürck explained that he had written to her about it on November 2, 1895, at the time that Elisabet had been in Münster. The Lower Court had upheld her claim, but the judgment was overturned by a Higher Court which concluded that the damage was done at the storage facility at the Chicago Exposition; therefore, the shipping company was not liable.[9] His efforts thus far to locate her statue of *Prometheus* had been unsuccessful except to learn that it had been removed from the *Residenz*, but had not been returned to her Schwabing villa. As she had requested of him, he had rented a studio for her where the other sculpture she had left behind was stored.

The news of the lawsuit and of *Prometheus* disappointed Elisabet, but did not overshadow her joy at being in the atmosphere of Munich once again. She was eager to see how well Friedrich Ochs had executed the King's statue, which Dr. Dürck had written was placed at *Schloss* Linderhof.

In an effort to locate *Prometheus,* Elisabet went to the Royal Palace as soon as possible in search of the statue, but no one she talked with knew anything of its whereabouts. "After all," Elisabet complained to Dr. Dürck, "it should be hard to accidentally misplace a monument weighing eight hundred pounds."[10] In her conversations with people in the *Residenz,* Elisabet was shocked to hear King Ludwig referred to as "the mad King Ludwig." She was even more shocked to hear that six weeks after his death his castles were opened to the public and attracted sightseers from all parts of the world. To know that his private dream castles had become tourist attractions would have horrified King Ludwig, who, as Elisabet well knew, abhorred crowds and was obsessed with his privacy.

In the Palace Elisabet learned that her bust of King Ludwig was in Hohenschwagau Castle near two of the castles that the King had built in the Bavarian Alps south of Munich. To make this journey, Elisabet rode a train to Oberammergau and from there hired a carriage to the valley of Graswang to Ludwig's Linderhof Castle. This palace, built in the years 1874 to 1878, was of white stone in the ornate Bavarian rococo style, decorated on the outside with statues, alcoves, and pillars and was set in the surroundings of a formal English garden, which included a moat and a high-spraying fountain at the entrance. In this garden, occupying a spot on a raised terrace as though greeting the visitors, Elisabet found the statue *King Ludwig II as a Knight of the Order of St. Hubert,* ecit Elisabet Ney, 1870.

The sight of her beautifully executed marble statue filled Elisabet with pride; yet also dismay because of its lack of protection from the elements. Although the marble was hard and durable, it would not stand years of exposure without deterioration. The statue must be moved inside and be protected.

After she had carefully inspected her statue, she walked about the grounds and was not surprised to encounter a Moorish kiosk. Inside the kiosk she was greeted with gaudy colors and gold rococo designs climaxed by a throne of Oriental splendor flanked by three enameled peacocks spreading their multicolored stained-glass tails. On the castle grounds was an artificial grotto built on the slope of a hill above the palace, a stage setting made real, a lake surrounded by shrubbery designed by a landscape architect against the backdrop of a mural illustrating the first act of Wagner's *Tannhäuser.*

After spending the remainder of the day in *Schloss* Linderhoff, Elisabet returned to Oberammergau for the night. Even though snow fell the next day, she continued her castle tour up the mountainside to Neuschwanstein, which Ludwig had begun building in 1869 when he was twenty-four, about the time that Elisabet had modeled his bust. But the castle, which cost 120,000,000 gold Marks, was not completed until seventeen years later, after his death, in 1886.[11] As she approached, this white castle with battlements and minaret towers like those of the middle ages, it rose like a stalagmite from the snow-covered forest below, appearing as if it, too, had come from a fairy tale of the Brothers Grimm.

Along with the other tourists, Elisabet walked up the steep path to the entrance of the castle. Once inside she recognized Ludwig's lavishly ornate style of decoration and realized that he had filled almost every room in the castle with murals and pictures illustrating scenes from Wagner's operas. She climbed the narrow winding stairway to the tower to admire the snowy Alps spread out before her and to view the neighboring brownstone, gingerbread castle of Hohenschwangau, where Ludwig had spent much of his childhood.

Eager to locate her bust of the young King Ludwig, Elisabet went the short distance to the neighboring ancient Hohenschwangau castle, which Ludwig's father, King Maximilian II, had renovated and decorated. At the end of a long room, the *Heldensaal* (heroes' room), decorated with battle scenes and pictures of old German heroes, she discovered a pedestal holding the bust of King Ludwig.[12] This room was filled with the history of ancient Bavaria and this castle that Ludwig had loved as a child was a proper setting for his statue, Elisabet thought as she gazed at the bust with fondness and sadness, sadness for the unfortunate King Ludwig and sadness for herself, no longer the young ambitious artist, but rather a disillusioned old woman.

After spending the day in the two castles, Elisabet decided to remain overnight in the nearby village of Füssen. All the evening and even after she went to bed, she felt the presence of Ludwig, felt that he wanted to communicate with her. Although she knew his presence could only be an illusion, or a dream, he, nevertheless, was very real — so real that she wrote of her experience in her journal:

> His Majesty and I were together again this evening. He only smiled compassionately when I fell on my knees and implored him to forgive my blindness of twenty-five years ago. He did not wish me to talk. He wanted to tell me that he was being persecuted in death as in life. He kept assuring me that he did not murder his physician-guard and then commit suicide. As though I had doubts — I who have always known that Ludwig could do no violence! Like Prometheus, he taught by example the lessons of peace and justice and artistic creation. Because he taught these lessons and not the les-

sons of greed and aggression and war, the world has pronounced him a mad king. It is the world which is mad — not Ludwig. I who know so much of him know that he was the most sane of persons — and a martyr, as surely as were Socrates and Christ and Jeanne d'Arc.[13]

Disturbed by this visitation from King Ludwig as well as the exposure of his statue to the elements, Elisabet informed Dr. Dürck as soon as she returned to Munich that King Ludwig's statue must be moved indoors and protected. He replied, however, that he thought that the garden at Linderhof was a fit setting, and was the location that Prince-Regent Luitpold had selected.

"Then I'll find whoever is in charge of public monuments and demand that my statue be moved indoors," Elisabet stated. The official in the Minister's office at the Palace was surprised to be confronted by an irate Miss Elisabet Ney, who had created King Ludwig's statue and then had disappeared for twenty-five years, and who was now demanding that the statue be moved inside Linderhof castle.[14] After hearing Elisabet's complaints, the official promised to do what he could about pollution to the sculpture.

This dreamed encounter with King Ludwig and the discovery of his bust and statue were still vividly in Elisabet's mind as she went about the streets of Munich, which was wearing the festive dress of the Christmas season: there were Christmas trees, bazaars, lights, and the *Christkindlmarkt* in the *Marienplatz* filled with handicrafts and holiday food, such as stollen, marzipan figures, *Kletzenbrot* and *Hutzelbrot* (fruit breads), all of which reminded Elisabet of her student days.

Elisabet's Christmas cheer was tempered this year by the deaths of many of her friends. In addition to King Ludwig's tragic end, others who had died were Max Widnmann, who had taught her sculpture at the Bavarian Art Academy; Johann Berdellé, who had taught her painting; Gottfried Keller, who had finally achieved fame as a writer; Baron George von Werthern, who had been assigned to Elisabet's dungeon of disliked persons; and Johanna Kapp, who had died isolated in a world of her own fantasy. With sadness, Elisabet also learned of the death of her friend Hans von Bülow, whose former wife Cosima, now Richard Wagner's widow, reigned over Wagner's legacies in Bayreuth.[15]

After Munich, Elisabet planned to go to Berlin, but she did not want to leave without visiting Ludwig's third castle, Herrenchiemsee, fifty miles east of the city, which was Ludwig's conception of a reproduction of Versailles. Although Ludwig was accused of bankrupting the country by building his castles, Elisabet learned that Bavaria was profiting from the tourists who were attracted to these extravagent citadels.

Ludwig's Herrenchiemsee castle, on an island in Lake Herrenchiemsee, was more ornate than any castle that Elisabet had ever seen except Versailles. The climax of Elisabet's visit to this castle was a concert by a string quartet that performed in the Hall of Mirrors, which consisted of one hundred mirrors illuminated by the light of more than four thousand candles reflecting from the looking glass walls. While she was in this hall, Elisabet again felt Ludwig's presence: she knew that he preferred night to day and illusion to reality, and this room made her feel as though she were part of Ludwig's dream world.

Before leaving Munich, Elisabet wrote to her friend Herr Anton von Werner, Director of the Berlin Royal Art Academy, who was delighted that she was returning to Berlin and offered his hospitality and use of a studio in the Art Academy. When he was a beginning student at the Berlin Academy, Elisabet had recognized his talent and had encouraged his efforts to become a painter. Over the years he became a well-known artist. His work *The Proclamation of the Empire of Versailles,* along with other paintings portraying the greatness of the Fatherland, resulted in his appointment as Director of the Art Academy. When Elisabet had asked him for assistance in 1892 in shipping King Ludwig's statue to the Chicago Exposition, he had been very helpful.[16]

In Berlin Elisabet found herself among friends, especially because the Director of the Academy recognized her as a fine sculptor. She revisited Rauch's old studio in the Lagerhaus, now converted into a Rauch Museum, and wandered among his *Plastik* with admiration and affection. She visited Friedrich Ochs to compliment him on his artistry in executing King Ludwig's statue into marble and to ask his guidance in finding a master craftsman to assist her in copying into marble the sculpture that she had brought from Texas.

Because of his position of influence, Director von Werner

procured a commission for Elisabet from Kaiser Wilhelm II to create a marble medallion of the standing portrait of a woman, who had donated anonymously a large sum of money to the Berlin Art Academy. This work Elisabet entitled *A Berlin Philanthropist.* At the Director's suggestion, Elisabet entered a contest, sponsored by His Majesty Kaiser Wilhelm, in which each contestant was expected to restore the head, shoulders, and arms to the same fragmented figure of a dancing girl, which had been unearthed at Pompeii. One of the three models selected for the final decision was Elisabet's; however, before the winner was chosen, Elisabet was disqualified when the judges discovered that she was no longer a German citizen.[17]

As a result of her work at the Academy, Elisabet received a commission for a bust of Paula Ebers, deceased sister of Georg Moritz Ebers, an emminent Egyptologist, from one of his friends as a gift to ease the brother's sorrow. From a photograph, Elisabet created a bust with excellent results. A letter that Herr Ebers wrote to his friend who had commissioned the bust, Elisabet treasured, wherein Ebers stated:

> When I am absorbed in contemplating this remarkable likeness, my eyes fill with tears. I feel, indeed, that my Paula is again with me. How happy would I be to have the privilege of kissing the hand of the great sensitive sculptress, the truly creative artist, who has brought forth a work so touching and masterful! . . . The sculptress, who has fashioned a beautiful *Prometheus Bound,* evidently believes that a sense of humor can alleviate human passion. This she has shown in her treatment of Paula's eyes and facial lines. I am eternally grateful to Elisabet Ney.[18]

Elisabet charged sizable commissions for the pieces of sculpture and, under the sponsorship of Director von Werner, her reputation flourished in artistic circles. The bust of Governor Sayers, which was executed in marble and exhibited with King Ludwig's statue, received favorable comment. In the past Elisabet had written to Dr. Dürck about her difficulties in raising sufficient money for her European stay and received a letter from him on March 24, 1896, in which he stated that during the past year he had sent no less than 46,000 Marks [approximately $11,500] to her American banker and could not understand why she needed funds.[19]

Elisabet realized that if she chose to remain in Berlin, she could be assured of recognition with no financial worries. Edmund could sell Liendo and join her; however, she knew that it could never be, for he could not physically withstand the cold winters and her son, no matter how he disappointed her, lived in Texas. In light of the sweeping changes that she saw in the German economy toward an industrialization that was controlled by cartels and the Prussian Junker class, who had little concern for the welfare of the peasants, Elisabet wrote to Edmund that since living in America, she could see the faults and repression in Germany even more clearly.

In a letter to Halley Bryan Perry, May 3, 1896, Elisabet wrote, "The proudness with which I used to say: 'such or such does not happen in Europe' is all gone. Besides the numerous crimes which remain undiscovered, the unsafety about life we do not find by far the progress towards abandoning prejudices as we have it in America. And clearsighted unbiased persons who come to know something about America are convinced: that she will outstrip European culture in the *nearest* future." [20]

As Elisabet had been in Germany for almost a year and had accomplished as much as she had planned, she wrote to Edmund to expect her in Liendo the last of the summer, that she loved and missed him and had been too long away from him. On her return journey to Texas, while on shipboard on September 8, 1896, Elisabet wrote the following to Bride Neill Taylor:

> I have spent the night in a deckchair, my Spanish rug wrapped around me, and above me the star–crowned skies. So, in fact, I have passed several nights, as though I were looking out upon the swinging gardens of Semiramis, with my heart filled with goodwill for all mankind and with a longing, *intense,* to devote all my strength during the counted days left to me to such as are now in need of what I can give.
>
> Though I am truly void of what one would call patriotism (I have had this to avow over and over again), the appellation of *Texas* has a charm of a peculiar kind, such as the name of no other part of the wide earth. . . . Oh, if you could be here at this moment! A rainbow with all its exquisite beauty stretches before. A rainbow, the ancient symbol of the promise of good! [21]

Putting down her pen, Elisabet realized, to her own amazement, that she had become a Texan.

21

Success and Castrophe

Why are we weigh'd upon with heaviness,
And utterly consumed with sharp distress,
While all things else have rest from weariness?
Alfred, Lord Tennyson

Warm sunshine and tropical flowers welcomed Elisabet to the Gulf Coast and Galveston in September, 1896, after a year's absence. She disembarked from her North German Lloyd steamship, collected her luggage, including marble busts of Governor Lubbock, Senator Reagan, General Hardeman, and Caroline Pease Graham, and proceeded to a customs inspection station. Elisabet informed the official who checked her declaration of personal properties that all four pieces of sculpture were unfinished and therefore not dutiable. Upon examination of the statues, the inspector informed Elisabet that he considered the busts of Reagan[1] and Graham to be finished and subject to full duty.

As she eyed him with haughty disdain, she exploded, "That's unreasonable. That's robbery. I'll not be intimidated. Keep the two statues until I get in touch with my lawyer. You'll

hear from me, Herr Inspector," Elisabet threatened as she hurried into a waiting carriage, taking the other two busts with
her.

As soon as she arrived in Austin from the long and tedious
journey on the Houston and Central Texas Railroad from Galveston, she announced her presence to the Pease family at
Woodlawn, rather than facing at that time the lengthy and
somewhat difficult task of opening her studio. After a visit at
Woodlawn, Elisabet called upon her attorney, Mr. Clarence
Miller, to tell him of her problems with the Galveston customs.
He advised her to leave the two pieces of statuary at the customs office, where they would eventually be auctioned to pay
the duty owed. He explained that Elisabet could have a representative buy them at the auction for much less than the duty
levied.[2]

Because Elisabet was yearning to return to her "best
friend" at Liendo, she completed her Austin business as quickly as possible and boarded the train which crawled from Austin
to Hempstead. Edmund was waiting at the depot when Elisabet arrived to happily greet him. Cenci was as eager as Edmund for Elisabet's report from the Old Country. Although
Lorne, Daisy, and their little son Edmund lived on the plantation, they did not appear at the big house, and Elisabet made
no mention of their absence.

Not until after dinner, when she and Edmund were seated
side by side on the veranda surrounded by the warm, fall twilight, did she ask about Lorne. Then, to Elisabet's sorrow and
disappointment, Edmond told her of their son's irresponsibil-
ity and of his apparent domestic difficulties. Edmund said that
he had not written to her in detail about the multiple problems
of Lorne and of the plantation because such news would have
caused nothing but useless worry.

To change the subject from the plight of Liendo, Edmund
told her about his work as Waller County Road Commissioner
after his reelection that year (1896). He explained that he was
responsible for increasing the tax evaluation on property in the
county to raise money for the construction of a much-needed
bridge across the Brazos on the road to Bellville in Austin
County. He had also served as secretary to the Waller County
Melon Growers Association in an effort to persuade the farm-

ers to switch from raising their over-produced cotton crops to the cultivation of melons.[3]

His interest in county affairs pleased Elisabet who was seeing Texas in a fresh way after her year in Europe. Edmund enjoyed Elisabet's revelations of her impressions and experiences of a militaristic Germany and shared her fears of the possibility of another war. She wished they could sell the plantation so Edmund could join her in Austin. They talked together in German until the first rays of morning hastened them to their respective bedrooms.

The following day, Elisabet did indeed discover problems at Liendo. One complication which demanded her immediate attention was the departure, shortly before her return, of the supervisor of the dairy. In a letter to her friend Bride Neill Taylor, November 17, 1896, Elisabet wrote: "Such devastation the dairyman left behind him. It became a simple question of more loss or immediate attention. I am a great deal on horseback trying to push matters and see it done well. Because you will find it almost invarably [sic] not done at all, or badly attended to, if you depend on those you charge to do the work."[4]

After hiring a new dairyman and attempting to stabilize affairs at Liendo, Elisabet noted in her journal, "under no circumstances do I wish to undergo once more the trials combined with a whiskey man or a passionate man."[5] After doing what she could at the plantation, Elisabet returned to Austin and Formosa to resume her neglected sculpture, still without seeing Lorne and his family.

In May, 1897, Elisabet received welcome news from Dr. Dürck that he had located *Prometheus,* although in a deplorable condition, in a storeroom of the Court Architecture Commission: a foot broken off and an arm cracked at the shoulder, but he felt sure that Elisabet could repair the damage. In the meanwhile, he placed *Prometheus* in storage until such time as Elisabet could ship it to Austin.[6] He also wrote to Elisabet that he was trying to interest an art dealer in purchasing Garibaldi's statue and had approached the Geisslinger Factory with the proposition of casting King Ludwig's statue in various sizes to be sold at the King's castles as souvenirs to tourists, with Elisabet receiving ten percent of the profits.[7] Even though she did need the money, Elisabet was not interested in commercializing the King or her art.

When Bernedette Tobin and members of the Committee for the Texas Exhibit in Chicago heard that Miss Ney had received generous commissions for work done in Germany, they filed suit in District Court, in 1898, as plaintiffs, for Elisabet to return their five hundred dollar advance and also claiming ownership of the Houston and Austin statues. Elisabet alleged that the statues were her property and that she was negotiating with the Daughters of the Republic of Texas to have them executed in marble. The Judge ruled that the evidence showed no contract of ownership between Elisabet Ney and the Women's Committee; consequently, Miss Ney owned the statues, but because she had failed in her agreement to deliver the Austin statue at the time required, she owed the Committee a refund of their five hundred dollar advance.[8]

Before Elisabet realized that she would be required to repay the five hundred dollars, she had spent a large portion that she had earned in Europe to pay expenses and indebtedness of the plantation. Then, as if her financial problems were not enough, on the first of December Cenci wrote that Herr Doctor was seriously ill with bronchitis. After receiving this letter, Elisabet and Horace Williams, a half-Indian man-of-all-work whom Elisabet had hired to work at her studio and who could also work at the plantation, hurried to Edmund, who developed complications of pleurisy soon after she arrived.

Elisabet described Dr. Montgomery's illness in a letter December 29, 1897, to Miss Julia Pease at Woodlawn:

> As the days wore on the beautiful constitution of this ideal person stood the terrible onslought victoriously, we considered the patient reconvalescent, but! Christmas-eve all hopes were violently shattered: the right side was doomed — Ah! it was pittyful to have to listen to such suffering of convulsive pain so that for nearly twenty-four hours not a drop of water could be taken. Up to this hour I have personally resisted all fatigue; the sleep I have taken since Dec. 2 was in an armchair, near the patients bedside, during the intervals between changing the heated flannels; it would not amount to $2\frac{1}{2}$ hours during the 24. It seems all necessity for rest is gone.
>
> I must confess I have an ideal patient to nurse back to health again.[9]

Edmund slowly regained his health, and as soon as he was stronger, Elisabet returned to Formosa. Sadly Elisabet's relationship with the Pease family came to a less than cordial end as a result of her dispute with customs in Galveston. Elisabet had left the bust of Carrie Pease Graham, along with that of John H. Reagan, in the customs office. The import duty, caused by a mistake in the invoice, according to Julius Runge, was $375.00.[10] When the auction of the statues occurred, Elisabet's agent discovered that another bidder, Henry Ladd, had purchased Reagan's statue. Elisabet was indignant when she learned that Senator Reagan had then bought his bust portrait from Mr. Ladd for one hundred dollars. She wrote to Senator Reagan that if she had known that he would be so deceiving, she would have left his likeness in plaster. Senator Reagan's reply was that he had made no agreement for the bust to be cut in marble in Europe. As far as he was concerned Elisabet should take action against Mr. Ladd for interfering with her agent at the public sale in Galveston, which Elisabet proceeded to do.[11]

When the Pease family heard of the auction of the statues, Miss Julia, not knowing of Elisabet's scheme to reclaim her sculpture, sent her own agent to bid for it. This misunderstanding led to the termination of their friendship.[12] After the Pease family acquired the bust, Mrs. Pease was further displeased to read the inscription beneath the bust "Julia Pease" —not "Carrie Pease Graham." Elisabet was to be reminded of another mistake that she had made in the inscription of "Arth" instead of "Arthur" Schopenhauer.

In an attempt to make amends for the errors and misunderstandings, on July 2, 1898, Elisabet wrote to Miss Julia:

> To solve the dilemma which thus confronts us both, I have a remedy to propose that would be in perfect harmony with my feelings, and that, I am led to believe, must also be in agreement with yours. And this is to annihilate the material embodiment in which my affectionate sentiments have sought so unfortunate an expression. I mean the complete destruction of both: the marble copy and the original in my possession. To leave no trail of material regret behind I shall with pleasure refund to all expenses incurred by you in the acquisition of the marble bust.[13]

Of course the Pease family did not accept Elisabet's offer of a refund, and because Elisabet did not receive payment for the statuary involved in litigation, her financial situation became desperate. She wrote letters to friends apologizing for her inability to pay her debts, even inserted the following announcement in an Austin newspaper: "To my creditors: Please do not bother to send me bills. I have no money. (signed) Elisabet Ney, Sculptor." [14]

Along with Elisabet's financial woes, both she and Edmund were saddened in the spring of 1898, by the death of their friend and benefactor, Governor Roberts. At this same time, Lorne announced that he was leaving the plantation, his pregnant wife and three-year-old son, to heed Colonel Theodore Roosevelt's call for volunteers to fight in the Spanish-American War in Cuba. To Elisabet, this seemed a gallant gesture; perhaps he would gain recognition as a military leader. Did not the blood of the great soldier Marshal Ney run in his veins?

In spite of Elisabet's attitude, neither Edmund nor Cenci were pleased with Lorne's action, particularly Cenci, who was left with the care of his family and the fear that some harm could come to her Lorne. Being an expert horseman, Lorne chose the cavalry, and without telling his mother goodbye, hurried to San Antonio to the enlistment depot, where he joined a regiment of cavalrymen, nicknamed the "Rough Riders," being assembled by Colonel Roosevelt. Lorne enlisted as a private on May 18, 1898, in Troop K, First Regiment, United States Volunteer Cavalry. [15]

Even though Lorne had made no attempt to see her before he left, Elisabet felt that she must see him before he was sent into combat and rode a train from Austin to San Antonio, where she hired a hack to take her to Troop K's encampment. As she started to the campsite, she was soon stopped by a sentry. Elisabet instructed him to inform his commanding officer, Colonel Roosevelt, that Miss Elisabet Ney, a sculptor, wished to speak to her son Lorne Ney Montgomery.

Elisabet's appearance and haughty bearing confused the young soldier, who delivered her message to the Officer-in-Charge. After a wait, a soldier returned with the report that they had no Lorne Ney Montgomery, only a Lawrence N. Montgomery, who listed Michigan as his birthplace. [16]

While this information surprised Elisabet, she insisted that that person must be her son and that it was important that she see him. The private disappeared into a tent, returned and escorted Elisabet to the tent of Captain Woodbury Kane, the Officer–in–Charge. After about thirty minutes, Lorne appeared, looking handsome in his cavalryman's uniform. Lorne saluted the Captain, who explained that the lady claimed to be his mother and had an important message for him.

Lorne looked at Elisabet and said bluntly, "I don't want to hear anything she has to say." Again he saluted, turned, and left the tent. Stunned and hurt, Elisabet's eyes filled with tears. The Captain spoke softly, "I'm sorry, Mrs. Montgomery, but there is little more I can do."

As Elisabet walked forlornly to the waiting carriage,[17] her anger and bitterness were lost in the sharp pain of heartbreak at her son's cruelty.

The "Rough Riders," a group composed of cowboys, college athletes, and hand–picked horsemen, on March 29, 1898 was sent to Tampa, Florida, then, on June 14, to Cuba. These cavalrymen however never received their mounts, and because of this, three weeks later, led by Colonel Roosevelt in their victorious charge up San Juan Hill, they were forced to fight as infantry.[18] Lorne, however, was not among them. Instead he was confined to a hospital bed with measles and dysentery. By the time he recovered, the war was over, and he returned to the United States.[19]

Lorne did, however, receive praise from Colonel Roosevelt for his ability as an interpreter in German, French, Italian, and Spanish, and for ability as an orator. A New York newspaper printed excerpts from his speech in Jersey City in a reply to an address of Commodore C. H. Benson at one of the farewell dinners given for Troops A, D, J, and K.[20]

After being mustered out of the army, Lorne returned to Liendo, where, shortly after, his wife bore a baby daughter named Ruth; however, less than two years later, Daisy Thompkins Montgomery divorced Lorne and left the plantation with their two children. When Elisabet was at Liendo, she ignored Lorne's presence, but her visits were infrequent because of her work with her sculpture and her work to organize a Texas Academy of Liberal Arts in Austin.

On one trip to Liendo, because of a mix–up in her time of arrival, she found no transportation available to take her to the plantation. She described this experience in an undated letter written to "My Beloved Woodlawn Friends" during the period

of their friendship: ". . . [On arrival in Hempstead] I was told
that the morning before I had been awaited and the man would
be back, if perhaps a little later 'if you set down, Miss Ney, in
the nice room at the hotel and watch for him,' the good old
darky said, who had been many years at the plantation. 'No,
Uncle Jim, I am no setting lady you know this; go I must at
once.'

"And with this I changed shoes, took umbrella and with
the formidable safeguard pistol, feeling well protected by the
latter and commenced my pedestrian tour highly elated to
walk the old path in the still moonlit night."[21]

As usual Edmund was delighted to see Elisabet, but he
could not approve of her walking five miles from Hempstead in
the middle of the night. Again as usual, his report of the situation on the plantation was discouraging. Edmund's term as
Road Commissioner had expired in January 1899, and he decided to retire from public life, for he realized that he needed to
devote more time to making the plantation economically via-
ble, which would be no small task, even with Lorne's help. He
also wanted to complete his book, which would be the most important contribution that he could make to the scientific
world. "We're growing old, *Meine Liebchen*. If we're to achieve
whatever means the most to us, we must do it now," he told
Elisabet.

She acutely missed the friendship and support of Governor
Roberts; moreover, since the unfortunate misunderstanding
with the Pease family, she was no longer in favor at Woodlawn.
She realized how much she needed someone as a patron and
sponsor. What influential woman of her acquaintances would
be a prospect? After perusal of the possibilities, the most likely
candidate appeared to be Mrs. Ella Dancy Dibrell, an Austin
native, an educated art lover, an energetic achiever, and wife of
Joseph B. Dibrell, State Senator from Seguin. By working together, she and Mrs. Dibrell could alert the State of Texas to
the need for the promotion of an Academy of Liberal Arts, and,
incidentally, of Elisabet Ney, Sculptor.

When Elisabet consulted with Mrs. Dibrell over the possibility of reactivating the Women's Committee (which had dis-
banded after Bernedette Tobin's lawsuit against Elisabet) and
of assisting in the foundation of a Texas Liberal Arts Association, Mrs. Dibrell was enthusiastic and also promised her hus-

band's support; furthermore, Elisabet won the friendship and sponsorship of the wife of Texas's governor, Joseph D. Sayers. In talking with these women and their friends, Elisabet expounded: "Generally one expects not much from us women, but I am so confident of our ultimate establishment of brain-powers at least equal if not superior, to most men that whenever a woman is concerned like it is with this committee, I am irresistibly pressed to feel one with her." [22]

In the same manner in which she had appraised her friends to select a mentor, she now reviewed prominent individuals in the United States for one who might become her next subject. After a careful scrutiny of the political scene, she chose William Jennings Bryan. Although Bryan had been defeated in his bid for the presidency by the incumbent William McKinley, he still had a large popular following and was considered a man of the people, and he also espoused a cause popular with Texans, agrarian reform. To follow up her selection, Elisabet wrote to Mr. Bryan of her admiration and of her desire to model his portrait. She mentioned their mutual friends and Mr. Bryan's supporters, Senator Dibrell and Governor Sayers, and invited Mr. Bryan to Austin for a sitting.

During Governor Roberts' regime, Elisabet had addressed the State Legislature to appropriate money for a Fine Arts Academy, but with little success, even though she offered to instruct in such an academy without salary. [23] This experience made her realize that she must devise some other means of influencing the lawmakers if she expected any success with her fine arts project. After consultation with her "lady committee members," Elisabet decided, in March 1897, to fête the members of the legislature with what Elisabet styled a "gypsy tea" at Bull Frog Lake on her studio premises. While they were planning the event, Elisabet specified that no refreshments could be served inside her studio because her sculpture might be damaged; so she wrote to her friend General Mabry at his military encampment and asked for a loan of a large tent in the event of rain, another for a cloak room for the ladies, and a third one for the musicians. [24] All of which the General supplied.

Early in the morning on the day of the tea, the members of the committee, including Mrs. Dibrell, came to the studio to lend assistance in such a large social undertaking and were horrified to find Elisabet in her basement kitchen, assisted by her helper, Horace Williams, cutting up unsqueezed lemons into a small barrel containing water, citric acid, and a little sugar.

"Where are the cakes and cookies? Do you plan to serve sandwiches? Do you have enough plates and cups and silverware?" the amazed ladies asked Elisabet.

Realizing that she probably had not given enough thought to planning this entertainment, Elisabet replied, unperturbed, that she did not have time to ask Cenci to bake cookies and cakes and to send them from Liendo; so the legislators would have to settle for lemonade.

"No," the ladies all agreed, "this party must be a success. We'll help." By teatime, the ladies had brought sandwiches, sweets, china, silverware, and napkins. One had enlisted her husband's aid in providing two blocks of ice and two jugs of claret wine, which she added to Elisabet's punch. Every one of the over 160 members of the legislature who could possibly attend did so, perhaps from curiosity, and filled the studio grounds with their buggies, phaetons, gigs, and horses.

During the party Elisabet talked individually with as many of the solons as possible while they strolled through the surroundings by the lake (pond), telling them of the need for a Texas Academy of Liberal Arts. As a climax to the entertainment, Elisabet invited them inside the studio, where, to the background music of a string ensemble, she displayed her latest artistic contribution to the State of Texas, a bust of the Confederate hero from Texas, killed in the battle of Shiloh, Albert Sidney Johnston.[25]

Elisabet's "gypsy tea" was a success, although hardly the sort of entertainment that the Texas lawmakers (whom Elisabet called the "lumberman's association")[26] habitually attended. After the party, the legislators, amazed at Elisabet's eccentricities, yet impressed with her artistic ability, were more inclined to take note of Elisabet Ney, Sculptor.

These state lawmakers were again impressed with Miss Ney when they learned that she would model William Jennings Bryan when he visited Austin in April, 1900, as part of his campaign as the Democratic candidate running against President McKinley's bid for reelection. That Texas was a strong Democratic state which had given him a majority in his last political race was undoubtedly a factor in Mr. Bryan's decision to come to Texas and to accept Elisabet's proposal for a portrait bust. Elisabet, however, informed her friends that he had come to Texas especially to have her model his countenance for posterity.

When Mr. Bryan and his wife arrived in Austin, they were the guests of County Judge Alexander S. Walker at 1802 West Avenue. Because of a full schedule, Mr. Bryan had limited time for sittings with Elisabet, so the Walker family invited her to set up a makeshift studio in their home. In a letter to Laura Bryan Parker, April 5, 1900, Elisabet wrote that even though she normally required twelve sittings of an hour each, Mr. Bryan had time for only ten sittings of thirty minutes duration.[27]

In spite of the shortened time for posing Elisabet was pleased with the bust, as was Mr. Bryan, who ordered it executed in marble. Elisabet noted in her journal: "Bryan's heart and thoughts are with the masses who suffer. I am convinced Bryan is a man of exceptionally pure morals, a man of high ideals for everyday matters which he follows out with utmost watchfulness."[28]

As was her custom, Elisabet talked with Mr. Bryan while she worked. "Modeling your strong features," she told him, "reminds me of modeling Garibaldi." She said that she had read his famous "Cross of Gold" speech and agreed with his idea of free coinage of silver and that she intended to work for his victory over McKinley.[29] She could visualize herself as being sponsored by the President of the United States.

Until after she had sculpted William Jennings Bryan, the members of the legislature had paid no serious attention to the unconventional German sculptress who had constantly petitioned them to establish a Texas Academy of Liberal Arts. To most of them, "art" was something for "foreigners." But because Miss Ney had created a bust of Bryan, a man of great political stature in Texas in 1901, they were more inclined to listen to and to approve the proposal of Senator Dibrell, which was also supported by Governor Sayers, for an appropriation for commissions to Miss Ney as follows: $5,000 each for a statue of Sam Houston and Stephen F. Austin to be placed in the State Capitol, with another $1,000 for two pedestals; $5,500 for a statue and for a second statue with pedestal of Sam Houston to be placed in the Hall of Statuary in the National Capitol to accompany a statue of Stephen F. Austin commissioned by the Daughters of the Republic of Texas, and

$10,000 for a marble memorial over the grave of Albert Sidney Johnston in the State Cemetery in Austin.

After two years of efforts to raise money for the marble statue of Austin, the Daughters of the Republic of Texas had collected only $1,500. Again, with pressure from these ladies added to the Governor's and Senator Dibrell's urgings, the legislature approved an additional $3,000 to be paid to Miss Ney to supplement the D.R.T. members' contribution.[30]

What a triumph for Elisabet! She now had commissions for $32,000. Although she would have to deduct the expense of executing the statues into marble, on the other hand, the work of creation was already completed on the Houston and Austin statues; furthermore, she had received the Johnston commission without even being asked to submit a model. She could not fail now. Finally, she had achieved recognition in Texas. Soon prominent people from all over America would commission her to immortalize their images in marble.

Elisabet's success, however, was almost overshadowed by disasters in Waller County. In 1899 the Brazos river flooded and swept away the bridge, which Edmund, as Road Commissioner, had sponsored. This flood also destroyed all of the year's cotton crop. In this same year at Liendo, the cattle and dairy herd, under Lorne's supervision, became infected with deadly diseases carried by cattle ticks and screw worms. Still more trouble hit the plantation in the following year, on September 8, 1900, when a great destructive hurricane brought death to six thousand people in Galveston and devastation to the Gulf Coast and inland throughout southeast Texas.[31] Floods and winds from the hurricane swept over Waller County, ruining the land, destroying tenant houses, and damaging the big house at Liendo; in Hempstead business houses and homes were battered or destroyed, as were the great trees in the Brazos riverbottom.

Following this disaster, Elisabet received word that Edmund was ill. After many difficulties and delays because of the storm, she finally reached Liendo. There she found a ruined country, decaying vegetation, damaged and destroyed houses, swarms of mosquitoes, and a sickening stench. Around her Liendo lay demolished, Edmund acutely ill with malaria, Cenci slightly ill with a recurrence of the fever, and Lorne unable to cope with the situation.

As a result of the hurricane, an epidemic of malaria was raging in Waller County, an area inhabited by fifteen hundred people with no hospital and only seven doctors, at least one of whom, Dr. Montgomery, was himself ill. Elisabet immediately took over Edmund's care, giving him quinine to reduce his fever and to prevent the often fatal black jaundice that was also prevalent in this stricken area. Elisabet sent for Horace Williams from Austin to help in her almost impossible task of trying to salvage what was left of the plantation.

To fight the infestation of the deadly mosquitoes, Elisabet ordered all possible water holes drained and the remaining filled with kerosene, the dead and decaying vegetation burned, and the green scum on the land plowed under or sprinkled with lime.[32] Elisabet stayed with Edmund night and day until Cenci's health improved enough for her to help with his care until his fever abated. As soon as Edmund showed signs of recovery, Elisabet attempted to rest, to supervise repairs to the house, and to deal with the uprooted trees stripped of Spanish moss, the decaying vegetation, and the ravished soil.

During this period, Lorne stayed away from the big house, repaired his own and what remained of the renters' houses, and tended the cattle still left alive. After his divorce, Lorne had married Alma Wietgen, the daughter of one of the German immigrants whom Elisabet had employed to manage the dairy at Liendo. This marriage to an immigrant dairymaid upset Elisabet even more than his first marriage. She felt that Lorne had purposefully married such a person merely to humiliate her. Elisabet refused to see the young bride, or Lorne, even after Cenci told her that Lorne's new wife had malaria and was pregnant. Cenci took over, as she had done with his first family, and assumed the care of Lorne's very ill young wife.

Surrounded by calamity at Liendo, Elisabet stayed to do what she could for the plantation until Edmund regained his strength. To heap even more misery onto the destruction of the hurricane, the next year brought a drought, which ruined the sugar–melon harvest, burned up the cotton crop, and dried the grass, leaving little feed on the plantation's land for the remaining 150 head of cattle.[33] Only money from Elisabet's commissions saved Liendo from total ruin. Both Elisabet and Edmund wrote letters and talked with agents in an effort to sell the plantation, but who would purchase ravished land in this depressed area? Edmund had no choice but to stay at Liendo, manage as best he could, and continue his writing and research, while Elisabet returned to Austin to work on her commissioned sculpture at Formosa.

After Elisabet had left Liendo in its hopeless state, Lorne realized that he had no future on the plantation and wanted a new start in Mexico. He asked Edmund to intercede to Elisabet to finance the venture, which she agreed to do. As had happened in the past, however, as soon as Lorne's cash was spent, he and his wife and new baby boy, named Theodore for Theodore Roosevelt, returned to Liendo.

Misfortune followed Elisabet from Liendo to Formosa in the form of an accident in January 1901, with her big, awkward horse Pasha, who overturned her carriage while trying to avoid a mud-hole, and according to Elisabet, "dumped me out, the driver on top of me, breaking my right arm."[34] After Edmund came to Formosa to set her arm, she settled down to recuperate, but she could do no modeling, a frustrating experience, especially because she had begun *Lady Macbeth* and the *Albert Sidney Johnston Sarcophagus.*

Before she had fully recovered, in trying to avoid a bumble bee, she slipped and fell, reinjuring her arm.[35] Another time the bungling Pasha stepped on her foot, sending her to bed for three weeks; yet she refused to blame the horse. Luckily Horace could drive her in the gig when necessary, prepare meals of clabber and vegetables, and brew endless cups of her favorite "Ceylon."

During this convalescence, Edmund wrote daily letters. A friend of Elisabet's, Mrs. Julia Fisher, handled her correspondence for her, but not the letters to Edmund. These letters Elisabet insisted upon writing with her left hand, often enclosing a sprig of mignonette or other flower.[36] When friends came to call, Elisabet often proudly read excerpts from Edmund's letters. In writing about him to Bride Neill Taylor, Elisabet commented: "Dr. M.'s power of influence is marvelous, has always been so, and in every situation, among the low & the high as well, among the ignorant & learned, among young and old, he has a very amicable way of entering into the opinions opposed to his own, meanwhile establishing his own opinions. . . ."[37]

After recovering from her injuries, Elisabet made a trip to Galveston to determine why her lawsuit against Henry Ladd, who had bought Reagan's statue at the customs auction, was still unresolved. For two weeks she "trashed [thrashed] straw," as she described it, and was frustrated because no settlement was reached. While in Galveston, Elisabet sent Edmund a telegram stating the time that she would arrive in Hempstead, but because the message failed to appear, no one met the train to drive her to Liendo.

Again Elisabet had walked the five miles to Liendo in the middle of the night, which she described in a letter to Bride Neill Taylor.[38] No one heard her arrival, not even Cenci, when she slipped into her room, which was always kept ready for her, and she surprised them in the morning. Edmund scolded, but he realized that Elisabet would do as she pleased, regardless. Now that she had money and because the past two years had been a nightmare for Edmund, she wanted to do something for his pleasure, and proposed a trip to the Old Country. "Perhaps I'll have my sculpture ready to be executed and can join you later."

The prospect of such a trip delighted Edmund, who, in June of 1902, before the hot Texas summer arrived, left for Europe with plans to visit the Swiss Alps, England, Austria, Germany, Italy, and as many other places as possible. After Edmund's departure, Elisabet worked with renewed vigor to complete the plaster statues to execute in marble in Berlin, and once again to join her "best friend" in Europe.

Recognition in Texas

So may it be that yesterday
No sad–eyed ghost
*   but generous and gay*
May serve you memories
*   like wine,*
When you are old.
                                        W. E. Henley

While Edmund was in Europe, Elisabet was busy in her studio, and as she worked she remembered that when she had visited the old Laugerhaus, now a Rauch museum, she had thought that one day there might be an Elisabet Ney Museum. Now that she had money, she could add enough space to Formosa to house such a museum.

After she assessed the studio for the best design for enlargement, she drew plans for an extra study–bedroom for Edmund in the form of a two–storied massive German–styled tower with a balcony and balustrade across the front adjacent to the west side of the Grecian–styled studio. Because she liked the Lone Star of Texas on the gable of her Liendo home, she added a large star to the grillwork of each of the four panels comprising the balcony's railing.

After arguments with workmen, frustrations, and delays, the resulting final effect of the building, combining the two styles of architecture, was an unconventional but interesting structure resembling a small fortress complete with battlements and a watchtower. From the tower Elisabet could view the University, the Capitol, and the hills surrounding Austin. This small, castle-like studio provided a distinctive German touch to this town filled with Victorian and Southern Colonial houses. When Elisabet surveyed the completed studio with its little pond and garden in 1902, she felt that she now had a building large and attractive enough to one day become the Elisabet Ney Museum.[1]

To the motto "Sursum" on the cornerstone she added the dates 1892-1902. The door leading to the sun deck on the tower was camouflaged as a cupboard. To modernize the facility, she immediately applied to the City of Austin for electricity. After two years of appeals, including a letter to the mayor, Elisabet finally had the use of an electric light hanging from the end of a cord;[2] also, she installed a telephone, but only for outgoing calls. "When I'm working, I do not want to be disturbed," she told her friends. "Neighbors will bring the message if you wish to talk to me."[3]

Because Elisabet's lawsuit against Henry Ladd, who had purchased Reagan's statue at the Galveston auction, was yet to be settled and Reagan still had possession of the bust, Elisabet filed a civil suit against Senator Reagan claiming ownership of the marble statue, contending that she had created the work, bought the marble into which she cut the original model, and had not received a cent from Senator Reagan. At the conclusion of the lawsuit, a jury awarded ownership of the bust to Elisabet.[4]

In retaliation, Senator Reagan objected to placing Elisabet's statue of Houston in the National Capitol because he claimed that she presented Houston wearing a buckskin coat, a woolen blanket, and high boots, and that even with a saber at his side, such Indian-like attire was demeaning to the General. Reagan, a former Confederate officer, also resented the fact that Houston, as governor, had opposed secession and had refused to take the oath of allegiance to the Confederacy.[5] On the other hand, Margaret Houston Williams, Houston's daughter, and her son Houston Williams, both wrote to Elisabet that they admired her statue of General Houston.[6] Dean Clarence Miller also wrote in defense of Elisabet's portrayal of Sam Houston.[7]

While Elisabet was entangled in controversies and legal battles in the hot Austin summertime, Edmund wrote cheerful and optimistic letters about the rejuvenating effects of mountain climbing in the Swiss Alps, where he was free of headaches and was able to climb for as long as seven hours without too much fatigue. He wrote of his visit to London, where he saw his old friend and mentor, Sir John Simon, and visited St. Thomas's Hospital, which had moved to Albert Embankment, and also had made a trip to Italy.[8] He was eager for Elisabet to join him so that they could be together in Germany. His letters encouraged her to complete the plaster models to take to Berlin. One work that she was anxious to finish was her *Head of Christ,* which she had begun after she conceived the idea as a tribute to Bishop Müller. In this work she seemingly blended the features of Bishop Müller, Edmund, and Rauch.

Although Elisabet had not allowed herself to return to the teachings of her Catholic upbringing, in this *Head of Christ* she expressed her appreciation toward the church and Christianity. She felt kindly toward the nuns, who taught art at nearby St. Mary's Academy, and who often visited Elisabet to observe her working in her studio, especially Sister Victoria, who became a friend.[9] At the same time that Elisabet was working on the *Head of Christ,* she also started fashioning the model of *Lady Macbeth,* using three different women as models.[10]

While Elisabet's energies were directed to her sculpture, she suffered a minor heart attack, and only because her friends insisted would she consult Dr. Ralph Steiner, brother of her friend Emma Burleson. Instead of explaining her symptoms of shortness of breath and swollen ankles to the doctor, Elisabet preferred to discuss humanitarian and scientific developments.[11] By late September, 1902, her work had progressed to the point where she decided to return to Berlin to oversee her statues being copied in marble and to join Edmund in Germany. She would leave Formosa in the care of her trusted helper, Horace Williams, and her financial affairs under the supervision of Mr.

Thomas Taylor, Bride Neill Taylor's husband, to whom she gave power-of-attorney.

A week before Elisabet was to depart for Europe, she became violently ill with food poisoning from tainted oysters. Dr. Steiner advised her against leaving, especially because of her heart condition, but she was determined not to miss her booking on the *S. S. Breslau,* North German Lloyd Line and undertook the long train ride from Austin to Galveston. By the time that she arrived, she was in such pain that she had to be carried aboard ship on a stretcher. Later in letters written on shipboard to her friends, Thomas Taylor and Ella Dibrell,[12] she wrote that she was still ailing on the ship, but, fortunately, was the only first class passenger and received every possible attention from the Captain and stewards; even so, a week passed before she could leave her cabin. Letters from Edmund greeted her upon arrival in Bremerhaven, relating his travels and his plans to join her in Munich.

From Bremerhaven, in the first part of October, Elisabet took her sculpture to Berlin to the studio of Franz Lange, a sculptor recommended by Ochs, who would assist in cutting Houston and Austin statues into marble. When the statues were uncrated, Elisabet was pleased with her Texas heroes. She told Herr Lange that when they were finished and polished in marble, she would ship them to America where they will be given a place of honor in to the Texas State Capitol and the National Capitol and she would be the first recognized sculptor in Texas.

From Berlin Elisabet wrote to Ella Dibrell October 1902 about her work in Berlin and that her sculpture was admired by the other artists. She wrote, "If I had not my time so intensely taken up with work I would not tarry long here. The new Berlin generation are odious to me."[13]

Before leaving Berlin for Munich, Elisabet made arrangements for the marble statues to be shipped from Bremen to Texas and booked passage for herself and Edmund on the same ship.[14] After going to Frankfurt to obtain a copy of the bust of Schopenhauer, Elisabet arrived in Munich on November 18, and spent the day with her "Counselor of Justice Dr. Dürck, my lawyer and always friends, and his wife, Josefa." Elisabet wrote in a letter to Mrs. Dibrell, that she had repaired the damage to her statue *Prometheus,* which had been in storage since Dr. Dürck had discovered it in 1897. She also made arrangements for it to be shipped to her Austin studio.[15]

After attending to her business affairs, Elisabet eagerly waited for Edmund's arrival. They were reunited, after six months apart, in Munich, a city that they both loved. When Elisabet saw Edmund, she was delighted by the improvement in his healthy appearance. "Ist gut" for them to be together again in Munich, she told him. "Let's enjoy this great old city and tell each other everything that has happened in the past months."

Hand-in-hand the old couple strolled through Max-Joseph Platz and admired once again the grandeur of the palacial *Residenz*. People in the streets stared curiously, but politely, at the older woman, still erect, wearing a dark Grecian-styled tunic topped by a small round hat, being escorted by a tall, distinguished gentleman with shoulder-length white hair, dressed in elegant, if slightly dated, evening attire as they entered the National Theater to attend Mozart's opera, *The Magic Flute*.

While in Munich, the two enjoyed themselves reliving pleasant memories. Even though the weather was cold, they walked through the *Englisher Garten* by the Isar River, had tea in the Japanese teahouse, and drove out Leopoldstrasse to Schwabing to Maria-Josepha-Strasse No. 8 to see *Steinheil Schloschen*, now overgrown with ivy and located on a busy street.

"I wish that we had time for you to see Ludwig's castles," Elisabet said, "but I feel that I must visit Fritz in Münster, especially because his wife died last year; also, we must conclude with the Lueders' home in Werne, for you to meet my *Tante* Elisabeth and my cousin Peter and his sister Maria's family."[16]

In the few days remaining before their steamer was scheduled to depart from Bremen, Elisabet and Edmund traveled to Münster, where they saw Fritz, and to Werne, where all the family living in the "Magic Hut" welcomed Elisabet and were happy to know Edmund. The Lueders' two children enjoyed Elisabet's games and stories; yet during this time, Elisabet never mentioned that she and Edmund had a son and grandchildren. Elisabet and Edmund unwillingly left the hospitable family and continued their trip to Bremen to cross the ocean once again to America, but this time they were going home.

It was after Christmas when Elisabet and Edmund returned to Liendo, where Cenci was delighted to welcome her Miss Ney and Herr Doctor home again and to listen eagerly to everything that they could tell her about the Old Country. "*Ach,* but I would like to see Munich, Innsbruck, and Vienna again before I die," Cenci sighed. "But I know it will not be. I'll die here in this foreign country. It has been very hard with both of you away, with Lorne's two babies and expectant wife to look after, and with all the worries that Lorne has had with the plantation."

"Everything will be better, Cenci, now that Dr. Montgomery is here to take charge," promised Elisabet, ignoring what Cenci had told her about Lorne, who waited until Elisabet had returned to Austin before he brought Alma and the babies to see Edmund.

Elisabet hurried to Austin because she wanted to personally supervise the unloading of the Houston and Austin statues and the placing of them on their pedestals in the main entrance to the rotunda of the Capitol. She was pleased with the placement and lighting after they were installed in their places of honor where they stood as if to greet all comers. Mrs. Dibrell unveiled the statues on January 19, 1903, to the satisfaction of the Governor and Mrs. Sayers, Senator and Mrs. Dibrell, the legislators, and the many visitors.[17] To show her appreciation for the help and encouragement of her Austin friends, Elisabet had modeled a likeness of Governor Sayers, which had been exhibited in Berlin, along with a bust of Senator Dibrell. She also hoped that these busts, including those of former Governors Oran Roberts, Francis Lubbock, and Sul Ross would find their niches in the Capitol.

Although she was seventy years old and subject to respiratory difficulties and heart palpitations, Elisabet worked in her studio as enthusiastically as ever. With so much still to accomplish, she realized that her time of achievement was running short. She must complete the medallion of Ella Dibrell, the large *Head of Christ,* the *Memorial to Albert Sidney Johnston,* her self-portrait bust that she had begun in Madeira, and, most important, the creation of what was to be her masterpiece, *Lady Macbeth.* The figure of *Lady Macbeth* embodied her dream of greatness, interwoven with disappointment and frustration. The creation of this *Lady* was a labor of love.

23

Seravezza, Italy

Elisabet Ney is one of the best equipped of women sculptors. There are few artists who think distinctly and invariably in terms of their art as does Miss Ney.

Lorado Taft

Another lady whom Elisabet learned to love was Madam Schumann-Heink, who arrived in Austin in May of 1903, two days before she was scheduled to present a concert at the University of Texas.[1] Austin had little to offer this world-traveled German opera star for entertainment, but because Elisabet was a German and an artist, Miss Ney's studio was included in her tour of Austin. When Madam Schumann-Heink entered the German-style castle studio in this backwoods environment and saw the grey-haired, distinguished-looking older woman standing among all her beautiful sculpture, she threw her arms around Elisabet, sobbing in German, *"Meine Freudin,* it's a miracle that I find you *here* — so far away from Europe. And such a fine artist!"*

Elisabet kissed her and in an instant they felt as if they

had always known each other. Madam Schumann-Heink's escorting ladies had to be content to sit stiffly in their chairs, while the two new friends conversed excitedly in German about the art and musical circles in Europe, as well as their own backgrounds and mutual interests. The next morning Elisabet sent a note to Madam Schumann-Heink at the Driskill Hotel asking her to return to the studio for another visit. She received the following note in reply:

> Good morning beloved person, Elisabet Ney —
>
> I cannot come because, pet — I talk too much, I have a lots to do — business letters to write and one to my poor invalid husband, who, if he does not receive his letters, is apt to relapse into another melancoly mood.
>
> *You* I love from the bottom of my heart and wish I could be with you a few weeks and draw from your noble art benefit for mine. How different our art and still how necessary one to the other, and to obtain mental stimulant from you, you so noble and dear. But now I have to control myself because I want to sing especially well tonight for Elisabet Ney.
>
> Now a hearty, Fervent kiss from your devoted
>
> Schumann-Heink [2]

This meeting began a friendship which lasted throughout the remainder of Elisabet's life. They corresponded regularly and called each other Elisabet and Ernestine, confided their problems and discovered that they had much in common besides their art: both had sons who disappointed them. Madam Schumann-Heink wrote on May 26, 1903, from Saginaw, Michigan that Elisabet's letter, her gift of a statuette of *Lady Macbeth,* and Dr. Montgomery's 'Sonnet on Lady Macbeth' have uplifted me so, and its contents have consoled me for the sorrow my oldest son has given me. [3]

Elisabet told Edmund that Ernestine Schumann-Heink was the only woman that she had met in America with whom she felt a genuine, understanding relationship. Because of her friendship with Schumann-Heink, Elisabet became even more of an Austin celebrity. When such visiting artists as Caruso, Pavlova, Paderewski, and Scotti came to Austin to perform, usually at the University, they paid their respects at the studio of Miss Elisabet Ney. Besides entertaining performing artists, Elisabet was active in community life and was generous in helping people less fortunate — especially immigrants from Germany. Through her efforts to assist a destitute family in

Waller County, Elisabet became reacquainted with Helen
Marr Kirby, now the first Dean of Women at the University of
Texas, who was also interested in helping the same family.

Because of Elisabet's act of charity, she and Mrs. Kirby
became friends. Later Elisabet received a commission from the
women students of the University for a life-sized medallion of
Helen Marr Kirby, presented as a gift to that institution in
honor of the first Dean of Women.⁴ Another commission was
for a bust of Dr. David T. Inglehart, a field surgeon for the
Confederacy and prominent Austin physician; still another
was for a second bust portrait of Sam Houston as he appeared
as an older man. Elisabet also executed a sensitively done medallion of Steiner Burleson, the son of Congressman Albert
Sidney Burleson, who had died as a young child. When the medallion was delivered, Elisabet wrote a sympathetic letter to
the Burlesons telling them that she, too, knew the sorrow of
losing a young son.⁵ She also modeled a death mask of the infant son of the Clarence Millers in gratitude for the Millers'
friendship.

While Elisabet was busily working on her plaster models
in her studio, Edmund arrived in Austin on October 28, 1903,
to deliver an address, entitled "Neovitalism," as President of
the Texas Academy of Science, a distinction that Elisabet was
proud that he had received. During his visit, she told him of
her plans to go to Italy, to Carrara, where the best marble existed, to have her latest sculpture reproduced and also to secure blocks of fine white marble for the *Johnston Memorial*
and *Lady M.* Although Edmund did not want to object, he was
mindful that she had suffered a slight heart attack and was af-
flicted with bronchitis and tried to discourage her from attempting another strenuous trip to Europe.

"You know how I hate to leave you, my very 'dearest
friend,' " she told him, "but we both know that there's not
much time left for either of us. My *Lady M.* must be projected
only in pure white marble, also I'm committed to sending the
Johnston Memorial and some of my other works to the St.
Louis Exposition in May of next year."

In spite of Elisabet's strenuous efforts, she was not able to
sail again on the North German Lloyd Line, *S. S. Cassel,* for
Bremen until December. When she arrived in Germany, she received a message from her cousin Maria Lueder that her

brother Fritz was seriously ill. Elisabet hurried to him and stayed to nurse him until he died before Christmas 1903. In the snow and cold she buried him in the old part of St. Mauritz Cemetery beside his wife, on the same lot with their parents.[6]

After the funeral, Elisabet returned to the silent house and stood before the meticulously hand-carved sturdy chest and handsome bed, which was dressed with her mother's handiwork with daintily embroidered sheets and pillow slips covered with a carefully quilted eiderdown *Steppdecke*. With an ache in her heart, Elisabet remembered her parents and realized how much her defiance of their way of life must have hurt them, as her son's behavior hurt her. Gently rubbing her hand over the fine grained wood of a cabinetmaker's carved headboard, in a wishful prayer, she asked for their forgiveness and wondered if Lorne would ever realize how much she loved him and would ever ask for her forgiveness for his cruel behavior. Next month she would be seventy-one. Would she die without knowing whether or not he understood her feelings?

During Christmas she visited her aunt and cousins in Werne in the "Magic Hut," where their vitality and affection and their Christmas spirit eased her heartache. No longer acclimated to the extremely cold weather, Elisabet contracted a severe cold and bronchitis, which kept her for three weeks in Werne, where the family looked after her.[7]

Elisabet regretted not being with Edmund not only during Christmas, but also on *Sylvester Eve* (New Year's eve), a celebration which meant much to both of them. She wrote of him to Mrs. Dibrell while aboard the *Bremen*:

> To think of Dr. M. keeping a lonely vigil on New Year's night, gives me pain. It is such a time honored custom that wherever we should be that night would find us together. . . . Perhaps you can find time to send him a flower for that day. It would be a warmful impetus for dispersing dark shadows which might try their powers for destroying the equanimity of so noble, lonely, & severe a mind.[8]

Before going to Berlin, Elisabet stopped in Hannover to obtain a copy of her bust of King George V. In Berlin she again visited her artist friends and discovered that Dr. Theodore Lewald, who as a young child had served as the model for the torchbearer in the *Genii* group, was now General Commissioner for the German Exhibit at the St. Louis International Expo-

sition of Arts and Science.[9] Dr. Lewald was delighted to see
Elisabet and promised his cooperation at the Exposition. To
inspect the work being done on her statues, Elisabet visited
Franz Lange's studio, where he was applying the finishing
work on Houston and Austin.[10] Herr Lange explained that the
reason he had done no work on *Lady Macbeth* was that the
statue was so beautiful that it deserved to be cut in the purest
white marble available. To find such a block, he suggested that
she go to Carrara, Italy where the finest marble was located.

Elisabet agreed with Herr Lange, and the Berlin stonecutter, who had been executing Elisabet's sculpture for twenty
years, accompanied her to Italy. They discovered that the finest marble was not found in Carrara, but in the small village of
Seravezza, the place where Pope Leo X sent Michelangelo in
1517 to open a quarry to secure marble for his statuary.

During her stay in Seravezza, Elisabet wrote many letters
to Edmund, to Bride and Thomas Taylor, to Miss Halley Bryan, to Mrs. Dibrell, and to others.[11] She wrote that she was fortunate to find lodgings in the establishment called a *Palaza* of
Signor Antonio Bocci, where twenty-five to thirty stonemasons and sculptors lived in adjoining apartments while they
worked in marble; furthermore, she was treated with the utmost kindness and respect, even to the extent of her host's sixteen-year-old daughter teaching her to understand Italian.
She reported that her bed — not a hammock — was such a delight that she named it *letto celeste* (heavenly bed) being soft
and warmed by a *scaldino* (a wooden arrangement filled with
smokeless charcoal which was placed in the bed in the early afternoon) making the bedclothes feel like "threads from
heaven" whenever she could find time to rest.

In Seravezza Elisabet secured pure marble for her *Head of
Christ* and the *Johnston Memorial* and could begin the process
of reproducing them. Because she pushed herself almost past
her endurance to meet the coming May date for the St. Louis
Exposition, and with her continuous inhalation of marble dust,
she became debilitated, but refused to rest.

In her letters she wrote that she had to "watch over four
men, work myself, learn Italian, & write three or four letters a
day, dress, sleep and take nourishment."[12] She also corresponded with Mr. Louis Wortham of Houston, Chairman of the
Texas Building Exhibits for the St. Louis International Expo-

sition, concerning the shipment of her sculpture from Italy to St. Louis.[13]

While still working at Seravezza, Elisabet received an advance review of a critique of her work by the sculptor Lorado Taft to be included in his book on *The History of American Sculpture*. Mr. Taft had previously visited Elisabet's Austin studio, and at that time had mentioned to her his conception of the "generous rivalry" existing between artists, to which she had replied, "Most of my works have been made in solitude, there one time, here another. I've seen *envy* and *unkindness* in art centers, but no *generous rivalry*." Later Taft stated in his book that because of her isolation from "generous rivalry," she may not have realized her greatest potential; nevertheless, he praised her work and wrote: "This [Memorial to Albert Sidney Johnston] is a work of high order, as is the promise of a sketch of *Lady Macbeth*, one of the most expressive and eminently sculptural conceptions among recent American ideals."[14]

At last in Seravezza, Elisabet found a block of pure white marble, fine enough for *Lady Macbeth*, but for a cost of two thousand Marks (approximately five hundred dollars).[15] No time was left in Seravezzo for *Lady M.* to be chiseled into marble before the St. Louis Exposition, a procedure which would have to be done perfectly to satisfy Elisabet; however, she did ship a plaster model of *Lady Macbeth* to St. Louis with the specification that it not be exhibited until executed in marble. In the middle of March, Elisabet shipped the *Memorial to Albert Sidney Johnston*, the *Head of Christ*, and the medallion of Helen Marr Kirby via New York to St. Louis.

These strenuous efforts left Elisabet exhausted. To Bride Neill Taylor, she wrote:

> What a "marble dust swallowing time" it has been!! It will take sometime to clear my lungs of it. Realy. — About 5 o'clock I get hoarse for some hours. And — tell Mr. Taylor — already in my "letto Celeste" (it still has to be warmed) I reach for a *little* flask to wash the dust down for good, and not having received from him a "mild" Christmas gift, it has a substitute in "Cognac."[16]

When she was younger, she would have welcomed the challenge of going to Rome in an attempt to be granted a commission to sculpt the Pope, but now she knew that she must abandon this lifetime dream and that the *Head of Christ* would be her tribute to her Catholic upbringing. *Lady Macbeth* would be her last and finest creation.

As she was contemplating these two works, she received a letter from Edmund telling her that he had completed his work, *Vitality and Organization of Protoplasm,* and was making arrangements for publication, but he was still writing *Philosophical Problems in the Light of Vital Organization,* which he considered would be his greatest achievement. Elisabet felt comforted. Perhaps they both could leave a lasting creative contribution to art and to science.

In May of 1904 Elisabet left Europe for the last time on the North German Lloyd *S.S. Bremen* bound for New York and from there proceeded to Washington, D.C. as the guest of Congressman and Mrs. Albert S. Burleson. When she arrived, she was ill with bronchitis and was forced to remain several days in bed.[17] While she was in Washington, the duplicate statues of Houston and Austin arrived and were placed in the Hall of Statuary, where heroes from the various states were exhibited in the Capitol.

As soon as she was well enough, Elisabet visited the Capitol to inspect the placement of Houston and Austin. When the Director of the Hall of Statues realized that Elisabet was the creator of the two statues, he remarked that they were excellent statues, but standing side by side, Houston was six feet two inches tall and towered over Austin.

"Sir," Elisabet said, giving him her "haughty stare," "God Almighty makes men. I only copy his handiwork. I suggest that you take your complaint to God."[18]

When Elisabet arrived in St. Louis on the last day of May, she found that her friend Dr. Lewald had arranged lodgings for her at the Inside Inn on the grounds of the Exposition. Elisabet checked the location and lighting of King Ludwig II's statue, the *Johnston Memorial,* and busts of Jakob Grimm and Giuseppe Garibaldi. She was not pleased with the placement of the statues and was further chagrined by the fact that *Head of Christ* and the bust of Governor Sayers were not accepted to be exhibited. *Lady Macbeth* remained covered. "But wait until she emerges," Elisabet predicted, "her resurrection in Washington will astonish the public."[19]

Other works in the Texas exhibit selected by Mr. Wortham

were several made by Elisabet's rival, Pompeo Coppini, which Elisabet criticized as being inferior to hers. To express her feelings, she approached a Coppini statue of General Rufus C. Burleson, dressed in an overcoat and holding a top hat into which Elisabet tossed a five-cent coin. She turned to a reporter from the *Houston Post,* who was standing nearby and remarked, "Consider this a fitting subscription and be sure to report that *Elisabet Ney* made the first contribution." [20]

During the Exposition, Elisabet received a bronze medal for her statury, which was small comfort when she discovered that ten other American women received bronze medals, one a silver, and another a gold. Wearily she boarded the train a few days later for the long ride back to Texas and was even more exhausted by a delay of four hours in Indian territory because of a washout of the tracks.

Not until the first week in June was Elisabet once again in Liendo with her "best friend," [21] recuperating in the quiet shade of Liendo's live oaks where she and Edmund talked for hours about the happenings of Elisabet's six months' absence: she told him about her problems in Italy, her illness, her disappointment with the St. Louis Exposition, and her great hopes for *Lady Macbeth;* Edmund spoke of his trials with Lorne and the plantation, his health problems, and his great hopes for his almost completed book *Philosophical Problems in the Light of Vital Organization.*

As they sat together on the shaded veranda, Elisabet took his hand and said, "My life shall soon have ebbed away — the youthful pleasures of renown, if they can exist at my age, would be short-lived, and my works speak for themselves where destiny placed them. My philosophy this!" [22] When she said this, Edmund leaned over and kissed her softly, "And I agree," he told her.

Lady Macbeth

Sonnet on Lady Macbeth

See how she steps with queenly flowing grace
Albeit her soul, with anguish dire distressed,
Drives her, in sleep, to flee the wild unrest
That meets the haunting quiet at every pace.
No wringing hands can wipe the gory trace,
Too deep it has defiled the living breast,
And left the tortured mind in dread, unblest;
In vain she turns from it her sightless face.

The night that wrought from dust her beauteous form
Ensouled it with the spark of righteousness —
With ruthless pride she quenched the sacred flame,
To shiver now, distraught and comfortless;
Bereft of all her winsome human claim,
A piteous sight of blasted haughtiness.

Edmund Montgomery

Although Elisabet did not want to leave Edmund at Liendo, the unfinished *Lady M.* demanded her return to Formosa. She ignored her difficulties in breathing and other health problems to immerse herself in creative work. While Elisabet was working in Austin, surrounded by a circle of admiring friends, Edmund, for health reasons, felt a need to leave the torrid Texas summer and rented a cabin at Troutdale-in-the-Pines in Evergreen, Colorado, where he could study and write in the cool mountain climate. He remained in the mountains until September 19, 1904, at which time he attended a meeting in St. Louis of the International Congress of Arts and Science, a part of the larger International Exposition. At this meeting Edmund met and compared ideas with the leading scientists and educators of the western world.[1] While in St. Louis, he visited the Texas Exhibit of the Art Exposition and agreed with Elisabet about the unfavorable placement of the *Johnston Memorial* and the insufficient lighting for the other works.

During the time that Edmund was away, Lorne managed the plantation. Ever since the 1900 hurricane, Lorne's wife Alma had been ill from time to time with malaria, which meant that most of the care of the three infants was left to Cenci, who had reached her seventieth birthday August 14. Because Edmund was in Colorado, Elisabet came from Austin to celebrate the *Geburstag Feier.* "I have to give a real festivity of good things to eat for "Miss Cenci," Elisabet wrote in her journal.[2]

When Edmund returned on the first of October, he was rested and refreshed from his vacation and was soon busy making arrangements with the publishing company of Gammel-Statesman in Austin to publish his eighty-two page monograph, "The Vitality and Organization of Protoplasm." Then in November, Lorne's wife became gravely ill with black jaundice and died on November 13, 1904,[3] leaving three babies entirely to Cenci's care, because Elisabet refused to recognize the unhappy situation.

At Formosa, Horace had departed because Elisabet would not accept his Negro wife and called her a "thieving woman," even though she was Uncle Archie's granddaughter. To secure another helper, Elisabet employed a kind, strong black man, Ben Morgan, who assisted with the heavy work in the studio and also prepared Elisabet's simple meals of clabber, vegetables, fruit, and "wind-dried" bread. When visitors came for tea, Elisabet seated them at a bare wooden table under the live oak trees in the studio garden by Bull Frog Lake, while Ben served tea or claret with clabber and dry bread. Regardless of the meager fare, Elisabet's friends came for conversation and to hear her lively tales.[4]

To welcome Congressman and Mrs. Burleson when they returned from Washington to Austin, Elisabet wrote to know the date of their arrival, stating, "Dr. Montgomery says, 'No bottle-opening without the donor — the Champain would not sparkle properly.'" In this letter to Mrs. Burelson, Elisabet explained that her helper, Ben, had left, but Horace had returned and had discarded his colored "cook." He was building a servant's house where he "shall in the future park ladies of color, and my inoffensive Pasha will have his abode with me in the yard."

Continuing the letter, Elisabet wrote, "And when I sometimes trye and have the house ring with my favorite: 'I build myself a lordly pleasure house,'[5] then Dr. Montgomery's answer comes from above: 'Oh! no, that won't do! That has not the right ring.'"[6] Later Horace left again, but Ben returned, to Elisabet's relief.

Not wanting to be away from Edmund during the holidays, Elisabet journeyed to Liendo where they were together for their *Sylvester Eve.* They built a fire in the fireplace and warmed themselves in front of it as they talked in German about their longing for an "ideal life and lordly pleasure house" that now seemed the substance of dreams; yet they continued to have great hopes for their projects not yet accomplished.

"When I look on my life's work," said Elisabet, "it was in my ideal creations, rather than the modeling of individuals, that I poured forth my inner feelings: *Prometheus* represents my fetters set by the conventions of society, *Sursum,* my faith for a better tomorrow, *Head of Christ,* my feelings for the eternal, *Lady M.,* my suffering and frustration. *The Young Violinist* is Lorne as I idealized him, but it is in your image, my 'dearest and best friend,' where I find my strength and love." They chatted together until the embers of the fire burned away and the room grew chilly in the small hours of the new year of 1905.

On this visit to Liendo, Elisabet experienced a second mild heart attack; Cenci became concerned enough to insist upon sleeping each night on a pallet outside Elisabet's door to be close at hand in the event that Elisabet should need her.[7]

After Elisabet's heart condition improved, she returned to Austin. In Washington the statues of Houston and Austin,

that had been patiently standing on their pedestals in the Capitol's Statuary Hall, were formally presented to the Fifty-eighth
Congress[8] on February 25, 1905, which occasion gave Representative John H. Pinckney from Hempstead a chance to deliver an address of grandiose political oratory. In speaking of
the sculptor Miss Elisabet Ney, Congressman Pinckney said:
"They [Houston and Austin] are the artistic creation of one in
whose veins flows the proud blood of a marshal of France.
Texas is proud to claim her as a citizen of the Lone Star State.
She has brought fame to herself and honor to her state, and
these two creations will stand as deathless monuments to her
artistic powers."[9]

Being a friend of Mr. Pinckney, the most influential person
in Waller County, Elisabet enjoyed the reflected glory of his
flowery words of praise in his speech to the House of Representatives; however, this oration was his last. Two months after
he delivered it, Elisabet and Edmund were shocked to learn
that at a heated town meeting in Hempstead involving a bitter
political battle over prohibition, Representative Pinckney, his
brother, and two other prominent citizens, all leaders of the
Dry forces, were killed in a hail of gunfire from members of the
Wet constituency.

These senseless slayings disturbed Elisabet, who said to
Edmund, "*We* are above such people, but think of our son
spending the rest of his life with such stupid, uncultured, lawless criminals." She knew that even before the wanton shoot-
ing of the two Pinckney brothers, their young brother, who was
a friend of Lorne's, also had been murdered in an equally unjus-
tified manner.[10] She felt that Lorne's decision to associate with
the Hempsteaders was done deliberately to distress her. Elisabet did, however, grudgingly admit that there were *some* decent persons in Hempstead such as Judge Reece, Gaines Lipscomb, and Congressman Pinckney, but now he was dead.

After the Pinckneys' slaughter, Elisabet stayed busy at
Formosa and away from Hempstead. At the conclusion of the
St. Louis Exposition, the *Memorial to Albert Sidney Johnston*
was returned to Elisabet's studio. Some of the members of the
Daughters of the Texas Confederacy and the Confederate Veterans complained that ten thousand dollars was too much to
pay for a monument to be placed in a cemetery and that it
should be on the Capitol grounds. Elisabet, on the other hand,

wanted it placed in the State Cemetery above General Johnston's grave.[11] After much controversy the *Memorial* finally
was placed over Johnston's burial site.

With this dispute settled, Elisabet was embroiled, almost
immediately, in another disagreement over the *Memorial*.
When she inspected the monument in the cemetery, she discovered that the pillars and fence surrounding it were of cast iron,
although her contract specified "wrought iron." [12] After Elisabet's arguments with members of the Legislature, the Confederate Veterans, and the Daughters of the Texas Confederacy,
through the assistance of Judge Thomas Reese, Dean Clarence
Miller, and many Austin friends, the cast iron was replaced
with wrought iron.[13]

Before the *Memorial* was finally unveiled on September
26, 1906, Elisabet had to be assured that precautions had been
taken to prevent birds from nesting in the chapel and on the
statue "and give the white marble a calico tinge." [14] Such em-
broilments and controversies took their toll on Elisabet's vitality and caused her to realize that she was not strong enough to
make another trip to Italy to supervise *Lady M.*'s execution
into marble. She arranged to ship the large block of white marble that she had purchased in Seravezza to Formoa and hired
an Italian stonecutter, Cosimo Docchi, who had worked with
her in Italy, to come to Austin to help her bring forth a marmoreal *Lady Macbeth*. Signor Docchi had cut the *Johnston Memorial* and also had seen the model of *Lady Macbeth*.

When Signor Docchi arrived from Italy, Elisabet installed
him in the upstairs bedroom at Formosa; Ben stayed in the
small house on the grounds. Signor Docchi kept up his spirits
with the red wine that Elisabet provided, and he often cooked
his own spaghetti. Fortunately Elisabet had learned enough
Italian to communicate and insisted on supervising the chiseling, even doing some of it herself. When she began coughing,
Signor Docchi warned, "You see how careful I work. You do
not need to work so close. So much marble dust is dangerous.
For you, it is no good." But Elisabet ignored his warnings and
continued her daily work on the statue.

Elisabet enjoyed working with Signor Docchi, a gregarious
individual who liked to drink wine, sing Italian songs, and accompany himself on his guitar to entertain Elisabet and her
guests. "He excels in songs of sunshine," Elisabet noted. Sig-

nor Docchi also made friends with Max Bickler, one of Elisabet's young friends, who helped the Signor learn American-accented English rather than Elisabet's German-accented version.[15] When they were not working on the statue, Elisabet kept the *Lady* covered because "she shouldn't be viewed until she is ready."

Finally after hundreds of inspections, Elisabet looked over the *Lady* once more. "*Ja, ja, ja,*" she exclaimed. "This is my best work. Here is my *Lady Macbeth!*"

Standing before the *Lady,* Elisabet and Signor Docchi admired the graceful, anguished figure, with her face to the right, her arms and clenched hands to the left, lines of tension apparent upon her neck and realistic veins in her hands. The Italian took his chisel and carved on the pedestal: "Elisabet Ney fec. Austin, Texas 1905." He asked what price Elisabet had set for the *Lady.* "At least $35,000," replied Elisabet. When Signor Docchi said that she was worth even more, Elisabet smiled and said, "That's because you love her as much as I do."

In her friendship with the Bicklers, Elisabet recalled an incident with Max Bickler when she asked for his help for an unusual task. When William L. Prather, President of the University of Texas, died in 1905, his family and the Board of Regents asked Elisabet to make a death mask so that a marble bust could be produced from it. Elisabet refused, saying that she had done a death mask three years previously for her friend Jacob Bickler, Max's father, and had been touched too deeply to do it again. When she was pressed to recommend someone, she had suggested that her friend Max Bickler, with the help of her Italian assistant, should be able to accomplish it.

Max knew nothing of sculpture and Signor Docchi was a stonemason, and to further complicate the situation, they did not speak each other's language very well. But Elisabet insisted and promised to give them explicit directions:

> My dear Maxy:
>
> I send my 2 books for you to look in when a understanding is needed.
>
> You see to:
>
> (1) Getting some old sheets and pieces of sheets to cover floor and bed.
>
> (2) Plenty water in a bucket.
>
> (3) Nobody to enter.

(4) Warm water is best.
(5) Sure: warm water, to wash afterward the grease off.
I know you will be the greatest blessing there.
Senior Docci will also take a hand.

After the two had followed Elisabet's instructions, Max wrote, "The hardest part was removing the hardened plaster-of-Paris cast from Prather's moustache and beard. First we greased his face with sweet oil, and then applied plaster-of-Paris and let it dry. When dry, we removed the model from the face in three pieces, put it in a box of sand, and carried it out to Miss Ney's studio on the streetcar."[16] After the mask, still left in the sand, had dried, Elisabet created a marble bust of President Prather for the Main Building of the University of Texas.

Before Signor Docchi departed on September 4, 1905,[17] as a gesture of appreciation he carved the face of a woman, presumably Elisabet, on the stone wall beside the door. After he had left for Italy, Elisabet not only missed his abilities as a stonemason, but, along with his Austin friends, missed his warm personality. But he had left Elisabet with an alter-ego, a finely finished and polished *Lady Macbeth*.

During the summer that Elisabet was working on *Lady M.*, Edmund had not been well and realized that he should find a cooler climate for the summer. He selected Morelia, in the mountains of Mexico, as a pleasant place to study and to work. While he was there, however, he experienced a recurrence of malaria, which forced him to return to Austin in October, where Elisabet could look after him. She wrote to Mrs. Dibrell, "After having chills and fever and influency [influenza] in Mexico, he came here, slept in a tent and worked above in the tower and recuberated [recuperated]."[18]

After Edmund was well enough to return to Liendo, he wrote that during his absence, Lorne had married Sarah Campbell, daughter of a Hempstead contractor[19] and that Lorne and his third wife were living at Liendo, where Lorne attempted to raise cattle. After Edmund's letter telling her that Lorne had married another Hempsteader, Elisabet was bitter and felt even more estrangement from her son and avoided meeting her new daughter-in-law. At least with Lorne to supervise the plantation, Edmund could concentrate his efforts on his book, which was nearing completion.

To accomplish her ambitions, Elisabet knew that she must

ignore her poor health and push her aging body, although she felt as old as poor Pasha looked as Ben harnessed the ancient horse to the buggy. "Pasha appears as if he may die before I do," she told Ben. A short time afterward, Pasha did die. Elisabet had loved the horse and had his hide tanned so that she could be reminded of his faithfulness. To the dismay of some of her friends, she hung Pasha's hide over the stairrail in her studio and gently stroked it on occasion.[20]

Elisabet bought another horse to replace Pasha, and kept the pony Titus for her friends' children to ride. When Bride Taylor jokingly suggested that instead of buying another horse, Elisabet should purchase one of the new autos, which some people predicted would soon replace the carriage. Elisabet replied, "Not after what happened to me with my neighbor Monroe Shipe's automobile. He stopped by Formosa in his new Stanley Steamer to join me and some friends for tea to show off his auto. When he started to drive away, he went backward instead of forward and knocked over my picnic table and sent glassware and dishes flying all over the garden. I told him not to bring that contraption back to my studio until he had learned to drive it. But," Elisabet continued, "he appeared a few days later, told me that he now knew how to handle the contrary machine, and that he had come to take me for a ride. I wasn't eager, as I'd never ridden in a horseless carriage, but he insisted. After I climbed aboard and rode a short distance, I told him that the seat cushion was very hot. 'Don't be nervous,' he told me, but I lifted the cushion anyway. *'Mein Gott,'* I cried, 'the thing's on fire!'

"When Mr. Shipe saw the flames, he yelled, 'Miss Ney, run like hell.' And I need not tell you that's what we both did."[21]

After the completion of *Lady Macbeth*, although Elisabet suffered exhaustion, as well as other ailments, she did agree to design a tombstone for Elisabeth Emma Schnerr of Fredericksburg, Texas. In one of her letters to Madam Schumann-Heink, Elisabet wrote that she had not designed a tombstone since her student days, but agreed to the request because the family wanted to honor a daughter who died in infancy. "I, who have known the pain of losing a little daughter couldn't be so cruel, as to deny this poor father the comfort my work might bring."[22] Elisabet portrayed the child as an impish winged angel peering over the top of the stone.

After this work, Elisabet did no more sculpture. Even though she felt old and tired, she hid the extent of her illness from her friends who came to call, and even scolded one for sending a priest to see her. "I know I'm growing older, but I'm certainly not ready for any 'last rites' — or even confession." But Elisabet did continue to visit with the Sisters, who came frequently and once left her a rosary.[23]

In the summer of 1906, Edmund did not leave Texas because of Elisabet's poor health; and also because he was short of funds. He and Elisabet were paying all the expenses for the publication of five hundred copies of his book soon to be published by G. P. Putman's Sons, New York and London, a 462 page octavo volume bound in maroon cloth with gold lettering, *The Philosophical Problems in the Light of Vital Organization*. On Edmund's seventy-second birthday, March 19, 1907, the book was released.[24]

To celebrate Edmund's *Geburstag* and the publication of his ultimate opus, Cenci cooked her special German dinner. Elisabet added wine and champagne. "Ask Lorne to come," Elisabet told Cenci, secretly hoping that when he saw his father's book and her *Lady Macbeth* that he might realize his parents' accomplishments and feel proud to be their son. The dinner was gay with toasts to the success of the book and to Edmund's natal day. After dinner Lorne sat down with his father's book, slowly turning the pages. He uttered a hollow laugh and said, "You mean you two spent all that money for *this,* and you're selling it for two-and-a-half dollars? I'll bet no more than forty persons, including the two of you, will ever read it."[25]

Edmund took the remark as a joke. "Well, son, you could be right," he agreed.

But Elisabet was not amused; she rose from her chair, trembling, pale, "What do you mean!" she sobbed as she clutched her throat and fell to the floor.[26]

Edmund rushed to her, using artificial respiration to restore her breathing, telling Lorne to rush to Hempstead for digitalis. By ministering to Elisabet, Edmund was able to keep her breathing until Lorne returned with the heart stimulant that revived her; however, her breathing was difficult. Although Lorne was frightened, he made no apologies and left the house as soon as it appeared that Elisabet's breathing was slowly improving. For six weeks Elisabet stayed at Liendo under the loving care of Edmund and Cenci. Although her health improved, she had too much lung congestion from her years of inhaling marble dust to rest or sleep lying down and spent most of her time in a comfortable chair.

Finally so many unfinished business matters accumulated at Formosa that Elisabet felt compelled to return to Austin. After assuring Edmund and Cenci that she could make the trip, she rode the night train, sitting upright in the chair–car. When she arrived in Austin the next morning, Ben was waiting with the buggy at the depot. "I'll stop and have breakfast with the Burlesons," she informed him. The Burlesons' home was on the way to Formosa and because Elisabet often stopped for breakfast when she arrived from Hempstead on the night train, the Burlesons were not too surprised to see her that morning. Knowing Elisabet's eating habits, the maid brought her dry bread, tea, and raw eggs with sugar and cognac. When Elisabet started to leave, she asked Congressman Burleson not to accompany her to the buggy, because she did not want him to know that she was so feeble that Ben had to lift her into her seat.[27]

When Elisabet's friends learned of her weakened condition, they arranged for one of them to visit each day, usually bringing flowers, fruit, sweets, or some story to amuse her. By the last of May, Bride Taylor wrote to Dr. Montgomery that Elisabet seemed much weaker, in spite of the letters that Elisabet had written to him to the contrary. Edmund hurried to Formosa and found Elisabet almost helpless, more or less confined to her chair, relying on Ben to carry her up and down the narrow stairway.

Edmund moved into Formosa to take care of her. One evening a month later, Elisabet shambled through her studio, pausing before the bust of Edmund, her own self–portrait, the *Head of a Young Violinist,* the medallions of her mother and father, *Sursum,* the busts of Schopenhauer, Garibaldi, and the statues of King Ludwig, *Prometheus,* the *Head of Christ,* and finally a long, loving pause before *Lady Macbeth.*

"Now Ben, you can take me upstairs," she said, then turned to Edmund, "Never again will I leave that room upstairs. I cannot live this way — helpless, useless."

Edmund followed Ben as he carried Elisabet upstairs and

placed her in her chair; then Edmund gently kissed her good-
night. The next day, Saturday, June 29, 1907, Elisabet's friend
Nannie Huddle came to call, bringing cookies and wild flowers,
along with news of the Texas Fine Arts Association's projects.
Ben brought tea and clabber for Elisabet, Mrs. Huddle, and
Edmund, who had joined them. When Mrs. Huddle left at twilight, Edmund walked with her toward the streetcar line.

   Sitting alone in her chair in the darkening room, Elisabet
dozed, as her head dropped forward, she dreamed. She saw her
glowing white marble statue of *Lady Macbeth* unclasp her
hands and reach out her arms. "Elisabet, come with me," the
Lady said.

   "I'll come," was Elisabet's reply as she fell to the floor.

   Ben heard Elisabet fall and ran to overtake Edmund and
Mrs. Huddle a block away. They rushed upstairs and Edmund
bent over Elisabet as she lay on the floor in front of her chair,
but Miss Elisabet Ney was dead.[28] Edmund would not leave
her body that night, but sat beside her as she lay peacefully,
sometimes caressing her.[29]

   Sunday afternoon of June 30, in a memorial service, hundreds of Elisabet's friends paid tribute to her. Edmund requested Lorne and Cenci to stay at Liendo to prepare for the
burial. Afterward Elisabet's body journeyed on the night
train, as she had done so many times, from Austin to Hempstead. Lorne and a few friends met Edmund with a wagon to
transport the coffin to Liendo. Elisabet had wanted a sunrise
burial, but as usual the train was late. The time was ten o'clock
before they buried Elisabet in the "Sacred Grove" on the west
side of the plantation homestead, beneath the live oak trees
that she and Edmund had planted.[30]

   In a letter to Marie Lueder on the night of Elisabet's burial, Edmund wrote:

> Some thirty years ago, we together planted with our own
> hands some very young live oaks, which now have grown
> into a grove of stately evergreen trees. We resolved to use
> this grove as our last resting place. Therefore, I had her dear
> body embalmed and brought here, with a few of the numer-
> ous floral tributes, to be buried early this morning. For fifty-
> four years we have shared life's joys and sorrows in a closely
> knit union. During this entire period not a single week pass-
> ed, when we were not together, without a letter reporting the
> day-to-day events. . . .

Many of her friends want to persuade me to move to Austin to live in her art-dedicated studio home. This will scarcely be possible for me, since our presence at the plantation is after all necessary. Our son with his family lives on the place near our house, also our faithful housekeeper, now seventy-three years old . . . . Soon the two of us, to whom my dearly beloved wife had given so much joy through her love, shall be resting there beside her.[31]

In another letter almost a year later, Edmund wrote to his friend Alvin Lane: "Soon after I received your last letter I had to hasten to Austin to nurse my ever faithful and ever devoted life-companion, who has shared with me joys and sorrows ever since we pledged ourselves to lead an ideal life together. And . . . on the whole we have kept faithful to the ideals of our youth."[32]

After Elisabet's death, glowing tributes and obituaries to the prominent sculptor Miss Elisabet Ney appeared in newspapers in Texas and Germany.

Sometime after his mother's death, Lorne went to Formosa to the upstairs room where she had died. Beside the chair where illness had forced her to sleep, he noticed a small trunk that she had always kept beside her bed. Thinking that something valuable must be inside, he broke the lock and opened the lid: there lay a beautifully sculptured model of the body of a young child.[33] He knew. It was his brother Arthur. As he stared at the baby's likeness, he felt his mother's presence beside him. "He was your brother," she said. "Lorne, I loved you the same as I loved him. Now can you understand?"

Lorne was appalled. He grasped the small work of art, held it over his head, and smashed it to pieces on the floor.

Epilogue

ON HER FAMILY

Soon after Elisabet's death, a stroke partially paralyzed Edmund, who was cared for by the faithful Cenci. In 1910 he sold Liendo plantation, but reserved the right to live out his life in the homestead and to have "sepulture" in the one-acre graveyard.[1] When Edmund's death occurred on April 17, 1911, Cenci laid the ashes of his son Arthur in the coffin with him, as he had requested, to rest in the "Sacred Grove" beside Elisabet.[2]

Twenty years after Edmund's death, through the efforts of Professor I. K. Stephens, the owners of Liendo donated his library of five hundred volumes, pamphlets, and copies of his books and writings to Southern Methodist University in Dallas. In recognition of this gift and of Edmund's contributions to science and philosophy, in April of 1931, officials of Southern Methodist University, with two of Edmund's grandsons, a great-grandson, and other friends, placed a bronze plaque on Edmund's gravestone which read: "Southern Methodist University has engraved this tablet in memory of Edmund Duncan Montgomery, hermit philosopher of Liendo, March 19, 1835-April 17, 1911. Eminent scholar, gifted experimental biologist, and brilliant speculative philosopher."[3]

After Edmund's death, Cenci lived with Lorne, who remarried his first wife, Daisy Thompkins, after the unexpected death of his third wife, Sarah Campbell, who had given birth to a daughter after Elisabet's death. At age thirty-five, Lorne received a painful spinal injury as the result of an accident, and

Cenci nursed him through months of suffering until he died on June 15, 1913, leaving five young children. He was buried in the Spanish-American section of Arlington National Cemetery with Roosevelt's Rough Riders.[4]

Unable to assume responsibility for the children at her advanced age, Cenci made her home at Seton Infirmary in Austin until her death, November 12, 1916, at age eighty-two.[5] Fräulein Crescentia Simath was buried in an Austin cemetery and not, as she had wanted, in the Liendo graveyard with "Miss Ney and Herr Doctor."

When Elisabet's red-headed granddaughter, Lorne's youngest child, Elisabet Ney Montgomery Douthit, died October 3, 1964, she left a request, which was honored, that she be buried at Liendo beside her grandmother and namesake, whom she never knew.[6]

ON HER ART

Lady Macbeth, properly placed and well-lighted, stands in the Lincoln Gallery of the Smithsonian Institution amidst representations of nineteenth century painting and sculpture. In appraising the work, in 1904 W. H. Holmes, Curator of the National Art Gallery, wrote to Mrs. J. B. Dibrell: "It is a superb work displaying genius of the highest order. The distress, the agony, the despair and remorse are depicted in a completeness and subtlety that cannot be surpassed. The statue has the effect of making the other marbles assembled about it appear as the work of amateurs."[7]

In 1930 the city of Münster dedicated a room of memorabelia to each of its three most famous women, which included Miss Elisabet Ney. During the bombings of World War II 1941–1945, the building housing the memorial rooms was destroyed, as were the Ney homestead and the statues of the Westphalian heroes that Elisabet Ney had executed for the assembly hall.[8]

The statue of King Ludwig II can be found in Herrenchiemsee Castle, fifty miles east of Munich and the bust of the King resides in the castle of Hohenschwangau, south of Munich in the Alps.

The marble statues of Sam Houston and Stephen F. Austin grace the rotunda of the State Capitol with marble reproductions located in the National Capitol. The *Memorial to Albert Sidney Johnston* commands a place of honor above his grave in the State Cemetery in Austin. Excluding her statues at the University of Texas and a few scattered about Europe, the majority of Elisabet Ney's art works reside in the Ney Museum (formerly her studio, Formosa), 304 East Forty-third Street, Austin, Texas.

Through the efforts of the Texas Fine Arts Association, which Elizabeth Ney had founded, this museum was opened in 1928 and is presently administered by the City of Austin. After Elisabet's death, Edmund had presented her sculpture, now displayed in the museum, to the custody of the University of Texas. In March of 1973 Austin celebrated an "Elisabet Ney Centennial" to commemorate the one hundredth anniversary of Elisabet Ney and Dr. Montgomery's arrival in Texas. One of their grandsons accepted a plaque designating the Elisabet Ney Museum as a State and National Historical Landmark. During the ceremonies the Governor and Austin Mayor presented a memorial tablet to the German Consul-General to be sent from Texas to the *Bürgermeister* of Münster in honor of Elisabet Ney, an internationally recognized sculptor.[9]

Renovation of the museum by the City of Austin was started in June of 1980 and completed with reopening ceremonies on October 31, 1982. This refurbished museum is one of the three sculpture studios from the nineteenth century that remains with all the furnishings intact and is believed to have been the first fine arts museum in Texas,[10] and stands as a tribute to the sculptor Elisabet Ney.

Appendix

Chronology of Elisabet Ney

The Old World

1-26-1833 — Born, Münster, Westphalia
1839 — Attended St. Martin's Catholic schools
1850 — Father's workshop
1852 — Art Academy, Munich
9- 1853 — Edmund Montgomery, Heidelberg
1854 — Rauch, Berlin Art Academy
1855 — Visit, Münster; Varnhagen's circle, Berlin
4- 1-1855 — Montgomery, University of Berlin
1856 — Montgomery, University of Bohn
8-18-1857 — Marriage of Cosima Liszt and Hans von Bülow, Berlin
11- 7-1857 — Montgomery, University of Würtzburg
12- 3-1857 — Death of Rauch
1858 — Studio, Berlin
10-10-1858 — Death of Varnhagen
1859 — Montgomery, Prague and Vienna
5- 9-1859 — Death of Humbolt
10- 1859 — Schopenhauer, Frankfurt; Montgomery, London
11- 1859 — King George V, Hannover
1- 1860 — Portrait by Kaulbach; return, Berlin
9-21-1860 — Death of Schopenhauer
6- 1861 — Commissions, Münster, Heidelberg
2-15-1863 — Visit, London
6- 1863 — Return, Berlin, Münster
9-10-1863 — London
11- 7-1863 — Marriage, Funchal, Madeira
1864 — Rome; Montgomery, Riviera
3-10-1864 — King Ludwig II, Munich
5- 1865 — Garibaldi, Caprera
1866 — Innsbruck, Austria; Cenci
8-23-1866 — Prussian victory, (war)

       1867 — Rome; Montgomery, London
2-   1867 — Berlin; International Art Exposition, Paris; Hannover; Berlin
       1868 — Munich; Montgomery, Munich and Italy
2-24-1869 — Montgomery's legacy (Forbes)
4-21-1869 — Trip, Mediterranean countries
7-   1869 — Return, Munich
7-19-1870 — Franco-Prussian War
8-25-1870 — Marriage of Cosima von Bülow and Richard Wagner
12-   1870 — Visit, Münster
1-14-1871 — Departure for U.S.A.
1- 5-1872 — Death of mother
6-10-1872 — Death of Stralendorff
12-21-1879 — Death of father
6-13-1886 — Death of King Ludwig II
       1891 — International Art Exposition, Berlin
2- 1-1895 — Sale of Schwabing Villa
9-   1895 — Visit Münster, Munich, Berlin
10-   1902 — Europe with Montgomery
11-   1903 — Visit Europe
12-   1903 — Death of brother
1-   1904 — Seravezza, Italy

The New World

2-   1871 — Thomasville, Georgia
6   1871 — Birth of Arthur
6-10-1872 — Travel in U.S.A.
10- 9-1872 — Birth of Lorne, Red Wing, Minnesota
3- 4-1873 — Purchase of Liendo Plantation, Hempstead, Texas
       1873 — Death of Arthur
       1875 — Montgomery's legacy (Duncan McNeill, Lord Colonsay)
12-16-1875 — Sale of Thomasville property
       1881 — Friendship of Governor Roberts
       1887 — Lorne's education, Eastern U.S.A. and Europe
       1890 — Commission for Houston and Austin statues
       1891 — Formosa studio, Austin
       1893 — Columbian Exhibition, Chicago
7-13-1893 — Lorne's marriage
9-   1896 — Return, Texas
5-18-1898 — Lorne, Roosevelt's Rough Riders
5-   1898 — Death of Governor Roberts
4-   1900 — Lorne's divorce
9- 8-1900 — Hurricane, Liendo
       1901 — Lorne's second marriage
12-   1902 — Return, Texas
5-   1904 — St. Louis Exposition; return, Texas
11-14-1904 — Death of Lorne's second wife
       1905 — Lorne's third marriage
       1907 — Montgomery's book

6-29-1907 — Death in Austin studio
4-17-1911 — Death of Montgomery, Liendo
6-15-1913 — Death of Lorne, Austin
11-12-1916 — Death of Cenci, Austin

Sculpture

1850 — Ney's dog
1854 — Medallion heads of mother and father
4- 1-1855 — Gravestone figure
1856 — Hermann Weiss (bust)
12- 3-1857 — *St. Sebastian* (statue)
1858 — Varnhagen von Ense (bust)
10- 1858 — Jakob Grimm (bust)
10- 1859 — Cosima von Bülow (medallion)
10- 1859 — Arthur Schopenhauer (bust)
11- 1859 — King George V, Hannover (bust)
1- 1860 — Joseph Joachim (bust)
6- 1861 — Four Westphalian heroes (statues)
2- 1863 — Christian Kapp (bust)
6- 1863 — Tom Taylor (bust), George von Werthern (bust),
        Eilhard Mitscherlich (bust)
1863 — Edmund Montgomery (bust), Elisabet Ney (bust completed,
        1903)
1864 — Lady Alford (miniature)
1864 — Lord Brownlow (statuette), *Die Brüder Genii* or *Sursum* (statue)
5- 1865 — Guiseppe Garibaldi (bust and statuette)
1866 — *Prometheus Bound* (statue)
2- 1867 — Otto von Bismarck (bust)
1868 — Amalie Joachim (bust), Friedrich Wöhler (bust), Justus von
        Liebig (bust), Iris and Mercury (statues on Polytechnic Building)
2- 1869 — King Ludwig II (bust)
7- 1869 — *King Ludwig II as a Knight of the Order of St. Hubert* (statue)
1881 — O. M. Roberts (bust)
        Lorne Montgomery, *Head of a Young Violinist* (bust)
1887 — Johanna Runge (bust), Julius Runge (bust)
1891 — Sam Houston (statue)
1893 — Stephen F. Austin (statue)
1894 — Bernedette Tobin (bust)
1895 — Carolyn Pease Graham (bust)
9- 1896 — John Reagan (bust)
1897 — W. P. Hardeman (bust), Bride Neill Taylor (medallion),
        Paula Ebers (bust), *Berlin Philantrophist* (medallion),
        Dancing Girl of Pompeii (restoration)
5- 1898 — Margaret Runge Rose (medallion)
4- 1900 — Albert Sidney Johnston (bust), Swante Palm (bust),
        Joseph B. Dibrell (bust), Ella Dancy Dibrell (medallion),
        William Jennings Bryan (bust)
9- 1900 — Jacob Bickler (bust)
1901 — Death mask, infant son of Clarence Millers

12-   1902 — Steiner Burleson (medallion)
11-   1903 — L. Sullivan Ross (bust)
12-   1903 — *Head of Christ* (bust)
 1-   1904 — David T. Inglehart (bust)
 5-   1904 — Albert Sidney Johnston (memorial sarcophagus)
11-   1904 — Sam Houston (bust as older man)
       1905 — Stephen F. Austin (bust)
       1907 — Guy M. Bryan (medallion), Lillie Haynie (medallion),
Lady Macbeth (statue), Helen Marr Kirby (medallion),
William L, Prather (bust), Elisabet Emma Schnerr (tombstone)

Simplified Chart Showing
Elisabet's Relationship to Marshal Ney

Pierre Ney
    -1836
    (Lorraine)

Michel Ney (Marshal of France)
1-10-1769 - 12-7-1815
(Saarlouis,   (Executed:
 Lorraine)   Paris)

Adam Ney (Cousin of Marshal Ney)
                            1769 - 1826
(Lorraine)

    Johann Adam Ney
    3-3-1800 - 12-21-1879
    (Lorraine)   (Münster)
              m
    Anna Elisabeth Wernze
      1799 - 1-5-72
    (Poland)   (Münster)

    Clara   & Friedrich   Elisabet
10-8-1830 10-8-1830 - 12-1903   1-26-33   -   1-29-1907
(Died in   (Münster)   (Münster) (Austin, Texas)
 infancy)   m
                                          11-7-1863
                                      (Funchal, Madeira)

                              Edmund Duncan Montgomery
                               3-19-1835   -   4-17-1911
                               (Edinburg,   (Liendo,
                                Scotland)   Texas)

            Arthur   Lorne
6-1871   -   1873   10-9-72 - 6-5-1913
(Thomasville,   (Liendo,   (Red Wing,   (Austin,
  Georgia)   Texas)   Minnesota)   Texas)

Notes

Abbreviations Used in Notes

Elisabet Ney, EN
Edmund Montgomery, EM
Austin-Travis County Collection-Austin Public Library,
  A-TCC-APL
Barker Texas History Center, University of Texas-Austin,
  BTHC-UT-A
Daughters of the Republic of Texas Archives-Austin, DRTA-A
Humanities Research Center-University of Texas-Austin,
  HRC-UT-A
Ney Museum Archives, NMA
Montgomery Collection-Fondren Library-Southern Methodist University, MC-FL-SMU
Texana Collection-DeGolyer Library-Southern Methodist University, TC-DL-SMU

1. Childhood in Münster

[1] Bride Neill Taylor, *Elisabet Ney Sculptor* (New York: The Devin-Adair Co.. rev. ed. 1938), pp. 2. 3
[2] Eugen Müller, Elisabeth Ney (Leipzig: Kroehler & Ameland, 1931): partial trans., NMA.
[3] Taylor (1916), p. 13.
[4] Ibid. (1938), pp. 6, 7.
[5] Müller, trans., NMA.
[6] Karl Baedeker, *Northern Germany* (London: 1897), (Pamphlet,) FL-SMU.
[7] Undated letter to Mrs. A. D. Goeth from relatives in Ger-

many giving information from German newspapers: name,
Franciska Bernadina Wilhelmina Elisabeth Ney, god-parents:
Wilhelm Breitenfeld and Franciska Berdina Schriker, NMA.

[8] Taylor (1938), p. 5.
[9] Vernon Loggins, *Two Romantics and Their Ideal Life,*
(New York: The Odyssey Press, 1946), p. 25.
[10] Ibid.
[11] Ibid., p. 20.
[12] Florence Crain Albrecht, "The Town of Many Gables,"
National Geographic Magazine, February, 1915, pp. 107-140.
[13] Brochure, NMA.

2. Munich Art Academy

[1] Eugen Müller, "Munchener Nauseten Nachten," *Presse
Allmanack,* Rev. Theodore Peterson of the Paulist Fathers,
trans., 1928, NMA.
[2] Taylor (1916), pp. 11-15.
[3] Loggins, p. 9.
[4] Ibid., p. 27.
[5] Ibid., p. 30.
[6] Ibid., p. 32.
[7] Taylor (1938), p. 8.
[8] Frank Roy Fraprie, *Little Pilgrimages Among Bavarian
Inns* (Boston: L. C. Page & Co., 1906), pp. 248, 249.
[9] NMA.
[10] Loggins, p. 36.
[11] Ibid., pp. 38, 39.

3. Edmund and Heidelberg

[1] Taylor (1938), pp. 10, 11. (Taylor states that the two met
in Munich; however, numerous letters from both EN and EM
testify that they met in Heidelberg in 1853.)
[2] John Stoddard, *Lectures,* (Chicago & Boston: George L.
Schuman & Co.), 7: 51.
[3] Loggins, p. 43.
[4] I. K. Stephens, *The Hermit Philosopher of Liendo* (Dallas: Southern Methodist University Press, 1951), p. 7.
[5] Ibid., pp. 17, 18.
[6] (As stated in the Preface, almost all correspondence between EN and EM has been lost.)
[7] Loggins, p. 51.
[8] Jan Fortune and Jean Burton, *Elisabet Ney* (New York:
Alfred A. Knopf, 1943), trans., pp. 29, 30: also trans., NMA.

⁹ Loggins, p. 48.
¹⁰ Document, HRC–UT–A.

4. Study with Rauch

¹ Stoddard, 6:23. (This statue, badly damaged in World War II, was not restored until 1980.)
² Loggins, p. 50.
³ Taylor (1838), p. 17.
⁴ Loggins, p. 52.
⁵ Ibid., p. 54.
⁶ Loggins, p. 60.
⁷ Ibid., pp. 61, 62.
⁸ Waldemar Kuhlman, article, *Today in Texas,* January 12, 1949, NMA.
⁹ Stephens, p. 54.
¹⁰ Ibid., p. 42.
¹¹ (Restored after World War II and is now known as Humbolt University in East Berlin.)
¹² Loggins, p. 66.
¹³ Ibid.
¹⁴ Geoffrey Skelton, *Richard and Cosima Wagner: Biography of a Marriage* (Houghton Mifflin Co., Boston: 1982), p. 14.
¹⁵ Ernest Newman, *Wagner as Man and Artist* (New York: Garden City Publishing Co., 1937), pp. 38–100.
¹⁶ Stephens, p. 46.

5. Deaths in Berlin

¹ Loggins, pp. 69, 70.
² Newspaper clippings, NMA.
³ Loggins, p. 71.
⁴ Fortune and Burton, p. 55.
⁵ Stephens, p. 49.
⁶ Ibid., pp. 50, 51.
⁷ Loggins, p. 74.
⁸ Ibid., p. 73.
⁹ Correspondence EN and Hoppe, 1859, DRTA–A.
¹⁰ Stephens, p. 64.
¹¹ Ibid., p. 69.
¹² Arthur Schopenhauer, *The World as Will and Idea,* R. B. Haldane & J. Kemp, trans. (London: Kegan Paul, Trench, Triber & Co. 1909).

6. Schopenhauer and King George V

[1] Loggins, pp. 78, 79.
[2] Ibid., p. 80.
[3] Encyclopaedia Britannica 11th ed., s.v. "Schopenhauer, Arthur."
[4] Dorothea W. Dauer, *Schopenhauer as Transmitter of Buddist Ideas* (Berne: Herbert Land & Co. Ltd., 1969), p. 5.
[5] Taylor (1916), p. 29.
[6] Schopenhauer's Correspondence, 1859, NMA.
[7] Loggins, p. 82.
[8] Müller, trans., A-TCC-APL.
[9] Stephens, pp. 64-70.
[10] Newspaper clipping, NMA.
[11] Loggins, p. 83.
[12] Ibid., p. 85.
[13] Schopenhauer to EN, NMA.
[14] Loggins, p. 86.
[15] Schopehauer to EN, NMA.
[16] Loggins, p. 87.
[17] Photographic copy, NMA.
[18] Müller, trans., ATCC-APL.
[19] EN to Schopenhauer, March 2, 1860, NMA.
[20] (This photograph was lost during the World War II destruction of the EN Memorial in Münster, only faded copies remain.)
[21] EN to Schopenhauer, August 11, 1860, NMA.
[22] EN to Schopenhauer, 1860, NMA.
[23] (This bust of Arth. Schopenhauer was later displayed in the Frankfurt City Library.)

7. Berlin and Münster

[1] Nora Bickley, ed., *Letters from and to Joseph Joachim*, Fortune and Burton, pp. 83-84.
[2] Loggins, pp. 95, 96.
[3] Müller, trans., NMA.
[4] Hermann Hüffer, *Lebenserinnerungen*, Ernst Sieper, ed., trans., NMA.
[5] Loggins, p. 99.
[6] Levin Schucking, letter in *Illustrirte* (Cologne: 1861), trans., NMA.
[7] Loggins, p. 105.

8.   Edmund in London

[1] Stephens, p. 14.
[2] Ibid., pp. 12, 13.
[3] Ibid., p. 13.
[4] Loggins, p. 44.
[5] EM to Lane, March 22, 1894, MC–FL–SMU.
[6] Stoddard, 9:236.
[7] Stephens, p. 64.
[8] Ibid., p. 87.
[9] Christopher Hibbert, *Garibaldi and His Enemies* (Boston: Little, Brown & Co., 1964), p. 331.
[10] Manuscript, TC–DL–SMU: Lieder in German signed, "M. B.," HRC–UT–A.
[11] Papers, MC–FL–SMU.
[12] Stephens, p. 88.
[13] Loggins, p. 83.
[14] Stephens, p. 89.
[15] Ibid., pp. 94, 95.
[16] Ibid., p. 97.

9.   Marriage in Madeira

[1] Copy, NMA.
[2] Loggins, p. 110.
[3] Letters stating that Theodore Lewald, Commissioner for the German exhibit at the St. Louis Exposition, as a child, had been one model for *Die Brüder Genii.*, NMA.
[4] EN notebook, HRC–UT–A.
[5] Loggins, p. 111.
[6] EN notebook, HRC–UT–A.
[7] Loggins, p. 113.
[8] Ibid., p. 114.
[9] Stoddard, 8:313–334.

10.   Garibaldi and *Prometheus*

[1] Hibbert, p. 363.
[2] Loggins, p. 115.
[3] EN journal, 1865, BTHC–UT–A.
[4] Ibid.
[5] Hibbert, p. 126.
[6] Ibid., p. 367. (A round hand–embroidered cap that his biographer Mme Swartz sent each year.)
[7] EN journal, BTHC–UT–A.

[8] Hibbert, p. 129.
[9] Ibid., p. 15.
[10] EN journal, BRHC-UT-A.
[11] Stephens, pp. 100, 101.
[12] Hibbert, p. 352.
[13] Loggins, p. 118.
[14] Taylor (1916), p. 49.
[15] Hibbert, p. 353.
[16] Stephens, p. 105.
[17] Ibid., p. 110.
[18] Loggins, p. 120.

11.   Berlin and Munich

[1] Newspaper clipping, NMA.
[2] Loggins, p. 122.
[3] Stoddard, 5:22, 23.
[4] Documents, NMA. (Placement of the two statues caused controversy after the two men were no longer allies.)
[5] Hüffer, *Lebenserinnerungen.*
[6] Encyclopaedia Britannica, 11th ed., s.v. "Ney, Michael."
[7] Loggins, pp. 124, 125.
[8] Ibid., 126.
[9] Wilfred Blunt, *The Dream King* (Middlesex: Penguin Books Ltd., New York: Penguin Books, 1973), p. 19.
[10] Newman, pp. 125, 126.
[11] Skelton, pp. 72, 73.
[12] Blunt, p. 29.
[13] Skelton, p. 63.
[14] Stephens, p. 23.
[15] Loggins, pp. 131, 132.
[16] Ibid., p. 132.
[17] Fortune and Burton, trans., p. 159.
[18] Correspondence, EN to King Ludwig II, Wilhelm A. Pauly, Director of the State-Administration of Herrenchimsee Castle Archives, trans., DRTA-A, NMA.
[19] Ibid.
[20] Loggins, p. 137.

12.   Travel in the Near East

[1] Blunt, p. 22.
[2] Luise von Kobell, *Konig Ludwig II von Byern und Die Kunst* (Munich: 1900), 2 pp. trans., HRC-UT-A.
[3] Taylor (1916), p. 37.

⁴ EN to Neureuther, undated, DRTA–A.
⁵ EN to King Ludwig II, NMA.
⁶ Notes, NMA.
⁷ Loggins, p. 138.
⁸ Stephens, p. 114.
⁹ Diaries of EN & EM, BTHC–UT–A.
¹⁰ EM dairy.
¹¹ Ibid.
¹² Ibid.
¹³ Ibid.
¹⁴ Stoddard, 2:53-59.

13. King Ludwig II

¹ Kobell, trans., Loggins, pp. 142–144.
² Blunt, p. 125.
³ Stephens, p. 124.
⁴ Dr. Bauer, Director, Land Office, Munich State Archives, to author August 31, 1982: Taylor (1938), p. 34. (Other biographers state that King Ludwig built this villa for EN.)
⁵ Fortune and Burton, p. 138.
⁶ Stephens, p. 117.
⁷ Blunt, pp. 256, 12–19.
⁸ *Augsburger Zietung* No. 194, July 7, 1886, trans., HRC–UT–A.
⁹ Blunt, p. 18.
¹⁰ Julius Desing, *King Ludwig II; His Life–His End* (Munich: Kienberger, 1976), p. 14.
¹¹ E. J. Passant, *A Short History of Germany, 1815–1945* (London: Cambridge University Press, 1959), pp. 85–87.
¹² Hibbert, p. 354.
¹³ Blunt, pp. 203–216.
¹⁴ Henry Channon, *The Ludwigs of Bavaria* (London & New York: E. P. Hutton, 1933), p. 110.
¹⁵ EN to King Ludwig II, HRC–UT–A.
¹⁶ Ibid., undated, trans., Fortune and Burton, pp. 184, 185.
¹⁷ (Bride Neill Taylor 1916, p. 52, and Fortune and Burton, p. 182, state that Liebig requested *Sursum* as his gift; however, the material quoted contradicts this.)
¹⁸ Passant, p. 58.
¹⁹ Blunt, p. 125.
²⁰ Hibbert, p. 360.
²¹ Skelton, p. 139.
²² Blunt, p. 128.
²³ Ibid., p. 130.
²⁴ Stralendorff to EM, 1870, NMA.

[25] EN to King Ludwig II, 1870, Fortune and Burton, trans., p. 188.
[26] Dürck to Neureuther, October 14, 1886, NMA.
[27] Friedrich Ney to Alexander Simon, March 10, 1881, HRC–UT–A.

14. Flight to Thomasville

[1] Loggins, p. 157.
[2] Ralph Waldo Emerson, *Essays* (New York: Thomas Y. Crowell, 1926), p. 33.
[3] Loggins, p. 159.
[4] Ibid., p. 164.
[5] Stephens, p. 130.
[6] Passant, p. 62.
[7] Loggins, pp. 166, 167.
[8] Merle Curti et al., *An American History* (New York: Harper & Bros., 1950), 1:588: Encyclopedia Americana, 4th ed., s.v. "Washington, D.C."
[9] Loggins, p. 167.
[10] Ibid., p. 168.
[11] Curti, p. 555.
[12] W. Irwin MacIntire, *History of Thomas County, Georgia* (Thomasville: 1923), p. 3.
[13] Stralendorffs' letters and photographs, NMA.
[14] Loggins, p. 169.
[15] Ibid., p. 172.
[16] Ibid., p. 173.
[17] MacIntire, p. 18.
[18] Edward Russell to Mary Norton, February 21, 1871, NMA.
[19] Loggins, p. 174.
[20] Stephens, p. 138.
[21] Ibid., p. 137.
[22] EN notebook, NMA.
[23] Stephens, pp. 139, 140.
[24] Loggins, pp. 178, 179.

15. Travel in America

[1] Edward Russell to Mary Norton, February 21, 1871, NMA.
[2] Loggins, p. 183.
[3] Stephens, pp. 141, 142.
[4] Ibid., p. 143.

[5] Loggins, p. 181.
[6] Ibid., p. 182.
[7] Stephens, p. 147.
[8] Loggins, p. 186.
[9] Ibid., p. 188.
[10] Newspaper clipping, NMA.
[11] Letters, NMA.
[12] Loggins, p. 190.
[13] Stephens, pp. 150, 151.
[14] Curti, pp. 1:343–345.
[15] Bride Neill Taylor, April 9, 1930, NMA.
[16] Stephens, p. 151.
[17] Curti, pp. 1:343–345: (Because the Mississippi steamboat was a popular means of transportation at this period and Lorne was born at a place near the terminus of the steamboat route, this means of travel for Elisabet and Edmund was not unlikely.)
[18] Stephens, pp. 151, 152.

16.   Plantation in Texas

[1] Texas Almanac, 1956–57, s.v. "History of Texas."
[2] Passant, p. 81.
[3] Stephens, p. 157.
[4] Willie B. Rutland, ed., *Sursum! Elisabet Ney in Texas* (Austin: Hart Graphics and Office Center Inc., 1977) p. 5.
[5] Loggins, p. 197.
[6] Stephens, p. 159.
[7] Ibid., p. 163.
[8] *Waller County Survey Committee, A History of Waller County* (Hempstead: 1973).
[9] Walter Prescott Webb, ed., *The Handbook of Texas* (Austin: The State Historical Association, 1952) 1:662, 663.
[10] Eusibia Lutz, "Liendo: The Biography of a House," *Southwest Review,* Vol. XVI, no. 2, (1931), p. 196.
[11] Taylor (1938), p. 57.
[12] Loggins, p. 201.
[13] Stephens, p. 165.
[14] Loggins, p. 203.
[15] EM to Lueder, July 1907, NMA.
[16] Loggins, pp. 213.
[17] Ibid., pp. 214, 215.

17.　Death of a Son

[1] Rutland, ed., p. 194.
[2] "Diptheria not Murder," *Houston Post,* March 11, 1962, A-TCC-APL.
[3] Taylor (1938), p. 59.
[4] Loggins, p. 219.
[5] Ibid., pp. 219, 220.
[6] Neureuther to Ney, May 19, 1872: Adam Ney to Ochs, August 5, 1873, HRC-UT-A.
[7] Loggins, p. 223.
[8] Letter from Grace Norton, July 5, 1926, NMA.
[9] Luciano Alberti, *Music of the Western World* (New York: Crown Publishing Co., Inc., 1967), p. 241.
[10] Copy of deed, TC-DL-SMU.
[11] Loggins, p. 230.
[12] Stephens, p. 170.
[13] Loggins, p. 240.
[14] Notes, NMA.
[15] Rutland, ed., letter from Mattie Crook (Hempstead), p. 13.
[16] Loggins, p. 234.
[17] Ibid., pp. 235, 236.
[18] Letter from Mrs. Dora Gray Mueller, May 25, 1947, NMA.
[19] Copy, NMA.
[20] Loggins, p. 241.
[21] Stephens, pp. 251–254.
[22] Blunt, pp. 226–227.
[23] Auguste Schiebe, article, *Dresdener Tagblatt,* July 17, 1886, HRC-UT-A.

18.　A Son in Rebellion

[1] Joe B. Franz, *Texas, A Bicentennial History* (New York: W. W. Norton & Co., 1976), p. 127. (This land, the XIT Ranch at the time the world's largest, was later subdivided and sold for many millions of dollars.)
[2] Taylor (1938), p. 84.
[3] Loggins, p. 141.
[4] Hayden W. Head, member UT-A Development Board, to ex-students of UT-A, November 1980: "The first private gift to the University, made in 1893, was from the artist Elisabet Ney. It was a bust of Oran M. Roberts, who as Governor of Texas, signed the legislation establishing the University in 1881."

⁵ EN to Runge, May 31, 1887, NMA.
⁶ Loggins, pp. 245, 246.
⁷ EN to Runge, May 31, 1887, NMA.
⁸ Ibid., January, 1887, NMA.
⁹ Stephens, p. 183.
¹⁰ EM to Cenci, September 30, 1884, NMA.
¹¹ Neureuther to Ney, May 19, 1872, NMA.
¹² Dürck to Neureuther, October 14, 1886, DRTA-A:
Fisher, Munich State Archives, to author, March 9, 1982.
¹³ EN to Runge, August 19, 1888, NMA.
¹⁴ Loggins, 253.
¹⁵ Ney to a school in Switzerland, undated, NMA.
¹⁶ Rutland, ed., p. 9.
¹⁷ Stephens, p. 283.
¹⁸ Taylor (1916), p. 45.

19.   Commissions in Austin

¹ Roberts to EN, October 1890, NMA.
² Taylor (1938), p. 95.
³ Sears & Roebuck Catalogue, 1897.
⁴ EN notebook, NMA.
⁵ Presently owned by former Governor Allan Shivers.
⁶ EN notebook, NMA.
⁷ Ibid.
⁸ Stephens, pp. 313, 314.
⁹ Taylor (1938), p. 77.
¹⁰ John P. G. McKenzie, "Elisabet Ney, Texas Legend,"
Austin American-Statesman, August 4, 1963, A-TCC-APL.
¹¹ Ochs to EN, December 16, 1890, NMA.
¹² Werner to EN, April 14, 1893, HRC-UT-A.
¹³ EN notebook, NMA.
¹⁴ Photograph, NMA.
¹⁵ Mattie Lee Seymour, "Interview of Mrs. J. W. Rutland,"
January 12, 1966, A-TCC-APL.
¹⁶ EN draft in notebook, to Margaret Lea Houston Williams and to Judge D. D. Clairborne.
¹⁷ Loggins, p. 258.
¹⁸ Stephens, pp. 317, 318.
¹⁹ Roberts to EN, January 4, 1889, NMA.
²⁰ Stephens, p. 314.
²¹ EN to Judge Gould, August 28, (1894?), NMA.
²² Loggins, p. 261.
²³ EN to Lorne, HRC-TU-A.
²⁴ EN notebook, HRC-TU-A.
²⁵ Stephens, p. 315.

²⁶ Tobin to EN, August 11, 1893, NMA.
²⁷ Loggins, p. 265.
²⁸ Agreement between EN & Tobin, HRC–UT–A.
²⁹ McKenzie article, A–TCC–APL.
³⁰ EN to Mrs. Pease, Pease Collection, APL.
³¹ Ibid.
³² Taylor (1938), list of friends of EN.
³³ EN to Mrs. Pease, January 12, 1885, NMA.
³⁴ Loggins, p. 276, 277.
³⁵ EN to Thomas Taylor, January 22, 1895, HRC–UT–A.
³⁶ Stephens, p. 317.
³⁷ Ibid., pp. 318, 319.

20.   Return to Europe

¹ Dürck to EN, April 29, 1895, HRC–UT–A.
² Dürck to EN, November 2, 1895, HRC–UT–A.
³ EN to various friends, September 1895, NMA.
⁴ Friedrich Ney to Alexander Simon, March 10, 1881, NMA. (This letter gives Ney address as Bohlweg 101 rather than 34.)
⁵ Henrietta Leisewitz's visit with Eugen Müller, 1897, NMA.
⁶ Data, NMA.
⁷ EN to Lueder, trans. Fortune and Burton, pp. 274, 275, also NMA.
⁸ EN to Mrs. Dibrell, November 18, 1902, NMA.
⁹ Dürck to EN, November 2, 1895, HRC–UT–A.
¹⁰ "A Grandniece of Marshall Ney and Her Lost *Prometheus*," newspaper clipping from Munich, HRC–UT–A.
¹¹ Blunt, p. 141, 142.
¹² (This statue remains to date at this location.)
¹³ Loggins, pp. 285, 286.
¹⁴ Ibid., p. 283.
¹⁵ Newman, p. 153.
¹⁶ Werner to EN, April 24, 1892, HRC–UT–A.
¹⁷ Loggins, pp. 285, 286.
¹⁸ Ebers to Mathlde L., 1896, HRC–UT–A.
¹⁹ Dürck to EN, March 27, 1896, HRC–UT–A.
²⁰ EN to Halley Bryan Perry, May 3, 1896, NMA.
²¹ EN to Bride Neill Taylor, September 8, 1896, NMA.

21. Success and Castrophe

[1] (John H. Reagan was Post Master General of the Confederacy and later U.S. Senator.)
[2] EN notebook to Clarence Miller, HRC–UT–A.
[3] Stephens, p. 319.
[4] EN to Bride Neill Taylor, November 17, 1896, NMA.
[5] EN notebook, NMA.
[6] Dürck to EN, May 1897, NMA.
[7] Ibid.
[8] Documents, HRC–UT–A.
[9] EN to Julia Pease, December 29, 1897, NMA.
[10] Julius Runge, note, 1888, NMA.
[11] Correspondence EN and Senator Reagan, HRC–UT–A.
[12] Rutland, ed., p. 67.
[13] EN to Julia Pease, July 2, 1898, NMA.
[14] Loggins, p. 292.
[15] Letter from U.S. Army, NMA.
[16] Ibid.
[17] Samuel E. Gideon, "Elisabet Ney, Noted Eccentric Sculptor Lived and Worked in Austin," *Austin Daily Tribune,* May 5, 1941: "Few People Understood Austin's Greatest Artist," *Austin American–Statesman,* December 8, 1940, A–TCC–APL.
[18] Irving Werstein, *The Spanish American War* (New York, Cooper Square Publishing Co., Inc. 1966), p. 41.
[19] Stephens, pp. 322, 323.
[20] Data, NMA.
[21] EN to Pease family, undated, NMA.
[22] EN notebook, HRC–UT–A.
[23] EN to Governor Francis Lubbock, (1900?), NMA.
[24] EN notebook, undated, NMA.
[25] Ettie M. Doughty, "Elisabet Ney, the Enigma of the Nineteenth Century," *Naylor's Picture Century,* November, 1939, NMA.
[26] EN to Mrs. Rebecca Fisher, April 25, 1897, NMA.
[27] EN to Laura Parker, April 5, 1900, HRC–UT–A.
[28] EN notebook, HRC–UT–A.
[29] Encyclopedia Americana, 4th ed., s.v. "Bryan, William Jennings."
[30] Copy, Gammel's *Laws of Texas* Vol. 2, 1898–1901, appropriations made by the Legislature of Texas in favor of Miss Ney, 27th Legislature, 1901, TC–DL–SMU.
[31] Franz, pp. 159–300.
[32] Loggins, pp. 299–301.
[33] Ibid., p. 300.
[34] EN to Miss Dawson, January 13, 1901, NMA.

[35] EN to Mrs. Dibrell, February 7, 1901, NMA.
[36] Rutland, ed., p. 93.
[37] EN to Bride Neill Taylor, November 28, (1901?), NMA.
[38] Ibid., October 3, 1901, NMA.

22.   Recognition in Texas

[1] (The original Ney Museum was renovated by the City of Austin in 1980–82.)
[2] EN to Mayor E. White, 1902, HRC–UT–A.
[3] Data, A–TCC–APL.
[4] Notes, HRC–UT–A.
[5] Judge Julius Schutze, ed. "An Answer to Judge Reagan," trans., *German Peoples Texas Vorwarts,* Austin, March 6, 1902, HRC–UT–A.
[6] Margaret Houston Williams and Houston Williams to EN, 1903, NMA.
[7] Clarence Miller, undated newspaper clipping, "People's Forum," NMA.
[8] Stephens, pp. 330, 331.
[9] EN to Thomas Taylor, October 5, 1902, NMA.
[10] Rutland, ed., p. 138.
[11] Ibid., p. 95.
[12] EN to Thomas Taylor, October 5, 1902: to Mrs. Dibrell, October 6, 1902, NMA.
[13] EN to Mrs. Dibrell, October 6, 1902, NMA.
[14] Ibid., (written October 2), NMA.
[15] EN to Mrs. Dibrell, November 18, 1902, NMA.
[16] Loggins, p. 302.
[17] Documents, A–TCC–APL.

23.   Seravezza, Italy

[1] Loggins, pp. 305, 306.
[2] Schumann–Heink to EN, May 8, 1903, NMA.
[3] Ibid., May 26, 1903.
[4] EN to Bride Neill Taylor, October 28, 1903: Documents, NMA.
[5] EN to Adele Burleson, May 5, 1900, NMA.
[6] To Mrs. A. C. Goette, information from German newspapers, NMA.
[7] EN to Halley Bryan, January 1, 1904, NMA.
[8] EN to Mrs. Dibrell, undated, aboard the *Bremen,* HRC–UT–A.
[9] EN to Bride Neill Taylor, March 13, 1903, NMA.

[10] Sarah Lee Norman Wood, "The Heroic Image: Three Sculptures by Elisabet Ney," (Master of Arts Thesis, UT-A, 1978).

[11] EN various letters from Seravezzo, 1904, NMA, HRC-UT-A.

[12] EN to Bride Neill Taylor, February 28, 1904, NMA.

[13] Ibid., March 13, 1904.

[14] Lorado Taft, *History of American Sculpture*, (New York, The Macmillian Co., 1924.), p. 214.

[15] EN to Bride Neill Taylor, March 7, 1904, NMA.

[16] Ibid., Arpil 2, 1904, NMA.

[17] Ibid., May 8, 1904.

[18] Mattie Lee Seymour, "Interview with Mrs. J. B. Rutland, January 12, 1966: Florence Baldwin, "The Inscrutable Sculptor," Texas Star Supplement, *Dallas Morning News*, January 16, 1972, A-TCC-APL.

[19] EN to Bride Neill Taylor, May 26, 1904, NMA.

[20] Ibid., May 31, 1904.

[21] EN to Thomas Taylor, June 8, 1904, NMA.

[22] EN to Bride Neill Taylor, May 3, 1904, NMA.

24. *Lady Macbeth*

[1] MC-FL-SMU.

[2] EN notebook, HRC-UT-A.

[3] Loggins, p. 321.

[4] Taylor (1938), p. 97.

[5] "The Palace of Art," Alfred Lord Tennyson.

[6] EN to Emma Burleson, August 24, (1904?), NMA.

[7] Rutland, ed., p. 192.

[8] Concurrent Resolution of the U.S. House and Senate granting the State of Texas the privilege of placing statues of Houston and Austin in the Hall of Statuary in the Capitol, HRC-UT-A.

[9] Loggins, p. 314, (Congressional Record, February 15, 1905).

[10] Ibid., p. 316.

[11] EN to Bride Neill Taylor, November 10, 1904, NMA.

[12] Specifications for *Johnston Memorial* from the Legislative Committee, HRC-UT-A.

[13] Article, *Austin American-Statesman*, October 8, 1905, HRC-UT-A.

[14] EN to Mrs. Dibrell, June 22, 1906, NMA.

[15] Loggins, pp. 320, 321.

[16] "Max Bickler Remembers Elisabet Ney," A-TCC-APL.

[17] EN to Mrs. Dibrell, October 16, 1905, NMA.

[18] Ibid.
[19] Stephens, p. 348.
[20] Loggins, p. 323.
[21] Rutland, ed., p. 20: "Elisabet Ney's Ride in Auto Dangerous," *Austin American-Statesman*, July 19, 1936, A-TCC-APL.
[22] Loggins, p. 329.
[23] Taylor (1938), p. 110.
[24] Stephens, pp. 350, 351.
[25] Loggins, p. 331.
[26] Taylor (1916), p. 122.
[27] Loggins, pp. 339, 340.
[28] Rutland, ed., p. 101.
[29] Loggins, p. 342.
[30] Ibid., p. 343.
[31] EM to Lueder, June 30, 1909, NMA.
[32] EM to Lane, April 1908, MC-FL-SMU.
[33] Taylor (1938), p. 59.

Epilogue

[1] Stephens, p. 365.
[2] Taylor (1938), p. 59.
[3] MC-FL-SMU.
[4] Documents, NMA.
[5] Documents, TC-DL-SMU.
[6] Clipping, *Austin American-Statesman*, March 8, 1973, A-TCC-APL.
[7] Letter from W. H. Holmes, Curator of the National Gallery of Art, Washington, D.C. (1904) to Mrs. Dibrell, NMA.
[8] Rutland, ed., p. 198.
[9] Article in *Austin American-Statesman*, March 8, 1973, A-TTC-APL.
[10] Dave Goska, "High Dry Roof: Elisabet Ney Museum reopening with formal celebration Sunday," *Austin American-Statesman*, October 30, 1982.

Bibliography

Abernethy, Francis Edward, ed. *Legendary Ladies of Texas.* Dallas: E-Hart Press, 1981.

Alberti, Luciano. *Music of the Western World.* New York: Crown Publishers Inc., 1967.

Baedeker, Karl. *Munich and Environs.* London, 1950, New York: 1956.

____. *Northern Germany.* London: 1897.

____. *Southern Bavaria.* London & New York: 1953.

____. *Southern Germany.* London: 1902.

Blunt, Wilfred. *The Dream King.* Middlesex: Penguin Books Ltd. New York: Penguin Books, 1973.

Channon, Henry. *The Ludwigs of Bavaria.* London & New York: E. P. Hutton, 1933.

Curti, Merle; Shylock, Richard H.; Cochran, Thomas C.; Harrington, Fred H. *An American History,* Vol. 1. New York: Harper & Brothers, 1950.

Dauer, Dorothea W. *Schopenhauer as a Transmitter of Buddist Ideas.* Berne: Herbert Land & Co. Ltd., 1969.

Desing, Julius. *King Ludwig II, His Life–His End.* Lechbruck: Kienberger, 1976.

Emerson, Ralph Waldo. *Emerson's Essays.* New York: Thomas Y. Crowell Co., 1926.

Flemmons, Jerry, and Muench, David (photographer). *Texas.* Chicago, New York, San Francisco: Rand McNally & Co., 1980.

Fortune, Jan, and Burton, Jean. *Elisabet Ney.* New York: Alfred A. Knopf, 1943.

Franz, Joe B. *Texas, A Bicentennial History.* New York: W. W. Norton & Co., 1976.

Fraprie, Frank Roy. *Little Pilgrimages Among Bavarian Inns.* Boston: L. C. Page & Co., 1906.

Hibbert, Christopher. *Garibaldi and His Enemies.* Boston: Little, Brown & Co., 1965.

Holley, Mary Austin, et al. *Women of Texas.* Waco: Texian Press, 1972.

James, Marquis. *The Raven, A Biography of Sam Houston.* Indianapolis: Bobs Merrill Co., 1929.

Keeton, Morris T. *The Philosophy of Edmund Montgomery.* Dallas: University Press in Dallas, 1950.

Loggins, Vernon. *Two Romantics and Their Ideal Life.* New York: The Odyssey Press, 1946.

MacIntire, W. Irwin, *History of Thomas County, Georgia.* Thomasville: 1923.

Mann, Thomas. *The Living Thoughts of Schopenhauer.* New York & Toronto: Longmans, Green & Co., 1939.

Müller, Eugen. *Elisabeth Ney.* Leipzig: Koehler & Ameland, 1931.

Newman, Ernest. *Wagner, As Man and Artist.* New York: Garden City Publishing Co., 1937.

Passant, E. J. *A Short History of Germany 1815–1945.* Cambridge, England: The University Press, 1966.

Rogers, Mary Beth; Winegarten, Ruthe; Smith, Sherry. *Texas Women, A Celebration of History.* Austin: The Texas Foundation of Women's Resources, 1981.

Roosevelt, Theodore. *The Rough Riders.* New York: Charles Scribner's Sons, 1899.

Rutland, Mrs. J. W. (Willie B.), ed. *Sursum! Elisabet Ney in Texas.* Austin: Hart Graphics & Office Centers, Inc., 1977.

Schopenhauer, Arthur. *The World as Will and Idea.* trans. Haldane, R. B. and Kemp, J. London: Kegan Paul, Trench, Triber & Co., 1909.

Skelton, Geoffrey. *Richard and Cosima Wagner: Biography of a Marriage.* Boston: Houghton Mifflin Co., 1982.

Stephens, I. K. *The Hermit Philosopher of Liendo.* Dallas: Southern Methodist University Press, 1951.

Stoddard, John L. *John L. Stoddard's Lectures.* 10 Vols. Chicago & Boston: George L. Shuman & Co., 1915.

Taylor, Bride Neill. *Elisabet Ney, Sculptor.* New York: The

Devon-Adair Co., 1916, rev. ed. 1938.

Taft, Lorado. *The History of American Sculpture.* New York: The Macmillian Co., 1924.

Waller County Survey Committee. *A History of Waller County.* Hempstead: 1973.

Watterson, Henry. *History of the Spanish-American War.* New York: The Werner Co., 1898.

Webb, Walter Prescott, ed. *The Handbook of Texas,* Vol. 1, Austin: The Texas State Historical Association, 1952.

Werstein, Irving, *The Spanish-American War.* New York: Cooper Square Publishing, Inc., 1966.

Windsor, Bill. *Texas in the Confederacy: Military Installations, Economy, and People.* Hillsboro: Hill Junior College Press, 1978.

Zimmern, Helen. *Schopenhauer, His Life and Philosophy.* London: George Allen & Unwin, 1932.

Magazine Articles

Albrecht, Florence Craig. "The Town of Many Gables." *National Geographic Magazine,* February, 1915, pp. 107–110.

Doughty, Ettie M. "Elisabet Ney: The Enigma of the Nineteenth Century." *Naylor's Pictorial Century Magazine,* November, 1939.

Lutz, Eusibia. "Liendo: The Biography of a House." *Southwest Review,* Vol. XVI 2, 1931, pp. 190-99.

Unpublished Material

Garwood, Ellen St. John. "The Wild Heart." Staged in Austin,
June 1970. HRC–UT–A.
Seymour, Mattie Lee. "Interview with Mrs. J. W. Rutland,
Former Curator of the Ney Museum." January 12, 1966.
A–TCC–APL.
Wood, Sarah Lee Norman. "The Heroic Images: Three Sculp-
tures by Elisabet Ney." Master of Arts Thesis, University
of Texas–Austin, August 1978.

INDEX

A

Achtermann, Wilhelm, 912
Alexandria, 116, 117
Alcott, Bronson, 167
  Louisa May, 167
Alford, Lady Marion (mother of Lord Brownlow), 87, 88, 89, 90, 97
Alta Vista Plantation. *See also* Prairie View College, 181, 208
Asher, David, 63
Assig, Ludmilla (niece of Varnhagen von Ence), 36, 37, 39, 47, 48, 92, 93
Austin, Texas, 172, 177, 182, 199, 200, 208, 210–212, 214, 218–222, 234, 235, 238, 240, 245, 246, 249, 250, 251, 253–256, 263, 264, 266, 268, 271, 272, 273, 276
Austin, Stephen F., 211, 212, 214, 218

B

Bayrhoffer, Karl, 168
Bavarian Art Academy. *See also* Royal Bavarian Academy of Fine Arts, Munich, 9, 15–17, 22, 23, 25, 27, 29, 34, 252
Bayreuth, 229
Berdellé, Johann Baptist, 16, 18–20, 106, 229
Berlin, 1, 2, 28, 30, 31, 33, 36, 38, 39, 41, 44, 45, 48, 49, 52–55, 57, 61, 64, 66, 70, 73, 90, 101–103, 105, 124, 128, 165, 213, 230, 231, 247, 250, 251, 253, 257
Berlin, University of, 32, 39, 41, 42, 83
Berlin Art Academy. *See also* Royal Academy of Fine Arts, Berlin, 30, 31, 33, 34, 39, 43, 44, 46, 54, 63, 90, 213, 223, 230, 231, 250
Bermondsey Dispensary, 76, 77, 80

Bickler, Jacob, 267
  Max, 267, 268
Bismarck, Count Otto von, 70, 99, 101–103, 105, 106, 115, 122, 124, 125, 150
Blind, Karl, 77
  Mathilde, 77
Bocci, Signor Antonio, 258
Bonaparte, Louis Napoleon. *See also* Napoleon III, Emperor of France), 77, 103, 104, 124
  Napoleon. *See also* Napoleon I (Emperor of France), 14, 103, 104, 188
Bonn, Germany, 43, 69, 71
Bonn, University of, 42, 68
Boston, 126, 160, 166, 167, 196, 203
Brazos River, 176, 244
Bremen, Germany, 73, 129, 147, 252, 256
Brenham, Texas, 172, 174–176, 178–180, 185, 192, 195, 206, 207
Brothers Grimm (Jakob and Wilhelm). *See also* Grimm, Jakob, 47, 175, 225, 228
Brownlow, Lord (son of Lady Marian Alford), 87, 88, 90, 97, 103, 164
Bryan, Miss Halley, 258
  William Jennings, 241–243
Bülow, Cosima Liszt von. *See also* Liszt, Cosima 37, 41, 45; married Bülow, 47, 70, 89, 106, 124, 129; married Wagner, 125, 129
  Frau Franziska von, 37
  Gertrude von (wife of George von Werthern), 70
  Hans von, 37, 41; marriage 45, 47–49, 70, 107, 124; divorce 125, 189, 229
Burleson, Congressman Albert Sidney, 220, 260, 264, 271
  Emma, 220, 250
  Steiner, son of Albert Sidney

Burleson, 256

C

Cairo, 116
Campbell, John Southerland, Marquis of Lorne, 151, 169
    Sarah (Lorne's third wife). *See also* Montgomery, Sarah Campbell, 268, 274
Capitol Building, Austin, Texas, 199, 211, 212, 249, 253, 265, 276
Capitol Building, Washington, D.C., 260, 265, 276
Caprera, 92, 95, 97, 149
Carnival in Munich, 18–23
Carrara, Italy, 205, 256, 258
Carus, Paul, 208
Cathedral School, Münster, 11, 14
Chappaqua Mountain Institute, Claverack, N.Y., 207
Chateau de Laucy (boys' school near Geneva, Switzerland), 207
Chicago, 167, 209, 211, 213, 217
Cologne, 68, 71, 72
Columbian Exposition, 1893, Chicago, 209, 211, 213, 216–218, 221, 226, 230, 236
Concord School of Philosophy, 196
Cone, Uncle Archie, 160, 161, 164, 170, 171, 179, 184, 189, 190, 191, 263
    Aunt Nelly (wife of Uncle Archie Cone), 164, 170–172, 179, 190, 191
Constantinople (Istanbul), 117, 118
Coppini, Pompeo, 261

D

Darwin, Charles, 77, 100
Daughters of the Republic of Texas, 236, 243
Daughters of the Texas Confederacy, 265, 266
Dibrell, Ella Dancy (wife of Joseph B. Dibrell), 240, 241, 251, 253, 257, 258, 268, 275
    Senator Joseph B., 240, 241, 243
Dickens, Charles, 77
Dietrich, Karl and Emma (names fictitious), 14, 15, 18
Docchi, Signor Cosimo, 266–268
Dolly, Aunt (fictitious character), 162, 163, 169

Doss, Adam von, 55, 61
Douthit, Elisabet Ney Montgomery (daughter of Lorne and Sarah Campbell Montgomery), 275
Dresden, 46, 47, 50
Dumas, Alexander, 77, 92
Duncker, Franz, 48
Dürck, Dr. Karl, 205, 206, 213, 223, 224, 226, 228, 231, 235, 252
Dürck, Josefa (wife of Dr. Karl Dürck), 226, 251

E

Ebers, Georg Moritz, 231
    Paula (sister of Georg Ebers), 231
Edinburgh, Scotland, 27
Eisenhardt, Baron August von, 110, 112, 113, 115, 119, 121–123, 125, 127
    Luise von (wife of Baron Eisenhardt). *See also* Luise von Kobell, 119, 121
Elisabeth, Empress of Austria, 61, 82
Emerson, Ralph Waldo, 148, 167
Emmerich, Theodor, 10
Ence, August Varnhagen von (Varnhagen), 36, 37, 39, 41, 43, 45–50
    Rahel von (wife of Varnhagen von Ence) *See also* Rahel, 36, 38
Eugénie, Empress of France (wife of Napoleon III), 103, 104

F

Fashing (last three days of Munich's Carnival), 18, 20
Feuerbach, Ludwig, 22, 37, 48
Fisher, Julia, 246
Forbes, Mrs. Mary Jane, 97, 115, 120
Formosa studio, (Austin), 212, 214, 215, 218, 221, 235, 236, 246, 248, 252, 259, 263, 266, 269, 271, 273, 276
Formosa studio, Funchal, Madiera, 86, 89, 212, 262
Frankfurt-am-Main, 27, 28, 50, 52, 54–57, 59, 61, 64, 73, 75, 81, 151, 168, 251
Friedrich, Crown Prince of Prussia, 124

Funchal, Madiera, 85–87, 90, 196
Fürtzwangler, Adolph, 223

G

Galveston, Texas, 172, 174, 175,
177, 180, 195, 203, 204, 224,
233, 234, 237, 244, 246, 249,
251
Garbaldi, Guiseppe, 77, 91–101,
103, 106, 122, 149, 243
George V, King of Hannover, 57–
59, 61, 63, 65, 70, 100, 105
German Hospital in London, 49, 50,
56, 76, 80
Gibson, John, 30, 89, 90
Goethe, Johann Wolfgang von, 30,
54, 55, 68, 121, 159, 208
Gould, Judge R. S., 216
Governor's Mansion, Austin, 199,
211
Graham, Caroline Pease (deceased
daughter of Mrs. Elisha M.
Pease), 220, 237
Margaret and Niles (grandchil-
dren of Mrs. Elisha M.
Pease, nicknamed "The
Brownies"), 219, 220
Grant, President Ulysses S., 152
Gray, Miss Dora, 195
Grimm, Jakob. *See also* Brothers
Grimm), 47, 175, 225
Groce, Colonel Leonard Wharton,
176–180, 182, 213

H

Hamburg, 224
Hankins, Benjamin F., 191
Hannover, 57, 58, 60, 61, 65, 66,
105, 226
Hawthorne, Nathaniel, 89
Heidelberg, 23, 26–28, 32, 43, 48,
70, 82, 176
Heidelberg, University of, 21–26,
29, 32, 35, 69
Helmholtz, Professor Hermann von,
42, 43, 46
Hempstead, Texas, 175, 176, 179–
183, 185, 187–189, 192–194,
199, 201, 203, 206, 207,
214–216, 218, 234, 240, 244,
265, 268, 270, 272
Hempstead News, 216
Herrenchimsee Castle, 230, 275
Hohenschwagau Castle, 227, 228,
275

Holzlotzschloss (Log Castle), Thom-
asville, 159, 160, 161, 162,
165, 171, 179, 190, 191
Hoppe, Gerhard, 48, 49
Hornstein, Robert von, 56
Hosmer, Harriet, 30, 89, 90
Houston and Central Texas Rail-
road, 174, 175, 180, 234
Houston, Sam, 177, 199, 211–214,
249, 250
Houston, Texas, 174, 185, 186
Huddle, Nannie Carver, 220, 272
Hüffer, Hermann, 68, 69, 71, 72,
104
Humbolt, Alexander von, 37, 39, 41,
43, 48, 49
Hyde Park (Austin suburb), 212

I

International Art Exposition of
1867, Paris, 103, 209
International Art Exhibition, Ber-
lin, 213
Iphigeneia in Tauras by Johann von
Goethe, 121, 159

J

Joachim, Amalie Weiss (wife of Joseph Joachim), 105
Joseph, 58–61, 65–67, 70, 97,
104, 105
Johnston, General Albert Sidney,
242, 244, 266

K

Kane, Captain Woodbury, Officer-
in-Charge, U.S. Cavalry
Troop, 239
Kant, Immanuel, 46, 55, 120, 128,
160
Kapp, Hofrat Christian (father of
Johanna), 21, 23, 24, 27, 29,
70, 71
Johanna, 16, 18, 20–25, 28, 36,
37, 39, 48, 70, 71, 106, 229
Kaulbach, Friedrich, 19–21, 57, 58,
60–62, 65, 66, 68, 226
Wilhelm von (Director of the
Bavarian Art Academy), 15,
16, 18, 30, 31, 46
Keller, Gottfried, 37, 38, 68, 229
Kirby, Helen Marr (widow of Jared
Kirby), 181, 182, 185, 252
Kobell, Luise von (wife of Baron
August von Eisenhardt),

119, 121
Kropsberg Castle, 98, 99
Ku Klux Klan, 187

L

Ladd, Henry, 237, 246, 249
Lagerhaus, das, 34, 47, 53, 57, 65, 83, 230, 248
Lane, Alvin, 273
Lange, Franz, 251, 257, 258
Lefevre, Arthur, 185
Leipzig, 54, 55
Leisewitz, Henrietta (daughter of Robert Leisewitz), 192, 195, 207, 215
   Robert, 174–179, 185, 192, 195
   Mrs. Robert, 179, 185, 192, 195, 207, 215
Lewald, Frau Elisabeth, 88
   Dr. Theodore, 88, 257, 258, 260
Liebig, Justus von, 106, 108, 110, 114, 115, 124
Liendo Plantation, 175–178, 180–183, 185, 188–191, 200, 202, 204–207, 211, 213, 214, 217, 218, 221, 232–235, 239, 242, 244–246, 248, 253, 261, 262, 264, 268, 271, 272, 274, 275
Lincoln, President Abraham, 95, 152
Linderhof Castle, 122, 224, 226, 227, 229
Lipscomb, Abner Gaines, 179, 180, 185, 187–189, 265
Liszt, Blandine (daughter of Franz Listz), 37, 41, 45, 70
   Cosima (daughter of Franz Listz). *See also* Bülow, Cosima von and Wagner, Cosima von Bülow, 37, 41, 45, 47, 70, 89, 106, 124, 125, 129
   Franz, 37, 39, 45, 46, 48, 107, 189
London, 49, 51, 56, 61, 66, 71–73, 75–77, 80, 81, 83, 84, 85, 89, 90, 106, 151, 250
London Royal Art Academy. *See also* Royal Art Academy, London, 81, 97, 105
Lorraine, France, 11, 14
Louis XIII, King of France, 104
Louis XIV, King of France, 26
Louise, Princess (daughter of Queen Victoria), 151
Ludwig I, King of Bavaria, 23, 120,

121
Ludwig II, King of Bavaria, 105–115, 118–125, 127, 150, 157–159, 196, 205, 224, 226, 228–230, 252
Lueder, Dr. Joseph, 225, 252
   Marie (wife of Joseph Lueder), 225, 252, 256, 272
Luitpold, Regent-Prince of Bavaria, 205, 223, 229

M

Macbeth, Lady (character in Shakespeare's *Macbeth*), 35, 98
McKinley, President William, 241–243
McNeill, Duncan, Lord Colonsay (father of Edmund Montgomery), 27, 74, 75, 78, 87, 188
Maddaleno, La, 93
Madeira, 82–86, 90, 165, 181, 212, 214, 253
"Magic Hut," (Lueder's home), 225, 252, 257
Marcus, Eli, 67
Maria Theresa, (wife of King Ludwig I), 23
Marie, Queen of Hannover (wife of George V), 59, 61, 157
Maximilian I, King of Bavaria, 16, 121
Maximilian II, King of Bavaria (father of King Ludwig II), 106, 120, 228
Mechlenburg, 126, 165, 166
"Mechlenburg Farm," 156, 158
Menton, (Lady Alford's villa on the Mediterranean), 90, 97, 103
Miller, Clarence, 234, 250, 256, 266
Mississippi River, 168, 169
Mitscherlich, Dr. Eilhardt, 83
Montez, Lola, 121
Montgomery, Alma Weitgen (Lorne's second wife). *See also* Wietgen, Alma, 245, 263
   Arthur, Arti (son of Ney and Montgomery), 163–171, 181, 185, 187, 188, 190, 273, 274
   Daisy Thompkins (Lorne's first and fourth wife). *See also* Thompkins, Daisy, 216–218, 221, 274, 275

Edmund Duncan, meets Ney in Hiedelberg, 25–29; childhood, 27, 28; correspondence with Ney, 35–39; medical studies at various Universities 42–49, meets Dr. Simon from St. Thomas's Hospital, London, 50, 56; work in London hospitals, 73–78; illness 79–81; Ney joins him in London; marriage in Madeira, 86–88; joins Ney in Munich, 107; Forbes's legacy and trip with Ney to Near East, 115–118; emigration from Europe to Thomasville, GA., 126, 147, 159; book on Kant, 160; journey with Ney through the United States, 166–172; birth of Lorne, 169; return to Thomasville, 171, 172; purchase of Liendo Plantation, 180; death of Arthur, 185, 186; legacy from father and citizenship 188, 195; enrolls Lorne in Swathmore, 201–204, becomes active in Waller County affairs, 206–208, 215, 216, 221, 222, 234, 240; hurricane and illness at Liendo, 244, 245; return to Europe, 247, 250; Ney joins him, 252; publication of book, 263, 268, 270; Ney's death, 272; Montgomery's death at Liendo, 274
Edmund (son of Lorne and Daisy Thompkins), 221
Elisabet Ney (daughter of Lorne and Sarah Campbell), born after Ney's death. *See also* Douthit, Elisabet Ney Montgomery, 275
Lorne Ney, Lore, (son of Ney and Montgomery), childhood at Liendo, 169–171, 181, 185, 188, 189, 191; rebellion against mother, 192–194, 201; schooling, 202, 204, 207, 215, 216; elopment with Daisy Thompkins and life at Liendo, 216–218; joins Roosevelt's "Rough Riders," 238, 239; divorce and remarriage 239, 245, 253; wife's death and third marriage, 246, 263, 268; death following an accident, 274, 275
Hugh (son of Lorne and Alma Wietgen), 263
Isabella Davidson (mother of Edmund Montgomery), 27, 73, 74, 75, 188
Ruth (daughter of Lorne and Daisy Thompkins), 239
Sarah Campbell (Lore's third wife). *See also* Campbell, Sarah, 268, 274
Theodore (son of Lorne and Alma Wietgen), 246
Wanda (daughter of Lorne and Alma Wietgen), 263
Morgan, Ben, 263, 269, 271, 272
Mossbauer, Karl, 120
Müller, Bishop Johann Georg, 6–10, 14, 31, 38, 44, 67, 90, 128, 225, 250
Professor Johannes, 39
Valentin, 68
Munich, 9, 12–15, 18, 23, 27–30, 33, 50, 55, 57, 60, 70, 105–110, 114, 115, 118–121, 125, 127, 128, 165, 189, 205, 211, 213, 223, 226, 227, 229, 230, 251, 252
Munich Academy of Fine Arts. *See also* Royal Bavarian Academy of Fine Arts, 9, 15–17, 22, 23, 25, 27, 29, 34, 252
Münster, Westphalia (birthplace), 1, 2, 4, 7–11, 13, 15, 20, 22, 27, 32, 38, 39, 66, 68, 69, 83, 128, 129, 175, 191, 219, 224–226, 252, 275

N

Napoleon I, Emperor of France. *See also* Bonaparte, Napoleon, 14, 103, 104, 188
Napoleon III, Emperor of France. *See also* Bonaparte, Louis Napoleon, 77, 103, 104, 124
"Napoleonic lace," 14, 69
Neureuther, Gottfried von, 108–110, 113–115, 187
Neuschwanstein Castle, 122, 227

New York, 128, 148, 150, 151, 167
Ney, Anna Wernze (mother), 1, 2,
    4–7, 9, 10, 13, 15, 67, 69,
    128, 165, 225
  Elizabet, Elise, hunger strike
    and early education, 1–4;
    eccentricities of dress as a
    child, 4–6; counsel with
    Bishop Müller, 7–10; com-
    promise for Munich Art
    Academy, 14–21; Kaulbach
    and Carnival, 20, 21; meets
    Montgomery in Heidelberg,
    22–33; scholarship to Berlin
    Art Academy, study with
    Rauch, 34, 35; life in Berlin,
    36–39, 45–49; King George
    V of Hannover and Kaul-
    bach, 58–63; Schopenhauer,
    50, 51, 61–64; joins Montgo-
    mery in London, 80–85;
    marriage in Madeira, 87,
    88; Garibaldi 93–101; Mun-
    ich and King Ludwig II,
    105–115; political upheaval,
    119–126; emigration to
    Thomasville, GA., 126–129,
    147–158; friendship with
    the Stralendorffs and birth
    of Arthur, 160–165; journey
    through America and birth
    of Lorne, 166–172; Liendo
    Plantation in Texas and
    death of Arthur, 174–189;
    problems with Lorne, 192–
    197, 201–204, 207; meets
    Governor Roberts 198–207;
    commissions for statues of
    Houston and Austin, 209–
    211; studio in Austin 212,
    213; Lorne's elopement,
    215–218; life in Austin,
    219–223; return to Europe,
    224–231; Lorne joins Roose-
    velt's "Rough Riders," 238,
    239; the State Legislature
    and William Jennings
    Bryan, 243, 244; destruction
    at Liendo 244-246; joins
    Montgomery in Europe,
    250, 252; work in Italy, 256–
    259; St. Louis Exhibition
    and Washington, D.C., 260,
    261, 265, 266; *completion of*

  Lady Macbeth 266–268;
    health problems and death,
    270–272
  Friedrich Fritz, (brother), 1, 3,
    10, 14, 38, 67, 69, 128, 191,
    224, 225, 252, 257
  Johann Adam (father), 1–7, 9–
    13, 38, 66, 67, 69, 87, 128,
    187, 191, 225
  Leonore Stoetmann, (wife of
    Fritz Ney), 128, 224, 225
  Marshal Michel (Marshal of
    France under Napoleon I),
    4, 21, 33, 54, 55, 97, 103,
    104, 188, 238, 265
North German Lloyd Line, 147,
    224, 233, 251, 252, 260
Nutt, Dr. Conway, 185, 186

                O

Ochs, Friedrich, 128, 187, 188, 205,
    213, 226, 230
Octoberfest, 23
Oterendorp, Herr Captain von, 147
Otto, Prince of Bavaria (brother of
    King Ludwig II), 114, 122
Owens, Richard, 100
  Robert, 148

                P

Paris, 49, 56, 103–105, 124, 125,
    148, 150, 209
Parker, Laura Bryan, 243
Pease, Mrs. Elisha M., 219, 220,
    234, 237, 239, 240
  Miss Julia, 219, 236, 237
Pease Mansion. *See also* Woodlawn,
    211, 219–221, 234, 236, 240
Perry, Halley Bryan, 232
Pinkney, Congressman John H.,
    265
Pope Pius IX, 90, 91, 96, 259
Prague, 47, 49, 99
Prairie View College. *See also* Alta
    Vista Plantation, 207, 208
Prather, William L. (former Presi-
    dent, The University of
    Texas), 267, 268
"Prelude," poem by William Words-
    worth, 26
Pre-Raphaelite Brotherhood, 81
Prometheus, 96, 98, 228

                R

Rahel, (philosopher wife of Varnhagen von Ence). *See also* Ence, Rahel von, 36, 48

Rauch, Christian Daniel, (mentor and teacher), 2, 4, 8, 9, 16, 30, 31, 33–36, 38, 39, 41, 43–51, 53, 54, 56, 58, 67, 70, 89, 90, 216, 230, 248, 250

Reagan, Senator John R., 237, 247, 249

Red Wing, MN. (birthplace of Lorne), 169, 170

Reece, Judge Thomas, 179, 180, 185, 187, 188, 190, 265, 266

Reid, Dr. James R., 161, 162, 169

Residenz. See also Royal Bavarian Palace, 110, 121, 127, 128, 226

Rhine River, 69, 72, 169, 174

Rietschel, Ernst, 47, 50

Rome, 90, 97–100, 115, 118, 259

Roberts, Governor Oran M., 198–200, 209, 211, 212, 215, 218, 220, 238, 240, 241

Roosevelt, Colonel Theodore, 238, 239

Röper, Peter (son of Elisabeth Röper-Wernze), 225, 252

Röper-Wernze, Frau Elisabeth, 225, 252

Royal Academy of Fine Arts, Berlin. *See also* Berlin Art Academy, 27, 30, 213, 230, 231

Royal Art Academy, London. *See also* London Royal Art Academy, 81, 97, 105

Royal Bavarian Academy of Fine Arts, Munich, 9, 15–17, 23, 25, 29, 34, 252

Royal Bavarian Palace. *See also Residenz,* 110, 121, 127, 128, 226

Royal College of Physicians in London, 79

Runge, Johanna (wife of Julius Runge), 203–205

Julius (German Consul in Galveston), 174, 195, 202, 203, 205, 206, 237

Ruskin, John, 57, 81

Russell, Mr. and Mrs. Edward (parents of Margaret von Stralendorff), 160, 166, 167

Mrs. Frances E., 210

S

"Sacred Grove," 181, 186, 272, 274

Saint Lambert's Church, Münster, 11

St. Louis, Mo., 260

St. Louis International Exposition of Arts and Science, 256–261, 263, 265

Saint Martin's Church, Münster, 8, 10

Saint Martin's Girls Seminary, Münster, 3, 7

St. Mauritz Cemetery, Münster, 225, 257

Saint Thomas's Hospital, 49, 73, 76, 79, 97, 204, 250

San Antonio, Texas, 238

Sanborn, Frank B. (Montgomery's proxy), 196, 203

Sayers, Governor Joseph D., 241, 253

Mrs. Joseph D., 241, 253

Schnerr, Elisabeth Emma, 269

Schopenhauer, Arthur, 28, 46, 50–59, 61–66, 70, 73, 75, 123, 237, 251

Schumann-Heink, Madam Ernestine, 254, 255, 269

Schwabing (suburb of Munich), 21, 120, 127

Schwawbing Villa. *See also Steinheil Schlosschen,* 120, 122, 123, 205, 226, 252

Seravezza, Italy, 258, 259, 266

Sherman, General William Tecumseh, 153, 156

Shipe, Monroe, 269

Simath, Fräulein Crecentia, Cenci, employed by Ney, 99, 100; housekeeper in Munich villa, 107, 108, 115, 118, 120; emigrates to America 127, 128, 147, 149–155, 158, 161–164; care of Arthur in Thomasville, 166, 168, 170, 171, 172, 179; housekeeper at Liendo, 180–182, 185, 186, 188, 190, 192, 204, 206, 215, 217, care of Lorne's family at Liendo, 221, 234, 236, 238, 242, 244, 245, 247, 253; seventieth birthday, 263, 264, 270, 271; care of Ney, Montgomery, and

Lorne until their deaths, 272–275; dies at Seton Infirmary in Austin, 275

Simon, Lady Jane (wife of Sir John Simon), 76, 79–81

Dr. Sir John, 49, 50, 56, 66, 76, 77, 79–84, 100, 250

Steinbach, Sabine von, 8

Steiner, Dr. Ralph, 250, 251

Steinheil–Schlosschen (Little Stone Castle). *See also* Schwabing Villa, 120, 122, 123, 205, 226, 252

Stralendorff, Baroness Margaret Russell von (wife of Baron Vicco von Stralendorff), 126, 150, 153–160, 164–167, 177, 189

Baron Vicco von, 126, 150, 153–160, 164–167, 177

Studios. *See* Formosa, Funchal; Formosa, Austin; Das Laugerhaus, Berlin

Sursum, 208, 209, 212, 249

Swathmore College, Philadelphia, 202–204, 207

T

Taft, Lorado, 259

Taylor, Bride Neill, (wife of Thomas Taylor), 220, 232, 235, 246, 258, 259, 269, 271

Thomas, 221, 251, 258, 259

Tom (English playwright), 57, 71, 80, 81, 152

Texas, 171–180, 182, 183, 188–191, 196–200, 202–204, 207–211, 213–215, 230, 232, 235, 242, 243, 247, 248, 251, 263, 265, 270, 273, 276

Texas Academy of Liberal Arts. *See also* Texas Fine Arts Association, 214, 219, 240–243, 272, 276

Texas Academy of Science, 222, 256

Texas Fine Arts Association. *See also* Texas Academy of Liberal Arts, 214, 219, 240–243, 272, 276

Texas, The University of, 200, 209, 211, 212, 222, 249, 255, 256, 268, 276

Thames River, 75, 79

Thomasville, GA., 126, 149, 150, 153–155, 157, 158, 159, 161, 162, 164–166, 168, 170, 171, 178, 179, 181, 190, 212

Thompkins, Daisy (Lorne's first and fourth wife). *See also* Montgomery, Daisy Thompkins, 216–218, 221, 274, 275

Tobin, Bernedette (Mrs. William B. Tobin), 209, 211, 213, 214, 217, 218, 220, 236, 240

V

Veterans of the Confederacy, 265, 266

Victor Emmanuel, King of Italy, 77, 98, 99

Victoria, Queen of England, 56, 58, 77, 81, 151, 200

Victoria, Sister (teacher at St. Mary's Academy, Austin), 250

Vienna, 49, 54, 55, 101

W

Waldhorn Estate (home of Dr. Christian Kapp, Heidelberg), 24, 25, 28, 70

Waller County, 177, 180, 182, 183, 187, 195, 196, 202, 206, 208, 215, 222, 244, 245, 256, 265

Wagner, Cosima Listz von Bülow. *See also* Listz, Cosima and Wagner, Cosima von Bülow, married Wagner, 125; widow, 229

Richard, 39, 49, 70, 106, 107, 119, 122, 124, 125, 189, 227–229

Siegfried (son of Richard and Cosima Wagner), 125

Washington, D.C., 152

Weimar, 55

Weiss, Hermann, 44

Werne, Wesphalia, 225, 252, 257

Werener, Anton von (Director of Berlin Art Academy), 213, 230, 231

Werthern, Baron George von, 70, 101, 105–108, 110, 115, 122, 125, 126, 229

Whittlebach Dynasty, 120, 122

Widnmann, Max, 17, 29, 30, 31, 106, 229

Wietgen, Alma (Lorne's second wife). *See also* Montgomery, Alma Wietgen, 245, 263

Wilhelm, King Friedrich I, Em-

peror *(Kaiser)* of Prussia,
39, 41, 70, 101, 102, 125, 150
Wilhelm I, Emperor *(Kaiser)* of
Prussia, 231
Williams, Horace, 242, 245, 250,
264
Margaret Houston (daughter of
Sam Houston), 214, 250
Wöhler, Friedrich, 106, 108, 110,
114
Woodlawn (home of Mrs. Elisha M.

Pease. *See also* Pease Man-
sion, 211, 219, 220, 221, 234,
236, 240
Woolner, Thomas, 81
Wordsworth, William, 26
Wortham, Louis, 258, 260
Wright, Frances, 148
Würtzburg, University of, 47, 79

Z

Zumbusch, Julius, 106, 107, 114